D0649931

In the Shadow of the Giant

In the Shadow of the Giant

The Americanization of

Modern Mexico

Joseph Contreras

RUTGERS UNIVERSITY PRESS

NEW BRUNSWICK, NEW JERSEY, AND LONDON

Library of Congress Cataloging-in-Publication Data

Contreras, Joseph, 1957–
[Tan lejos de Dios. English]
In the shadow of the giant : the Americanization of modern Mexico / Joseph
Contreras.
    p. cm.
  Includes bibliographical references and index.
  ISBN 978–0-8135–4482–3 (hardcover : alk. paper)
    1. Mexico—Politics and government—1988–2000.   2. Mexico—Economic
  conditions—1994– 3. Mexico—Social conditions—1970– 4. Mexico—Foreign
  relations—United States.   5. United States—Foreign relations—Mexico.
  6. Mexico—Civilization—American influences.   I. Title.
  F1236.7.C6613 2009
  303.48'27207309045—dc22

                                                                2008026171

A British Cataloging-in-Publication record for this book is available from the British
Library.

Visit our Web site: http://rutgerspress.rutgers.edu

Manufactured in the United States of America

For Claire, Francesca, and Dominic

Contents

Preface   ix

Introduction   The United States of Mexico   1

PART I

1   A Chicano Comes to the Big Enchilada:
     Mexico City, 1984–1987   19
2   Not Such Distant Neighbors: Mexico in the
     Era of Vicente Fox   38
3   Looking Northward   63

PART II

4   NAFTA: The Double-Edged Sword of
     Free Trade   87
5   The New Breed of Mexican Businessmen   103
6   The Modern Mexican News Media   118

PART III

7   The Mexican Dream   135
8   The Gringo Riviera   151
9   The Umbilical Cord of Remittances   165
10   The Southernmost City in Texas: Monterrey,
     Nuevo León   183

PART IV

11   Made-in-the-U.S.A. Diseases   205
12   The Evangelical Challenge   220

Conclusion   An Invaded Country   235

Acknowledgments   245
Notes   247
Selected Bibliography   261
Index   265

Preface

One of the very first Spanish words I learned as a child was *pocho*. Though my Mexican immigrant parents, Joe and Olga Contreras, started speaking to me almost exclusively in English in the months prior to my entering kindergarten in the Los Angeles suburb of Pico Rivera in the early 1960s, Spanish was always in the air at home, especially when relatives came calling or Mom and Dad were quarreling. The word *pocho* literally means "overripe" or "rotten," as in fruit, and it would surface at the dinner table from time to time. But the context was very different when my father said it, for the term is a well-known slur used by native Mexicans to describe assimilated Americans of Mexican descent who have lost touch with their cultural roots.

And I certainly was a *pocho*. As a kid growing up in southern California, I spoke little Spanish and emphatically preferred hamburgers and French fries to tamales and menudo. I wasn't exactly thrilled when my parents announced we were pulling up stakes and moving to my father's hometown of Guadalajara upon his retirement in the winter of 1968. When I enrolled in one of that city's exclusive private schools, I found myself gravitating toward my American peers instead of the locals. To my considerable relief we went back to Los Angeles later that summer, and with a blend of amusement and mild shame I still recall trying to downplay if not outright deny my family's ethnic roots with my WASPy friends at the suburban junior high school I attended in the early 1970s.

Only in college did I begin to see Mexico, and by extension Latin America, in a vastly different light. As a teenager I had always taken Spanish courses in school, but only because they guaranteed an easy A on the report card; as an undergraduate, however, I started to toy with the idea of finding something to do south of the border one day, perhaps as a foreign correspondent for a leading U.S. publication if the long hours I spent at the student newspaper ever translated into a career. They eventually did—and when I moved to Mexico City in the winter of 1984 to take over *Newsweek* magazine's editorial bureau, I was full of both enthusiasm and apprehension. Enthusiasm, because I would be getting an enviable opportunity at the age of twenty-seven to cover Mexico as well as Central America's guerrilla wars—a foreign policy priority for the Reagan administration and therefore a major news story for my editors. Apprehension, because my rusty Spanish and discernibly foreign accent would undress me as a *pocho* before the political and business elites I would be meeting in the land of my forefathers.

A quarter-century later I have a perspective on Mexico diametrically opposite to that of my childhood and pubescence. I press upon my three college-age children the paramount importance of learning Spanish with the same zeal and, probably from their standpoint, repetitiousness that my parents conveyed to me four decades ago. I asked my editors to send me back to Mexico as *Newsweek*'s Latin America regional editor in 2005 and was elated when they approved the request. I have devoured dozens of books on Mexican history and culture and visited both of my parents' birthplaces, where I befriended relatives of whose existence I had not known. When the Mexican and U.S. national soccer squads periodically face off in a World Cup qualifying match, I find myself rooting for the guys in the green jerseys and white shorts. I revel in the glories of Mexican cuisine—and here I mean *real* Mexican food, not the Tex-Mex fare so familiar to most of my fellow Americans—though I'm still not big on tamales or menudo ("What kind of a Mexican are you?" my despairing mother has asked on more than one occasion when I have declined her offer to prepare those specific dishes).

The idea for this book sprouted primarily from two personal epiphanies. The first took place in June 2000 when I returned to Mexico City for the first time in twelve years for a series of interviews with the country's outgoing president and the two leading candidates vying to replace him. Both the lame-duck incumbent Ernesto Zedillo and Vicente Fox, the former Coca-Cola executive who would achieve a historic victory over the country's long-entrenched ruling party in that year's presidential election, agreed to conduct the interviews in English, something that would have been unheard of in Mexico not so long ago. As *Newsweek*'s special diplomatic correspondent Lally Weymouth and I waded through the Mexican capital's notorious traffic jams, I was struck by the many U.S. corporate logos dotting the cityscape. From Burger King and McDonald's to Marriott and Wal-Mart, many of the Fortune 500 big boys had established a high-profile presence that simply wasn't there when I had called Mexico City home in the mid-1980s.

The second moment of clarity occurred nearly three years later when I went to the Mexico City offices of Emilio Azcárraga Jean, the scion of Latin America's top broadcasting dynasty. The boyish-looking chief of the Televisa media conglomerate told me he was ready to apply for a U.S. passport if that would accelerate his company's penetration of the burgeoning Latino market on the other side of Mexico's northern border. This too seemed remarkable because Emilio's demonstratively patriotic father had gone to great lengths to conceal the inconvenient fact of the elder Azcárraga's birth in Texas—and here was his only male child telling an American correspondent he had no compunctions about acquiring U.S. nationality if it would benefit Televisa's bottom line.

Something profound and unprecedented about Mexico had changed during the years when I'd been living in other countries and continents. The ways in which its people viewed and were influenced by the United States seemed quite different from what I had seen as a schoolboy and a young man, and over the ensuing months a notion began to take shape in my mind about writing a book about the Americanization of modern Mexico. Such a book might provide a better understanding of how Mexico has evolved in the past, what makes the country tick today, and where it may be headed in the twenty-first century. This then is one California-born *pocho*'s attempt to make sense of the Americanizing land of his ancestors.

In the Shadow of the Giant

The United States of Mexico

Every modern society has catch phrases that become ingrained in the collective subconscious of its people. Ask any American of my generation to complete the sentence uttered by President John F. Kennedy in his 1961 inaugural address that began, "Ask not what your country can do for you . . ." and without missing a beat, most will answer ". . . ask what you can do for your country." For Britons, a similar example might be Prime Minister Winston Churchill's stirring tribute to the Royal Air Force at the height of the Nazi bombardment of London during World War II, when he declared that "never in the field of human conflict was so much owed by so many to so few." One of the quotations that Mexicans from all walks of life commit to memory from childhood is a wry truism that perfectly captures the mixed emotions they feel toward their imposing neighbor to the north: "Poor Mexico, so far from God and so close to the United States."[1]

The statement has been widely attributed to Porfirio Díaz, the military strongman who ruled Mexico for over thirty years in the late nineteenth and early twentieth centuries. There is no historical evidence that Díaz ever said those words, but the phrase has stuck to him, perhaps in part because of the country that Díaz helped fashion during his long tenure in power. Mexico embraced the contemporary equivalent of globalization under Díaz's stewardship, flinging open the doors of its economy, society, and culture to the outside world. In matters of style and taste, France was the foreign country most admired by Mexico's elites during the *Porfiriato*, as Díaz's reign came to be known. French was the foreign language of choice in high society. Mexico City's elegant thoroughfare Paseo de la Reforma aspired to become the regional equivalent of the Champs Elysées. And Paris was the world's undisputed trendsetter in the realms of fashion and architecture.[2]

But when it came to the more pragmatic and concrete fields of international trade and foreign investment, the United States was *the* dominant player in Porfirian Mexico. Díaz's seizure of power via an armed rebellion in 1876 prevented Washington from recognizing his government at first, but after full diplomatic relations were restored two years later the Mexican dictator actively cultivated a "special relationship" with the United States that took precedence over ties with European powers or other Latin American republics.[3] The first railroad link to the U.S. border was established in 1884 with the inauguration of the Central Mexican Railway connecting Mexico City to Ciudad Juárez across the Rio Grande from El Paso, Texas. With the active encouragement of the pro-business advisers who surrounded Díaz and were known as the *científicos* (the scientists), American companies in 1909 controlled nearly three-quarters of the country's active mines and over 70 percent of its metallurgical industries.[4]

By that year, the United States accounted for 42 percent of all direct foreign investment in the country (among foreign nations with a strong economic presence in Mexico, only Great Britain came close to challenging American supremacy).[5] From the vantage point of Wall Street, Mexico had no peer as a foreign haven for American capital in the early years of the twentieth century. Over half of the United States' entire overseas investment portfolio was concentrated in Mexico, and the prominent captains of industry with extensive interests in the country included the Guggenheims, J. P. Morgan, and the Rockefellers.

The country was completely integrated into the prevailing international order by the time the Mexican Revolution erupted in the fall of 1910. In 1904 the Mexican capital's ritziest neighborhood was called the American Colony (Colonia Americana);[6] only in later years would it be rechristened with the more patriotic surname of the country's first indigenous president, Benito Juárez. During a ceremony held in honor of a newly arrived American ambassador in 1897, the Mexican dictator positively gushed with praise for the United States. "Great is the admiration that your country inspires among the Mexican people," Díaz told the envoy, Gen. Powell Clayton, "who have taken it for a model for their political institutions, and who are attempting to imitate it in the development of their natural resources."[7]

THE RISE AND FALL OF THE *CIENTÍFICOS*

The credo of the Porifirian establishment was positivism, a philosophy rooted in the writings of the nineteenth-century French thinkers Henri de Saint-Simon and Auguste Comte that promoted scientific methodology as a means to analyze social, economic, and political issues and devise government policies. Its premier Mexican apostle was José Yves Limantour, Diaz's elegant, white-haired finance minister, who saw foreign investment and trade with the outside world as panaceas for much of the country's economic backwardness. In modern parlance Limantour would have been called a fiscal conservative, and he helped transform what had been a debtor country best known to international bankers throughout most of the nineteenth century for its repeated defaults into a showcase of prosperity and prudent government spending. At the height of the *Porfiriato*, Mexico boasted an excellent credit record and a silver peso that was accepted as hard currency in foreign countries as far away as China.[8] "Order and progress" became the signature slogan of the times, and in the context of Latin America, Mexico was every bit the darling of foreign investors a century ago that Chile is today. As Mexico prepared to celebrate the centennial of its declaration of independence from Spain in September 1910, the country's short- and medium-term outlook seemed to promise ever greater growth and profits for American and other foreign investors as well as the Mexican elites with whom they had made partnerships.

The outbreak of the Mexican Revolution shattered the Porfirian paradigm. A calamitous decade of civil war and economic depression destroyed the edifice of stability that Díaz had methodically built up during his long reign, and nationalism supplanted positivism as the guiding principle of the army generals who ruled Mexico in the 1920s and 1930s. The U.S.-dominated oil industry was nationalized in 1938, and over the ensuing four decades Mexican industrialists successfully lobbied their own governments to bar or limit the access of foreign companies and their competitively priced products to the domestic market. Under the tutelage of the long-ruling Institutional Revolutionary Party (PRI), Mexico assiduously culti-vated an image of independence from the United States in international affairs that verged on blatant defiance at times. Practically alone in the Western Hemisphere, Mexico resisted pressure from Washington to cut diplomatic ties with Fidel Castro during the early years of the Cuban Revolution, and in the 1970s Mexican governments rolled out the red car-pet for legions of left-wing politicians and guerrillas from South America who had fled U.S.-backed military dictatorships in their native lands.

AMERICANIZATION AND THE TECHNOCRATS

Mexico has now come full circle. In many ways the country today has more in common with the Mexico of Porfirio Díaz than with the Mexico forged by the PRI during its heyday in the mid-twentieth century. The nation's current president Felipe Calderón is the latest in a string of Ivy League–trained technocrats who make economic policy according to the precepts of free trade. The PRI-sponsored doctrine of economic national-ism that limited foreign investment throughout the middle decades of the last century has been supplanted by a dogma of open markets, export-driven growth, and the privatization of government-run enterprises. The principal pioneer of these free-market policies was Carlos Salinas de Gortari, a Harvard-educated cabinet minister who became president at the age of forty and jettisoned the party's traditional support for a vigorous government role in the economy. It was Salinas de Gortari who signed the 1994 North American Free Trade Agreement (NAFTA) that irreversibly linked the country's economic fortunes to those of the United States.

As Limantour had done a century before, Salinas de Gortari's U.S.-educated finance minister Pedro Aspe balanced the federal government budget after years of big deficits and extravagant spending, and in 1991 Aspe achieved the unthinkable—an operating budget surplus.

Salinas de Gortari and his top economic advisers—including his eventual successor as president, Ernesto Zedillo—completely bought into the neoliberal model of growth championed at the time by U.S. policymakers, the World Bank, and the International Monetary Fund (IMF). Their bible was the Washington Consensus, a checklist of free-market nostrums that touted among other things greater fiscal discipline in government, the privatization of money-losing public enterprises, and deregulation of developing-country economies.

If forced to make a choice, these young Mexican technocrats consistently placed economic development above democratic reform. "This emphasis was always at the expense of a concern with political freedom," wrote the historian Enrique Krauze. "In a very modernized form (and with polished methods of presentation), Salinas de Gortari and his generation shared that quality in particular with Porfirio Díaz. They were an imperious and impatient group, the new *científicos*, the 'enlightened despots' of the computer age."[9] Like their Porfirian predecessors, these Mexican policymakers professed an unshakable faith in the efficiency and bountiful rewards of U.S.-style capitalism. "They have a religious attitude to the free market, an economic fundamentalism," the Mexican writer Carlos Monsiváis told the American historian David Thelen in a 1998 interview. "President Ernesto Zedillo went to an Indian area of Oaxaca and made a speech in praise of the IMF. It's a crusade, it is amazing."[10]

In crafting the NAFTA accords, Salinas de Gortari also violated what Enrique Krauze once termed the "Eleventh Commandment of official Mexican mythology: Thou Shalt Not Trust Americans." During his six-year term in office, Salinas de Gortari laid the groundwork for a definitive break with the country's self-consciously nationalist past. Under his successors, Mexico's foreign policy gradually turned away from the rest of Latin America and came to emphasize the bilateral relationship with

Washington above all else, just as Don Porfirio had once done. In the new century Mexico's formerly chummy ties with Cuba deteriorated into a tense standoff under the conservative president Vicente Fox, and Castro's heir apparent as the Western Hemisphere's leading oracle of anti-Americanism, Venezuelan president Hugo Chávez, publicly berated Fox as a "puppy" of the American empire[11] and hurled similar insults at his successor Felipe Calderón.[12] In the process, Mexico has surrendered the distinctive role it once played on the world stage as an independent voice on foreign affairs and a haven for refugees from Nazi Germany, the Franco dictatorship in Spain, and the Pinochet regime in Chile. And as its recent governments have increasingly sided with Washington on matters like free-trade treaties and the dangers posed by populist leaders like Chávez, Mexico has lost much of its influence and clout within Latin America.

THE PRESCIENCE OF DON PORFIRIO

Porfirio Díaz's lapidary lament about Mexico's geographically determined fate has never resonated with greater force than today. To my mind, twenty-first-century Mexico is a significantly more Americanized country than the one I moved to in the mid-1980s. That statement might give pause to anyone who has ever crossed into Mexico from the United States by land; there is no shortage of outside observers who have remarked upon the stark, almost brutal contrasts between the opposite sides of the countries' shared border. But on a number of levels, Mexico is in the grips of a potent process of Americanization as defined by *Webster's Dictionary*: "1: to cause to acquire or conform to American characteristics. 2: to bring (as an area) under the political, cultural, or commercial influence of the U.S."[13] While some scholars might quibble on the grounds that Americanization should be limited to a discussion of strictly cultural penetration, I use the term in its broadest sense in these pages. By way of illustration, one example of Americanization is the pervasive impact of the United States on Mexicans at all levels of society, from the wealthy Arango family who sold off their supermarkets, discount stores, and restaurants to

Wal-Mart for $2 billion, to the small farmer who sees his livelihood endangered by rising imports of cheap Iowa corn.

The consequences of Salinas de Gortari's decision to embrace the free-trade paradigm have been truly far-reaching. Mexico has become a de facto economic colony of the United States in the NAFTA era. Since the trade treaty took effect, Mexican exports to the United States more than quadrupled, from $39.9 billion in 1993 to over $170 billion in 2005, and in most years they account for well over 90 percent of the country's total international trade. Annual U.S. exports to Mexico have nearly tripled, from $41.6 billion in 1993 to $120 billion in 2005, and as of 2006 American capital represented about two-thirds of the $122 billion in total direct foreign investment in Mexico.[14] The increasingly dominant role of U.S. companies in the Mexican economy is epitomized by the likes of Citigroup, which owns what was once the country's biggest bank, and Wal-Mart, the nation's largest private-sector employer with over 150,000 employees on its payroll who work at over 1,000 stores and restaurants nationwide.

But the Americanization of modern Mexico transcends mere dollars and cents. It can be seen in the influence of American traditions, resources, and values on Mexico's social mores, foreign policy, consumer tastes, health problems, and even everyday language. In the realm of politics, for instance, Mexico today has a functioning democracy that, for all of its flaws and foibles, provides the country's three main parties with a reasonably level playing field. Mexico has a freedom of information law modeled on a similar U.S. statute, and it has been widely hailed as an example for other developing countries. Rising awareness in the United States about global warming and other environmental issues has seeped into Mexico, and concerted efforts in recent years to combat the capital city's infamous smog have produced some modest improvement. For my purposes, the term "Americanization" encompasses the best values the United States has to offer—efficiency, accountability, respect for the rule of law—along with a number of its ugliest features—untrammeled consumerism, a surrender to the supremacy of big business, and the rising incidence of social diseases like AIDS, obesity, and drug use. The official name of the country in Spanish may be the United Mexican States, but the United States of Mexico might be a more apposite way of describing the country in this day and age.

"You Should Not Gringoize My People"

Mexicans by and large bristle when they hear the term "Americanization" applied to their proud nation. One of the most searing images from their country's turbulent history is the Carl Nebel lithograph depicting Gen. Winfield Scott's triumphant entry into Mexico City in September 1847 at the head of a U.S. expeditionary force to punctuate the humiliating conclusion of the Mexican War; in the background of the painting is a rendering of the Mexican capital's colonial-era National Palace with the Stars and Stripes flying above it.[15] For most Americans, the Mexican War of 1846–47 is the oldest and least remembered military conflict that the United States has fought on foreign soil. But cross to the other side of the border and the bitter legacies of the war—the sale of half the national territory for $15 million, the unbroken string of ignominious battlefield defeats inflicted on the Mexican army—remain incredibly vivid, the painful memories constantly renewed for successive generations by school textbooks and solemn monuments to the Boy Heroes, the six mostly teenaged military cadets who died in combat defending Mexico City's hilltop Chapultepec Castle in the final hours of the conflict.

Not surprisingly, the slightest inkling of encroaching Americanization has long produced resistance and rejection in Mexico. When one of Pancho Villa's top generals returned from a three-year exile in the United States in 1918 brimming with praise for American society and urging the revolutionary chieftain to seek better relations with the government of President Woodrow Wilson, Villa bluntly chided his comrade-in-arms: "General, as far as I can see, you have become gringoized. . . . Everything that you say is all right, except that you should not gringoize my people."[16] The terms Americanization and *agringado* (the Spanish word actually used by Villa) touch a raw nerve to this day, and in an era of rampant globalization the very notion that their nation might be acquiring the virtues as well as the vices of the United States forces many Mexicans to ask themselves what is happening to their country.

Over the decades, some of Mexico's greatest intellects have sought to highlight the cultural, social, and linguistic differences that distinguish the neighboring countries and the inherent inequalities in their relationship. That was an important theme in a lengthy article the renowned philosopher Octavio Paz published in *The New Yorker* magazine in September 1979. "We are two distinct versions of Western civilization," he wrote. "As for [Mexico's] relationship with the United States, that is still the old relationship of strong and weak, oscillating between indifference and abuse, deceit and cynicism. Most Mexicans hold the justifiable conviction that the treatment received by their country is unfair."[17] But the country that Paz wrote about back then was very different from twenty-first century Mexico. In 1979 the ruling PRI was completing its fifth consecutive decade in power, the Mexican government was still a robust actor in the national economy, and the country's authoritarian political system functioned so smoothly that the Peruvian author Mario Vargas Llosa would memorably dub it "the perfect dictatorship."

The conviction that cultural differences trump economic realities and shared political interests lives on more than a quarter-century later. One of the first persons I interviewed for this project was the highly respected historian Lorenzo Meyer of the government-funded Colegio de México in Mexico City. One of the political analysts most widely quoted in the foreign press, Meyer has written extensively about relations between the United States and Mexico throughout his distinguished career. When I met Meyer for lunch in the summer of 2004, he made it clear from the outset that he wasn't buying this book's central premise. Meyer had suggested we meet at a shopping mall in southern Mexico City called Perisur, one of the capital's first temples of U.S.-style consumerism, and as we scanned our restaurant menus he readily acknowledged the distinctly American look and atmosphere of our physical surroundings that afternoon.

But appearances can be deceiving, he maintained, especially in a place like Mexico. Meyer reminded me that there was nothing faintly Americanized about Andrés Manuel López Obrador, the Mexico City mayor who at the time looked like the prohibitive favorite to win the 2006 presidential election. The folksy left-wing politician from the Gulf Coast state of Tabasco spoke no English, had set foot on U.S. soil only once in his life, and had little in common with Mexico's technocratic ruling class apart from nationality. Carlos Slim, the son of Lebanese immigrants who had parlayed his acquisition of the state-owned Telmex phone monopoly into what is now one of the world's largest fortunes, had in recent times reoriented the foreign investment strategy of his Carso conglomerate toward Latin America after sustaining big losses from the acquisition of a U.S. computer products retail chain. In Meyer's view, these two men in their different ways personified an inescapable reality: the country was simply too Mexican at its core to ever justify description as an Americanizing society. "The middle class is nationalist, and the lower classes are far too Mexican to be able to understand the United States," he told me. "To be especially pro–United States is like a sin, it's not respectable. Mexico cannot Americanize itself."[18]

A similar argument was made by Jorge G. Castañeda long before he was named foreign minister by President Fox and helped forge the most pro-U.S. foreign policy of any government in modern Mexican history. In a 1988 book he coauthored with the former Carter administration adviser Robert Pastor, Castañeda identified what he called the "strong suits" of Mexican culture that served as breakwaters to the tsunami of American social, economic, political, and cultural influence. "Mexico possesses an extraordinarily rich, diversified, historically well-anchored cultural personality of its own," he wrote at the time. "It has its language and shapes, its rhythms and colors, its beliefs and its fantasies. All the McDonald's in the world could never submerge them."[19]

Indeed, there is no denying the profound imprint left on Mexico by its indigenous and Spanish heritage. It is evident everywhere you turn—in the mixed-race physiognomy of its people, in the unique cuisine they prepare, in the temples, churches, and buildings they have erected, in the languages they primarily speak. It bears remembering that Mexico, or New Spain as it was then called, was the jewel in the crown of the Spanish empire for nearly three centuries. It only takes an hour-long stroll among the old convents and plazas in Mexico City's historic downtown to feel the weight of its colonial past, and the unctuously polite manners of its upper crust are a vestige of the fawning courtiers who sought the viceroys' favor. The indigenous civilizations that preceded the conquistador Hernán Cortés achieved levels of economic and social development their native American brethren in more northerly latitudes never remotely approached. The pull of Mexico's pre-Columbian era lives on in the pyramids of the sun and moon that tower over the ancient city of Teotihuacán near the Mexican capital and the Mayan-speaking communities that people the Yucatán Peninsula and the southeastern state of Chiapas.

But the rising influence of the United States cannot be ignored or wished away. Not that some Mexicans don't try: some politically correct types who can't stomach the word "Americanization" opt for more neutral terms like "hybridization" to describe the modernization of their country.[20] Others fall back on the argument that the dreaded A-word is just another way of saying globalization. To my way of thinking, those two words don't always mean the same thing: the BMW dealership and Salvatore Ferragamo boutique that sit astride the main boulevard in the resort city of Cancún are clear examples of European-flavored globalization in the heart of a U.S.-styled resort. But in the context of the North American continent, Americanization strikes me as being the more precise term by far. In a 1999 speech, the former finance minister Jesús Silva Herzog stated the self-evident: "To me, the globalization of Mexico signifies its Americanization."[21] In far more piquant language, the Tijuana poet and essayist Heriberto Yépez posed a pointed question in his irreverent Internet blog called e.n.s.a.m.b.l.e: "Is there any idiot who still believes we are not living in an era of accelerated Americanization?"

There are important limits to this broad trend in today's Mexico. And the country is hardly alone in having succumbed to the onslaught of

Americanization in the last twenty years. But as Paz suggested in his *New Yorker* essay and as any Mexican sixth-grader can readily comprehend, the implications of Americanization contain a special sting for a nation that has suffered so much at the hands of the United States. Those wounds pre-date the disastrous outcome of the Mexican War and stretch back to the rebellion of American settlers in Texas in 1835, which gave rise to an independent republic that would be annexed by the United States a decade later. Mexican governments could do nothing to prevent U.S. forces from occupying the port of Veracruz for seven months in 1914 nor could they halt the cross-border incursion two years later of an American expeditionary force in hot pursuit of Pancho Villa. As recently as the mid-1920s, Mexican presidents had credible fears of U.S. plans to forcibly occupy the country's oil fields. The scars left by that checkered history are reopened every time the Mexican news media reports on the physical dangers facing their countrymen when they clandestinely cross the U.S. border or the bigotry that not a few Americans harbor toward predominantly Mexican undocumented workers.

THE PULL OF *EL OTRO LADO*

There is one notable exception to the general reluctance to accept the Americanization thesis. For political purposes, some prominent figures in the modern Mexican left use it as a handy cudgel for critiquing the pro-capitalist, free-trade economic model adopted by Salinas de Gortari in the early 1990s. One of their most influential voices belongs to Carlos Monsiváis. "People used to think of Mexico City as the mecca, as 'the' city," Monsiváis said in the 1998 interview cited above. "Now it's Los Angeles. California offers jobs, not glamorous jobs, but the young people believe that there are jobs there. And California, to a young Indian from Oaxaca or to people with no real possibilities of jobs in Mexico, offers also a new way of life, a freer and smarter way of life that they don't have in the countryside or in the slums. Of course, that's all a utopian ideal. They're going to find humiliations and low wages. But what they think they have in

Los Angeles is the promise of modernity, being in tune with the changes at the end of the century. And that's what they don't find in Mexico."[22]

The appeal of *El Otro Lado* (The Other Side), as the United States is often called colloquially inside Mexico, is no longer limited to menial laborers who abandon the nation's impoverished hinterland for a better life across the northern border. The country's leading corporate moguls see in the swelling ranks of Mexicans living in the United States a limitless appetite for their tortillas or TV soap operas that will one day surpass their markets at home. Faced with the ongoing decline of what was once Latin America's premier movie industry, Mexico's best actors, filmmakers, and screenwriters flock to Hollywood in ever-growing numbers. Aspiring business executives covet a master's degree from one of the leading U.S. graduate schools of business administration. Cabo San Lucas hotel porters prize tips from American tourists as the primary source of their income. Millions of Mexican teenagers view *El Norte* as the ultimate arbiter in music, fashion, and high-tech gadgetry. Across the board, increasing numbers of Mexicans from all social strata see in Americans and the United States their best hopes for jobs, education, markets, role models, and even inspiration.

This is not a one-way street. Some scholars have identified a Mexicanization process that is gathering steam inside the United States. This is especially pronounced in traditional magnets for Mexican immigrants like California, the Southwest, and the Chicago metropolitan area. But states like South Dakota, Delaware, and Indiana have reported sharp jumps in the size of their native Mexican populations in recent years.[23] Corona displaced Heineken some time ago as the imported beer of choice throughout the country, and Mexican food restaurants have become common sights in much of the rural South. The ugly backlash against undocumented workers that poisoned the atmospherics of the 2008 U.S. presidential campaign was undoubtedly fueled by the influx of Mexican immigrants into parts of the country where few if any Latinos had lived ten or fifteen years before.

The evolving image of the United States in the minds of many Mexicans can be seen in the contrasting responses of two very different politicians to major crises confronting their administrations. When a massive earthquake struck Mexico City on the morning of September 19, 1985, President Miguel de la Madrid initially brushed aside all offers of emergency assistance coming from the United States, or any other foreign country for that matter. In those days, no self-respecting Mexican office-holder could be seen appealing to the United States for help in the face of a natural disaster. The Harvard-educated de la Madrid soon backtracked when the scale of devastation and loss of life wrought by the temblor became fully apparent. But his knee-jerk response in the initial aftermath of the disaster that killed an estimated 20,000 people spoke to a deeply entrenched nationalism that has defined most Mexican governments since the early years of independence.

Seventeen years later, the acknowledged leader of the country's largest left-wing political party had not the slightest qualms about seeking the crime-fighting expertise of a prominent American pol—and a Republican one at that. In 2002 that least Americanized of Mexico's current crop of politicians, Mexico City mayor López Obrador, accepted a proposal from a group of wealthy Mexican businessmen led by Carlos Slim to hire the services of former New York City mayor Rudolph Giuliani's security consulting firm. The success of Giuliani's "zero tolerance" approach to crime fighting on the streets of Manhattan evidently impressed López Obrador, who was under pressure to do something about an epidemic of lawlessness in Mexico City brought into sharp relief by the 2002 kidnapping of two sisters of the Mexican pop music diva Thalia. "Going to Giuliani was symbolic for López Obrador," notes political analyst Luis Rubio of the Mexico City–based Center for Development Research. "It was designed to show the private sector that he meant business."[24] If López Obrador was capable of handing over $4.3 million to Giuliani for advice on how to make Mexico City a safer place, then Mexicans today clearly have fewer inhibitions about asking their rich, powerful, and often insensitive neighbors for help and guidance. That by itself represents a sea change in attitudes and self-perception from the Mexico of a quarter-century ago.

The first part of this book will provide broad overviews of the Mexico I encountered in the 1980s and the country I rediscovered at the dawn of the new century, followed by a discussion of how Mexican attitudes toward the United States have evolved from the early years of independence to the present day. Part two will spotlight the historic transformation wrought by NAFTA inside Mexico and how some of those changes have played themselves out among the country's business elites and in the news media. Part three will analyze the impact of Americanization on four different cities and regions of the country: the immigrant-exporting state of Zacatecas; the can-do industrial titan of Monterrey; the towns of Ajijic and San Miguel de Allende, where hordes of American retirees and aging baby boomers are putting down roots; and the beach resorts of Cancún and Sayulita, which cater to the tastes and needs of gringo tourists. Part four will focus on selected sociological symptoms of Americanization, such as the spread of evangelical Christianity and soaring rates of obesity and substance abuse among the population at large. As he lay on his deathbed in Paris, where he spent his final years in exile, the old dictator Porfirio Díaz could have scarcely realized just how prophetic his legendary aphorism would turn out to be.

Part I

CHAPTER 1

A Chicano Comes to the Big Enchilada

MEXICO CITY, 1984–1987

Octavio Paz was in his late twenties when he won a Guggenheim scholarship to travel to the United States in the 1940s and pursue his studies at the Berkeley campus of the University of California. During his stay in the Golden State, Paz encountered the unique cultural phenomenon known as the *pachucos*, the flamboyantly dressed Chicano gang members who often scuffled with white U.S. Navy sailors in the streets of wartime Los Angeles and came to symbolize Mexican American youth culture of that era. Those zoot suit–sporting youngsters seem to have made quite an impression on the young Paz. The first essay in his masterly meditation on Mexican culture and character, *The Labyrinth of Solitude*, is entitled "The Pachuco and Other Extremes," and in those pages he reflects on what may have motivated those rebellious Mexican Americans to dress and talk in ways that set them apart from mainstream American society.

The language and tone used by Paz to describe these uprooted sons of his own country evoke a zoologist who has stumbled upon a new mutant species he finds faintly repulsive. "[T]he *pachucos* do not attempt to vindicate their race or the nationality of their forebears," wrote Paz. "Their attitude reveals an obstinate, almost fanatical will-to-be, but this will affirms nothing specific except their determination—it is an ambiguous one, as we will see—not to be like those around them. The *pachuco* does not want to become a Mexican again; at the same time he does not want to blend into the life of North America. . . . Whether we like it or not, these persons are Mexicans, are one of the extremes at which the Mexican can arrive."[1]

MIXED EMOTIONS

"Whether we like it or not." That phrase aptly captures the disdain bordering on contempt that many Mexicans of Paz's generation felt toward Chicanos in that era. By the 1970s, of course, it had become politically correct for the intellectual heirs of Paz to embrace the American-born children of Mexican immigrants and deplore the racism they and their parents suffered inside the United States. But as the son of a Mexican couple who entered this world in 1957, my personal memories predated the seventies. I accordingly had rather mixed emotions when my editors at *Newsweek* approached me in the fall of 1983 about the vacant position of Mexico City bureau chief.

From a professional standpoint, it represented a fantastic opportunity that would elevate me to the newsmagazine's team of foreign correspondents at a relatively early stage of my career. I stood to become one of the three *Newsweek* reporters primarily responsible for covering the armed conflicts raging to the south in El Salvador and Nicaragua. I had heard the horror stories about the smog and traffic of "*el D.F.*," the popular shorthand for the Mexican capital adapted from the Spanish-language initials for Federal District (the equivalent of District of Columbia in Washington's case). But as a native of Los Angeles, I was no stranger to either of those urban plagues.

As I contemplated the proposed move to Mexico City and what special circumstances might apply to a Chicano like myself, I recalled the Mexican American academic Julian Nava's account of his first meeting with Mexican foreign minister Jorge Castañeda y Álvarez de la Rosa after President Jimmy Carter named Nava to be U.S. ambassador to Mexico in 1980. "He kept talking to me in English even though I spoke to him in Spanish," Nava wrote in his memoirs. "I figured I should use Spanish since I was in Mexico, but he maintained the conversation in English. I was annoyed."[2]

I knew the feeling. Prior to being offered the Mexico City job, I had encountered a similarly condescending reception on several occasions while on assignment for *Newsweek* in Central America and along the U.S.-Mexican border. But instead of feeling grateful to an English-speaking Latin American for having saved me the tedious task of translating an interview conducted in Spanish, the insecure cub reporter inside me acquired a big chip on his shoulder over the language issue. This reaction was silly of me in hindsight: the reason I lacked a native Spanish speaker's accent was mainly owing to my parents' conscious decision to make English my first language before I started kindergarten. That had nothing to do with any shame they might have harbored about their origins. To the contrary: Joe and Olga Contreras always sought to instill in me their deep-seated pride in our Mexican roots. But they had also seen how the perfectly normal children of other immigrant couples in our working-class Los Angeles suburb of Pico Rivera had been shunted into "special education" classes for the mentally retarded simply because those kids arrived for the first day of classes speaking only Spanish. As practical people with high ambitions for their only child, my parents were not about to let that happen to me. So while they spoke to each other mostly in Spanish, their native tongue gradually took a back seat to the official language of my parents' adopted country in their everyday dealings with me.

In his own unwitting way, my father fed my ambivalence about Mexico. Born Crispín Contreras in the town of Jocotepec on the shores of Lake Chapala in 1902, he was a walking, breathing embodiment of the stereotype associated with natives of the central Mexican state of Jalisco. A diehard fan of the Guadalajara soccer club popularly known as *las chivas*, "Pepe" Contreras was Victorian in his social mores and a right-winger verging on reactionary in his politics. (A hardback copy of Adolf Hitler's *Mein Kampf* occupied a place of honor on the bookshelf, and after backing John F. Kennedy in the 1960 U.S. presidential election because the young Massachusetts senator was a fellow Roman Catholic, my father became a steadfast Republican voter for the rest of his life.) My father openly scorned Mexican Americans and the half-English, half-Spanish sentences many of them spoke. He mocked their allegiance to the Democratic Party, ridiculed their embrace of the term "Chicano" and detested the graffiti-daubing youth gangs who roamed the hardscrabble streets of East Los Angeles and Boyle Heights. In my father's eyes, Chicanos were a hybrid population of underachieving losers who were neither true Americans nor true Mexicans.

My mother was cut from different cloth. Born Consuelo Granillo in the northern Mexican city of Chihuahua in 1924, she was only three years old when she immigrated to El Paso with her mother Leonor and three older siblings. (As an adult, she changed her name to Olga when she became a naturalized United States citizen.) Unlike my father, who could never shed his thick foreign accent, Mom not only achieved a native speaker's level of fluency in written and oral English but also assimilated to a much greater degree with her adopted homeland. My parents were like oil and water even in their politics: Olga made a point of negating Pepe Contreras's unwavering support for Republican candidates by marking an x alongside the names of their Democratic rivals on her ballot.

When Dad would disparage Mexican Americans in our suburban Los Angeles home, he seemed to forget he was in the presence of one. But I didn't—and over time I became acutely sensitized to the differences separating Mexicans from Chicanos. Those were brought home to me on the schoolyard when our family moved to Guadalajara upon my father's retirement from a Los Angeles linen distribution company. I enrolled in the American College of that city in January 1968, and from day one I was treated as just another gringo by my Mexican classmates.

Looking back now, I realize that was completely understandable. After all, my Spanish was rudimentary and I had far more in common with the children of American expatriates attending that school than with the sons and daughters of Guadalajara's upper crust. But the cold shoulder I was shown by many of the Mexican fifth-graders at the American College rankled for many years afterward. When a light-skinned, upper-class undergraduate at the Monterrey Technological Institute for Higher Studies derided Mexican Americans as "border filth" midway through an interview for this book,

I held my tongue but found myself cringing inwardly. That patronizing atti-tude continues to reveal itself in different settings and even among senior Mexican government officials who should know better. When foreign min-ister Luis Ernesto Derbez was asked to explain why four in ten Hispanic vot-ers in the state of Arizona supported a controversial law that restricted state government services to illegal immigrants in a 2004 referendum, the Mexican official replied: "It's sad, and it gives an idea of how we have to work to educate even *our* own Mexican Americans"(emphasis added).[3] When my mom announced in the late spring of 1968 that she was fed up with life in Guadalajara and the sexist attitudes of my father's newfound buddies and was taking me back to Los Angeles, I felt both glad and relieved.

In the end it didn't take me long to accept the *Newsweek* editors' offer of a transfer to Mexico City. Whatever conflicted sentiments I had about mov-ing south of the border weren't going to get in the way of my career ambi-tions. In February 1984 my then wife Caroline and I flew into the Big Enchilada—the irreverent term used by a columnist of Mexico City's lone English-language newspaper to describe the sprawling metropolis—buzzing with excitement over the travel and adventures that would surely await us.

Feuding Neighbors

Through a stroke of pure luck, the house we rented in the elegant neigh-borhood of Lomas de Chapultepec belonged to Alan Riding, the veteran *New York Times* correspondent who was in the process of taking up a new assignment in Rio de Janeiro. An urbane and witty Englishman whose coverage was widely regarded as the gold standard of Mexico City's resi-dent foreign press corps, Riding had just finished writing *Distant Neighbors: A Portrait of the Mexicans*, the 1985 best-seller that instantly became required reading for anyone seriously interested in the country and its people. It soon became clear just how apposite that title was for Riding's seminal profile of late-twentieth-century Mexico.

In the realm of international affairs, for instance, Mexico in the mid-1980s was still charting its own distinctive course. The byproduct of a

fervent patriotism and genuine differences with Washington over national interests and worldviews, Mexico's independent foreign policy collided
head-on with the hawkish instincts of the Reagan administration.
Throughout most of my four-year stint in Mexico City, U.S.-Mexican
relations were a tangled web of tensions and mutual suspicion. When I
arrived in Mexico City in the winter of 1984 the main flashpoint of friction was Central America, where the government of President Miguel de
la Madrid was trying to negotiate a regional peace agreement under the
auspices of the recently formed four-nation Contadora Group. Consisting
of Mexico, Colombia, Venezuela, and Panama, the Contadora Group saw
diplomacy as the only enduring solution to the armed conflicts raging in
El Salvador and Nicaragua. That approach clashed directly with Ronald
Reagan's bellicose Central America policy, which essentially boiled down
to the overthrow of the Sandinista *comandantes* in Managua by any means
necessary, coupled with massive military and economic support for the
pro-U.S. government in El Salvador.

The opening salvo in what became an increasingly public war of words
was fired by an American general in the same month I landed in Mexico.
Testifying before a U.S. Senate hearing in February 1984, Gen. Paul
Gorman called the country a "one-party state" that had opened its doors
to Marxist guerrilla movements from El Salvador and become "the center
for subversion throughout Central America." The Panama-based head of
the U.S. Southern Command predicted that, in the absence of dramatic
change, Mexico would become Washington's "number one security problem" in the next ten years. The blunt language of the general, who
betrayed a limited understanding of geography when he branded Mexico
"the most corrupt government and society in Central America,"[4] blind-
sided the U.S. State Department, which hastened to disavow Gorman's
remarks as his "personal views." But the damage had already been done
south of the border. A foreign ministry spokesman hastily denounced
Gorman's assertion as a "stupidity" and "a danger to the security of
Mexico" that could be used by Washington as a pretext "to intervene in
our country."[5]

Gorman's congressional testimony was the first in a string of pronouncements and leaked memos by senior U.S. officials aimed at bullying the Mexican government into a change of course on Central America. *Newsweek* ran a brief story in April 1984 about a proposal by then U.S. National Security Council adviser Constantine Menges to devise "a diplomacy master plan" that would eventually convince the Mexican government to back the Reagan administration's obsessive war against communism in Central America.[6] The Menges initiative never got anywhere, but the timing of the story's publication, coming only a month before de la Madrid's first visit to Washington as president in May of that year, raised eyebrows in both capitals. On the eve of his arrival, the syndicated columnist Jack Anderson published a thinly documented story in the *Washington Post* claiming that de la Madrid had "stashed away" $162 million in a personal Swiss bank account. Anderson based the story on interviews with unnamed Reagan administration officials and classified U.S. intelligence documents he claimed to have seen.[7] As with the Menges memo, nothing concrete ever came out of the Jack Anderson column. But to de la Madrid and his aides, it all smacked of an elaborate, orchestrated effort by hard-liners in Washington to turn up the heat on the Mexicans over Central America.

The dissonance between the distant neighbors rose to a din nine months later after gunmen snatched a U.S. Drug Enforcement Administration (DEA) agent off the streets of Guadalajara in broad daylight. The kidnapping and subsequent murder of DEA agent Enrique "Kiki" Camarena Salazar in February 1985 brought a swift response from U.S. officials, who deliberately slowed traffic coming in from Mexico along the countries' 1,951-mile-long border. Code-named "Operation Intercept," the measure was portrayed by U.S. officials as part of the ongoing manhunt for the missing DEA agent. But the real motive behind the operation was to prod Mexico into cracking down on its "criminal elements, including drug traffickers," said John Gavin, the highly controversial U.S. ambassador to Mexico at the time.[8]

A preening second-rate actor who was the only U.S. envoy in my experience ever to insist that reporters rise when he entered the room for a news conference, Gavin became the living, breathing incarnation of the Ugly American for millions of Mexicans. Gavin's propensity to hold high-profile meetings with Mexican opposition party leaders and to lecture government officials on the need to make their country more democratic incensed de la Madrid and his cabinet secretaries. But this uniquely undiplomatic ambassador accurately reflected the Mexico-bashing views of several top officials back in Washington. Their ranks included CIA director William Casey, who fretted about a tidal wave of illegal immigrants washing across the Mexican border if communism ever established a lasting beachhead in Central America; U.S. Customs Commissioner William von Raab, who saw in Operation Intercept an excellent opportunity to punish Mexico for its sluggish response to the emergence of major drug trafficking rings; and Elliot Abrams, the pugnacious assistant secretary of state for inter-American affairs who once told a closed-door U.S. Senate hearing that Mexicans suffered from a tendency "to define their foreign policy in opposition to ours," a tradition he traced back to the Mexican War of 1846–47 and that mirrored "a desire to be distant from us in whatever policy we are taking."[9]

In this campaign of neighbor bashing, administration hard-liners were sometimes aided and abetted by American correspondents based in Mexico, and I don't exempt myself from that assertion. As the anti-Mexican chorus was reaching a crescendo in Washington in the spring of 1986, the international edition of *Newsweek* weighed in with a lengthy article under my byline about the tarnished credibility of de la Madrid at home and abroad. The cover image of that issue featured a destitute-looking street waif standing in a grimy Mexico City alley under the words "Broken Promises."[10] The story later earned *Newsweek* a formal motion of censure in the lower chamber of the Mexican congress that was introduced by a lawmaker of the ruling PRI party.

As I passed the midway point of my four-year stint in Mexico City in 1986, the distant neighbors seemed even more at loggerheads than had been the case when Riding was writing his book. Therein lay a certain irony: from the outset of his presidency de la Madrid, the first in a series of

Ivy League–educated technocrats who would govern Mexico in the 1980s and 1990s, adopted a far less indulgent stance toward the Sandinistas and the Cuban-backed Salvadoran guerrilla forces than had his radical-chic predecessor José López Portillo, who had openly sympathized with both rebel movements. De la Madrid had declined repeated invitations from the Sandinista leader Daniel Ortega to visit Managua, suspended heavily subsidized oil deliveries to Nicaragua, and demanded cash payments up front for future deliveries of Mexican crude. That policy shift won grudging praise even from Elliot Abrams. "They are distancing themselves from Nicaragua," the Reagan administration official conceded during a 1986 U.S. Senate hearing. "That we view, obviously, as a positive step."[11]

But that "positive step" went only so far in Ronald Reagan's Washington. To the saber-rattling anticommunists of the U.S. government, anything less than a total embrace of the crusade to unseat the Sandinistas was insufficient. "The problem lay in the fact that while Mexico may have stepped back from the left, the Reagan administration was moving even further to the right," wrote Jorge G. Castañeda. "As Mexico was toning down its peacemaking initiatives and muting its criticism of U.S. policy in Central America, Washington was raising the stakes and increasing its own commitment to bringing down the Sandinistas."[12]

De la Madrid's exasperation at the height of the American campaign against Mexico comes through loud and clear in his memoir *Cambio de rumbo* (A Change of Course). The president felt an almost visceral loathing for Gavin, whose strutting style de la Madrid likened to a "proconsul." But de la Madrid also recognized that the abrasive U.S. ambassador was no loose cannon on the deck of Ronald Reagan's ship of state. "It seems absurd that the United States would want to kick us around," noted de la Madrid. "And yet, that's exactly what it is doing." There were times when the Mexican president despaired of any improvement in relations with the United States during his term in office. "We are facing boorish people who, instead of seeking a mutual understanding, want to impose their will," wrote the gray technocrat with uncharacteristic candor. "That leads me to suspect that our relations will not change very much."[13]

STRANGER IN A STRANGE LAND

But it wasn't just differences over foreign policy that separated the neighbors. Economic policies and cultural values also deepened the divide. Given its relative proximity to the U.S. border, the Mexico City I got to know in the mid-1980s was a remarkably un-Americanized world capital. True, Fords and Chevrolets plied the streets of the city, the Coca-Cola logo was ubiquitous, and the latest Hollywood blockbusters dominated movie theater screens. Thanks to cable television, I could watch the *CBS Evening News* with Dan Rather, check out the latest MTV music videos, and frequently tune into live broadcasts of Los Angeles Dodgers baseball games—my hometown team whose roster featured the pride of Sonora, the screwball-hurling pitcher Fernando Valenzuela. "There is no question that consumption patterns among the urban middle class are increasingly 'American,'" wrote Castañeda in 1988. A political science professor at the time who would follow in his father's footsteps twelve years later when Vicente Fox appointed him foreign minister, Castañeda hedged that observation by arguing that middle-class Mexicans were adopting those consumption patterns not because they were American but because such tastes were most suited to people of their socioeconomic strata. "Hamburgers, jeans, rock music, a certain sexual liberation, are telltale signs of the apparent growth of American influence in Mexico in recent years," he noted. "Are all these trends essentially American, or did they originate in the U.S. because the underlying economic and social processes which gave birth to them first emerged there? Is [rock music] so popular because it is American, or because it is tailored for middle-class consumption? Are blue jeans American, or middle class?"[14]

The answers to Castañeda's rhetorical questions are pretty straightforward. The intrinsically "middle-class" properties of Levi's 501 jeans are a fiction, given the trousers' early history as a staple of the American working class well before the denim look became fashionable in the 1950s. The pelvic gyrations of the young Elvis Presley actually scandalized millions of middle-class parents in suburbs and small towns across the United States before the king of rock and roll became a mainstream celebrity suitable for Las Vegas stages. In fact, blue jeans, rock music, and hamburgers conquered the planet precisely because each represented in its own way a slice of the American way of life.

But however Americanized the Mexican middle class was becoming on a superficial level by the 1980s, the country still had a fairly closed economy that restricted the entry of U.S. companies and their products into the national marketplace. The banks were in the hands of the government and the major hotel chains were Mexican-owned, as were the supermarkets where Caroline and I shopped. The fresh produce and canned foods were nearly all homegrown, and the beer on offer came almost exclusively from local breweries. While hamburgers were plentiful, there was but one McDonald's in the entire country in 1985. Most American goods were either impossible to find in Mexico City stores or prohibitively expensive—to the point where my wife and I made a special trip to the border city of El Paso to purchase a changing table, baby stroller, playpen, and other related items when Caroline became pregnant with our first daughter. "When I was growing up," wrote the Mexican journalist Rossana Fuentes-Berain, "Mexico had one party: the PRI; one church: the Roman Catholic; and one brand available for every product: a Mexican one."[15]

Some of the rhythms and customs of Mexico City were unlike anything I had ever seen in the United States. Punctuality was still an alien concept for many *chilangos*—the originally pejorative nickname, now in vogue, for residents of the Mexican capital—to the point where I always took a magazine or book with me to an interview appointment in the almost certain knowledge I would not be received at the designated hour. Productivity was another American value that had not yet taken root in Mexico City, a fact of life affirmed on a daily basis by the traditional ritual of the leisurely, three-course afternoon lunch. Sources almost never returned phone calls, and the job title of government spokesman seemed like an oxymoron, since most of the ones I dealt with appeared to be under instructions never to speak to the foreign press. The air in Mexico City was dirty, the aromas from the sidewalk food stalls were pungent, and the noise of the traffic and car horns could be deafening. There was nothing bland or homogenized about the sights and sounds of the Mexico of that era. Its sheer otherness made a powerful impression on all outsiders, even to one like myself with strong ties to the country and its culture on both sides of his family.

Some Mexican institutions were little more than empty imperson- ations of their American counterparts. This was especially true of what passed for mainstream journalism in the 1980s. When I picked up the morning edition of the Mexico City newspaper *Excélsior* each day, I found myself marveling at how anyone could bring himself to actually read the rag. A typical front page of the broadsheet was an unsightly clutter of a dozen or more stories topped by a meaningless headline often lifted directly from the president's latest speech ("The Demands of the Majority Are Resolved without Demagoguery" was one of my all-time favorites).

Some Mexicans deluded themselves into thinking of Jacobo Zabludovsky, the evening news anchor for the country's dominant televi- sion network Televisa, as a local equivalent of the legendary *CBS News* broadcaster Walter Cronkite. But there was nothing about Zabludovsky's uncritical parroting of the official line from the Mexican presidential res- idence of Los Pinos that remotely approached the healthy skepticism of American television networks' news coverage. The cozy relationship of both *Excélsior* and Televisa with the government was summed up by a photo the newspaper published during de la Madrid's first foreign trip as president to four Latin American countries in March 1984: the grainy, black-and-white image showed Zabludovsky and *Excélsior* editor Regino Díaz Redondo hobnobbing with the president during a stopover in the Colombian capital of Bogotá. Only the weekly magazine *Proceso* and the tabloid *La Jornada* were worth reading on a regular basis in those years, but with both publications a discerning reader had to filter out the stri- dently left-wing editorial slant in their coverage of foreign affairs.

The spirited in-fighting among Democrats and Republicans for the pres- idential nominations of their respective parties was conspicuous by its absence in Mexican politics. De la Madrid came to power as the literally handpicked successor of López Portillo, and though he took office with a pledge to promote the "moral renovation" of Mexican society, the phrase soon rang hollow. I was one of many foreign correspondents who saw first-hand how the government engaged in blatant ballot box stuffing to ensure victories for PRI gubernatorial candidates in the northern border states of Sonora and Chihuahua. The last cover story I wrote out of Mexico for *Newsweek* was de la Madrid's anointment of Carlos Salinas de Gortari as the PRI's candidate in the 1988 election, thereby perpetuating the country's time-honored but thoroughly undemocratic means of choosing the next president of the republic.[16] However shrill some of Gen. Paul Gorman's remarks about Mexico may have seemed at the outset of my assignment, his characterization of the country as a one-party state was not entirely off the mark.

The ulterior motives of Mexico-bashers like Gorman were reprehensible in many instances. But much of what they said needed to be said by somebody. To the Mexico City intelligentsia, North Carolina's xenophobic Republican senator Jesse Helms must have seemed a walking, breathing caricature of the bigoted American white southerner. But some of his frank criticisms of Mexico's bogus democracy at a 1986 U.S. Senate hearing were way overdue. "I would say to the Mexican government, open up your electoral process to review and inspection," declared Helms, to the dismay of even some Reagan administration officials. "Mexico deserves no help from the international community until this is done. And let the press in Mexico speak with an open mind. Let all of the political parties in Mexico criticize the process and recommend reforms."[17]

Damn Yankees

The hostility that dominated U.S.-Mexican relations in that period was by no means a one-way street. Reams have been written about the conflicted feelings that their northern neighbors evoke among Mexicans, and one of de la Madrid's senior cabinet ministers recalls the mid-1980s as a time when anti-gringo sentiment ran particularly high at all levels of society. "There was an anti-American sentiment not only in the foreign ministry and the government but also in Mexican public opinion," said the former cabinet secretary. De la Madrid later accused his own diplomats of allowing emotion to prevail over reason when it came to the United States. "They feel hatred toward the United States," he stated in his memoirs, "because throughout our history the governments of that country have exploited and abused the dependence we have on them. Naturally, our relations have not been helped by the stance of the current U.S. administration."[18]

No issue, it seemed, was too peripheral for Mexican diplomats who wanted to display their defiance of Washington. The African colony of Namibia was a case in point: the Mexican ambassador to the United Nations incurred the Reagan administration's wrath when he voted for a resolution sponsored by several black African countries that censured the United States and other Western powers for not doing more to help Namibia gain its independence from the white minority government of South Africa. Among Western Hemisphere countries, only Cuba and Sandinista-ruled Nicaragua voted against the United States on more occasions at the U.N. than Mexico in the mid-1980s. That displeased both the Reagan administration and de la Madrid, who later chided his foreign minister Bernardo Sepúlveda Amor in print. "The problem is that Sepúlveda has fallen into the trap offered by the relationship with the United States," wrote de la Madrid. "No matter what the motive might be, we cannot pick fights with the United States."[19]

The nadir of de la Madrid's presidency came on the most public of stages. On May 31, 1986, over 100,000 soccer fans filed into Mexico City's Azteca Stadium for the first match of the sport's ultimate showcase event, the World Cup. And when de la Madrid took the microphone to formally inaugurate the quadrennial tournament, much of his prepared speech was drowned out by a prolonged din of jeers and catcalls. The president's humiliation in front of the world's television cameras capped what was probably de la Madrid's single worst month in office. The money-losing Fundidora de Monterrey, the oldest steel mill in Latin America, declared itself bankrupt on May 8. Its rusting smokestacks overlooking the northern industrial city of Monterrey instantly became a demoralizing symbol of the recession de la Madrid inherited from his predecessor and which seemed to have no end in sight. The ongoing U.S. Senate hearings chaired by Jesse Helms stoked outrage in the

Mexico City press and prompted the de la Madrid government to deliver a rare diplomatic note of protest to the State Department.

But it was the Azteca Stadium episode that really touched a nerve inside the usually imperturbable Mexican president. Recalling that the assembled fans were drawn largely from the country's middle and upper middle classes on account of the expensive price of game tickets, de la Madrid in later years blamed the booing on "a new Mexican bourgeoisie" whose most noticeable trait was "its penchant for expressing its dissatisfaction with the realities facing us." In his memoir, he asserted that the conservative National Action Party (PAN) owed much of its improving political fortunes during his presidency to those petulant upper-middle-class Mexicans. De la Madrid held this nouveau-riche class responsible for encouraging the once timid Mexican right to accuse him of needlessly straining relations with the United States in recent months. The president attributed those allegations to a "frankly pro–United States affiliation" among "wide segments of the private sector and . . . the wealthy classes."[20]

From my seat in the press section of the Azteca that afternoon, de la Madrid looked like a spent political force. He was still on the defensive over his bungled handling of the catastrophic Mexico City earthquake of the previous year, and the PRI was facing an unusually stiff challenge from the PAN in an upcoming gubernatorial election in Chihuahua. The Contadora Group's peace initiative in Central America had all but expired in the face of the Reagan administration's single-minded drive to overthrow the Sandinista regime in Nicaragua. With two and a half years still left in his presidential term, de la Madrid had become a national laughingstock for many of his countrymen: some wags referred to him as *Presidente Mas de la Misma Historia* (President More of the Same Story), a sarcastic nickname derived from his full name, Miguel de la Madrid Hurtado.

A Warming Trend

But the crisis atmosphere that soured U.S.-Mexican relations during the first two years of my Mexico City stint quietly dissipated in the months after the

Azteca Stadium debacle. John Gavin's decision to resign as U.S. ambassador in the summer of 1986 removed one particularly irksome thorn in de la Madrid's side. In July Mexico finally concluded an agreement with the International Monetary Fund (IMF) that would provide the country with $1.6 billion in new credits. Perhaps spooked by the very real possibility of a default on Mexico's massive foreign debt, the U.S. Treasury Department had played a constructive, behind-the-scenes role and urged IMF officials to relax some of the rigid spending and fiscal targets they routinely imposed on developing nations. De la Madrid encountered an altogether different reception at the Reagan White House in August of that year. The cast of characters had not changed—Abrams was among the senior officials in the entourage who accompanied Reagan—but de la Madrid's hosts uncharacteristically emphasized the modest progress Mexico had made in the war against drugs. "The atmosphere . . . was surprisingly positive," de la Madrid later recalled. "I have the impression that Reagan was anxious about the level of tension that relations between Mexico and the United States had reached."[21]

The warming trend went unnoticed by most of us in the Mexico City foreign press corps, however. Throughout most of my four years, the Mexican capital served primarily as a launching pad for recurring trips to Central America, and I could informally gauge the state of bilateral ties by the number of days I physically spent inside Mexico. The more time I spent at home, the greater the strains in the relationship—and by that yardstick 1985, the year of DEA agent "Kiki" Camarena's murder in Guadalajara and the Reagan administration's retaliatory crackdown along the Mexican border, was surely the time when the distance separating the neighbors became a gaping chasm.

By the end of 1986, however, the Reagan administration found itself on the defensive over its Nicaragua policy. White House officials had their hands full with allegations that the administration had circumvented congressional restrictions on channeling more money to the anti-Sandinista guerrillas known as the contras by secretly selling arms to Iran. There was little enthusiasm left in the White House for continued arm-twisting of Mexico on behalf of a Central America policy under siege on Capitol Hill.

By the winter of 1986–1987, the same country that had been treated as a whipping boy by the Reagan administration on drug trafficking issues two years ago was being touted to the U.S. Congress as a success story for its counter-narcotics efforts. When Jesse Helms introduced a resolution in the Senate that year calling for the imposition of sanctions against Mexico, some of his fellow Republican senators, with the tacit backing of the Reagan White House, openly opposed the proposal. The proposed Helms amendment was defeated in due course.[22]

HEADING FOR THE EXITS

When I left Mexico at the beginning of 1988, the country's short-term prospects didn't inspire great hope in me. De la Madrid was still struggling to pull the economy out of its worst downturn since the Great Depression, and his talk of "moral renovation" had been exposed as so much empty sloganeering. Drug trafficking ranked as one of Mexico's few growth industries.

As had been the case twenty years earlier when my parents moved back to Los Angeles from Guadalajara, I wasn't particularly sorry to be leaving—and we also had plenty of new incentives for a change of scenery. The birth of our daughter Claire had crystallized our anxieties about the health hazards that smog-infested Mexico City posed to its inhabitants. The news story in Central America was fizzling as Reagan went into crisis-management mode over the Iran Contra scandal. On a professional note I was discovering that a foreign correspondent starts to lose his energy and freshness of perspective by the fourth or fifth year of covering the same patch of turf. The time had come to move on.

I felt immense gratitude for the opportunity to have traveled around the country and make the acquaintance of some of my mother's relatives who were still living in Chihuahua state. I was leaving the country with more blood ties, through the birth of our two daughters, than when I had arrived. But I had found the formality of upper-class Mexicans to be stifling at times. The crude racism of the country's predominantly white elites could be difficult to swallow: I vividly recall an incident in our neighborhood supermarket when a light-skinned, well-dressed Mexican mistook my swarthy and somewhat informally attired *Time* magazine colleague Ricardo Chavira for a manual laborer and spoke to him accordingly. As the day of our departure approached, I realized that my ambivalence about Mexico had not appreciably diminished. I felt about the country the way I imagined some liberal American Jews feel about Israel—a homeland with a host of problems, injustices, and hypocrisies. But there was no getting around the fact that it was still the homeland, warts and all.

The American imprint on Mexico had spread over the course of our four-year stay despite all the recent political tensions. U.S. companies accounted for over two-thirds of all direct foreign investment in the country in the mid-1980s. The number of in-bond assembly plants known as *maquiladoras*, most of which were U.S.-owned or -affiliated, had nearly doubled in six years, from 600 in 1981 to over 1,000 by the middle of 1987. The de la Madrid government's decision to join the General Agreement on Trade and Tariffs treaty in 1986 represented the first step on the path toward economic integration with the United States that would culminate in the NAFTA accords eight years later. A significant degree of Americanization had also penetrated Mexican youth culture.

But the identity of the homeland remained as vibrant and unique as ever. At the end of the day, Mexican-ness was very much alive and well south of the border. The country's approach to relations with the Great Colossus hadn't changed much, either. Miguel de la Madrid had many faults as president, but he never wilted in the face of the Reagan administration's pressure tactics on Central America. Looking back on that period, I now believe that the mid-1980s bore witness to the worst deterioration in relations between the distant neighbors since President Woodrow Wilson dispatched U.S. troops to occupy the Gulf Coast port of Veracruz at the height of the Mexican Revolution in 1914. And to their credit, de la Madrid and his aides largely stood their ground. "In foreign policy and the way both countries view the world," concluded

Jorge G. Castañeda in 1988, "the differences between the two countries are not fading."[23] But those differences would narrow significantly many years later after Castañeda became foreign minister under Vicente Fox—and the elitist intellectual widely known as *El Güero* (The Blond) would wind up steering Mexico's policy toward the United States in a new, friendlier, and often controversial direction.

CHAPTER 2

Not Such Distant Neighbors

MEXICO IN THE ERA OF VICENTE FOX

Twelve years elapsed before I next set foot in Mexico. My career trajectory at *Newsweek* had taken me to South America, southern Africa, and the Middle East, and during that time I had only casually followed events in Mexico. I had seen the headlines: the 1988 presidential election brazenly stolen by the Mexican government on behalf of the ruling PRI party's handpicked nominee Carlos Salinas de Gortari; the signing of the North American Free Trade Agreement (NAFTA), which was supposed to represent Salinas de Gortari's crowning achievement as president; and the outbreak of the left-wing Zapatista rebellion in the southern state of Chiapas on the first day of 1994 when NAFTA took effect. Though I registered these events, I never really delved into them for a simple reason: at that point in time I had no reason to believe I would ever go back to Mexico as a reporter in the foreseeable future. I had moved on to different continents, cultures, and wavelengths, and I was not in the habit of keeping abreast of news in old stomping grounds.

That changed quite suddenly when the magazine transferred me to its Miami bureau in the summer of 1999. Latin America was now firmly back on my radar screen, and a year later an editor in the New York headquarters asked me to accompany the magazine's special diplomatic correspondent, Lally Weymouth, on a mission to Mexico City ahead of what would turn out to be a presidential election of absolutely historic proportions.

Weymouth had three overriding objectives for that visit—to sit down with the two leading candidates in the campaign, National Action Party (PAN) nominee Vicente Fox and Francisco Labastida of the PRI, and also land a rare interview with the outgoing incumbent, Ernesto Zedillo. These meetings would not represent my first encounter with the high and mighty of Mexico: that had occurred in 1984, when the office of Manuel Alonso, the dour press secretary of Miguel de la Madrid, offered *Newsweek* an unsolicited interview with his boss ahead of the Mexican president's ill-fated trip to Washington. With a smartly dressed military aide standing at attention behind his chair in a wood-paneled office inside the presidential residence of Los Pinos, de la Madrid lived up to his image as a dull, starchy technocrat: his answers had a rehearsed, prerecorded sound to them. The interview was conducted in Spanish from start to finish, with an official translator on hand, even though the Harvard-educated president was known to speak good English.

Lally's first appointment was with Fox, whose support as measured in the latest polls appeared to be dropping with the election still more than three weeks away. Looking tired and a bit harried, the PAN candidate arrived late for the interview at his campaign headquarters in the Fiesta Americana hotel along Mexico City's majestic boulevard, the Paseo de la Reforma. But from the outset it became clear that Fox was a very different breed of politician from the ones I had covered in the 1980s. His craggy good looks and towering height had earned Fox the nickname The Marlboro Man, and his business background as a former president of Coca-Cola's Mexican operations reinforced the image of a man ready to lead the country into the twenty-first century. He turned up for the interview in his trademark cowboy boots and answered all of Lally's questions in flawless English.

My lord, how times had changed. For politicians of de la Madrid's generation, the notion of doing an interview with an American reporter in English would have been unthinkable. "Protocol required a president to speak Spanish in public," de la Madrid told me at his private residence in Mexico City many years later.[1] I still recalled how some Mexican pundits wondered at the time whether de la Madrid's government minister, Manuel Bartlett, one of the top contenders within the PRI for the party's presidential nomination in the 1988 elections, could ever reach Los Pinos with a surname like his. By the summer of 2000, no such musings were being heard about the electoral prospects of a candidate like Fox, the grandson of an American who had immigrated to Mexico from Cincinnati in the late nineteenth century. For his part, President Zedillo also had no qualms about answering Lally's questions in her native language, and while Labastida did speak to her in Spanish through an interpreter, the PRI's anointed candidate was already on the record as saying that all Mexican children should learn English.

The undercurrents in U.S.-Mexican relations had also changed noticeably. In his meeting with Lally, Labastida opined that relations with the United States were experiencing "a magnificent moment"[2]—a sharp departure from the frictions that had overshadowed so much of de la Madrid's presidency in the mid-1980s. Zedillo went one step further, declaring that in outgoing President Bill Clinton "Mexico had a very good friend,"[3] praise that no Mexican politician would have ever lavished on Ronald Reagan in 1988.

NEGROPONTE'S VISION

The failure of government officials to anticipate events is an endless source of grist for journalistic mills around the world. Whether it be the 9/11 attacks on New York and Washington, the disastrous course that the war in Iraq would follow, or the collapse of levees in New Orleans in the wake of Hurricane Katrina, reporters rise to the pinnacle of their profession by documenting how those in power ignored signs of impending disaster or downplayed the threat posed by a foreign government or terrorist organization.

But every so often there comes to light a document revealing the foresight of a public servant who grasped the full consequences and implications of a particular government measure or policy. Such a document was written in the spring of 1991 by the then U.S. ambassador to

Mexico, John Negroponte, to the State Department's top official on Latin American affairs. The topic of the confidential memo was NAFTA, which was then under negotiation by the United States, Mexico, and Canada. Subsequent events would amply bear out Negroponte's prediction of how such a trade accord would reshape the perennially prickly relationship between Washington and Mexico City.

"Mexico is in the process of dramatically changing the substance and image of its foreign policy," began the memo, which was addressed to then U.S. Assistant Secretary of State for Western Hemispheric Affairs Bernard Aronson and later leaked to the Mexican weekly magazine *Proceso*. "It has switched from an ideological, nationalistic, and protectionist approach to a pragmatic, outreaching, and competitive view of world affairs. The compelling factor in this change was the failure of the previous approach to respond to the real needs of the Mexican people, but better and more responsible leadership was also clearly an indispensable factor.

"Next, the economic dimension," wrote Negroponte. "Concurrent with the replacement of Third-World demagoguery by responsible internationalism, was the decision to reform the internal economy to make it more open to foreign investment and competition. Hence, privatization, revision of investment rules and a genuine turn-around in attitudes towards foreign investment in most sectors of the economy. Again, the compelling factor was to create conditions of business confidence and economic growth more responsive to the needs of the Mexican people."

The American envoy envisioned a seismic shift in Mexico's policy toward the United States. "The prospect of an FTA [free trade agreement] must be seen in the context of these reformist trends which started in the mid-1980's and were dramatically accelerated by Salinas after he came to office in 1988. The proposal for an FTA is in a way the capstone of these new policy approaches. From a foreign policy perspective, an FTA would *institutionalize acceptance of a North American orientation to Mexico's foreign relations.* Just think of how this contrasts with past behavior. Previously, as now, 60 or 70 percent of Mexico's business would be with the United States; but if you listened to us in the U.N. or debating Central America,

you would have thought we were archenemies. The fact that the preponderance of Mexico's foreign dealings were with the United States was carefully masked through various defensive mechanisms [emphasis added]."
The conclusion reached by Negroponte spoke to a new paradigm in the
bilateral relationship. "In a way, therefore, adoption of an FTA would help
put on an open and legitimate footing what many feel should have been
the reality of U.S./Mexico relations a long time ago."[4]

The career diplomat knew whereof he wrote. Negroponte was serving
as U.S. ambassador to Honduras in the mid-1980s when tensions between
the de la Madrid government and the Reagan administration spiked over
drug trafficking and Central America. From his perch in Tegucigalpa,
where he helped oversee Washington's covert campaign to topple the
Sandinista regime in neighboring Nicaragua, Negroponte was well positioned to monitor the public jousting over foreign policy that had soured
U.S.-Mexican relations. As a onetime protégé of Henry Kissinger,
Negroponte viewed those bilateral ties through his mentor's prism of
Realpolitik. And as Negroponte's prescient memo argued, the two countries had come to share too many mutual interests to justify the arm's
length remove that had separated them throughout most of the previous
eight decades after the fall of the Porfirio Díaz regime.

". . . AND SO CLOSE TO THE UNITED STATES"

The high marks given to Bill Clinton and the willingness of leading politicians to give interviews in English were but two of the many signs of rising American influence I noticed upon my return to Mexico in the late
spring of 2000. Once a rare sight on city sidewalks, the Converse All-Star
sneaker had become de rigueur footwear for millions of young Mexicans.
Chilango college students sipped cups of white mocha frappuccino and
caramel macchiato espresso at the Starbucks opposite the famous Angel
monument to Mexican independence on the Paseo de la Reforma. Parents
took their kids to a sprawling Six Flags amusement park on the southern
outskirts of Mexico City.

Valet parking had become a standard service at fashionable restaurants. At the other end of the gastronomic spectrum, millions of Mexicans feasted on Big Macs at 292 McDonald's outlets nationwide and ate up Whoppers at nearly 200 Burger Kings. So tight had the Mexican embrace of American junk-food culture become that it was blamed for a 50 percent drop in the sale of Mexican sandwiches known as *tortas* over a ten-year period and a 25 percent decline in the consumption of tortillas between 1998 and 2004.[5] (There were limits to that embrace, however: Taco Bell had to close its four branches in Mexico City within a year of entering the market when its insipid version of Tex-Mex fast food found little favor among consumers.) I later discovered a restaurant in the Mexican heartland whose owners had introduced a complete and heretofore inconceivable ban on smoking, a decidedly American trend. The tobacco-free policy seemed all the more noteworthy because the restaurant, Dorados de Villa, was located in the city of Zacatecas, a jewel of colonial-era architecture that for some reason is rarely visited by most American tourists.

The country had become wired—and wireless. From the coffee-growing town of Coatepec in Veracruz to the immigrant-exporting city of Jerez in Zacatecas, every community of any reasonable size seemed to have conveniently located internet cafes where I could check my e-mail. Wireless access for laptop computers was fast becoming a commonplace feature of cafes and major airports throughout the republic. Ads sponsored by the world's telecommunications giants vied for the Mexican yuppie's attention, such as the poster touting a so-called smartphone from Nokia that read, "For the workaholic inside us whom we all deny." While the waistlines of some Mexicans were getting noticeably bigger, others were heading in the opposite direction after absorbing the American physical fitness ethic: on weekday mornings, Mexico City's Chapultepec Park played host to dozens of local residents dressed in sweatsuits and running shoes who jogged, rode bicycles, or simply walked to stay healthy. In major cities more schoolchildren celebrated Halloween than the traditional religious holiday that falls on November 2 and is known as the Day of the Dead. American-style malls had become entrenched fixtures of the suburban landscape.

The television screen had become almost as ubiquitous in some parts of Mexico as in the United States: from *taquerías* to elegant Mexico City restaurants like Villa María and Los Canarios, screens bombarded diners with music videos, sporting events, and CNN's Spanish-language newscasts at all hours of the day. When I boarded a bus in Mexico City for the seventy-five-minute ride to the city of Cuernavaca one afternoon, my fellow passengers sat glued to the TV monitors hanging from the ceiling of the vehicle that were screening an inane Hollywood comedy called *Jersey Girl* starring Jennifer Lopez and Ben Affleck. On the return trip to the capital city, a different group of passengers was equally transfixed by the latest James Bond film, *Die Another Day.*

No example of what passes for American pop culture in the twenty-first century seemed too vulgar or mindless for the tastes of some Mexicans. *Big Brother* and other programs inspired by American "reality TV" racked up high ratings. The popular TV talk show host Adal Ramones wore a baseball cap during tapings of his program in a studio that looked like a replica of *The Tonight Show* sound stage where the American comedian Jay Leno delivered nightly monologues on the NBC television network. The Miami-based Univision TV anchorman Jorge Ramos once told me that, with the exception of soccer broadcasts and the durable workhorse of Mexican television known as the *telenovela* (soap opera), nearly all of the programming he saw on his periodic trips back to his native Mexico City seemed modeled on American television.

That most monotonous and redneck-friendly of American sports, the NASCAR stock car races that feature overpowered Chevrolets and Fords and Dodges endlessly spinning around oval tracks, made their debut in Mexico City in March 2005 before a sellout crowd of nearly 100,000 cheering fans. A rendition of the Mexican national anthem was followed by three young pop music crooners who sang the American national anthem a cappella while U.S. flags fluttered from poles above the race track. The implications of Mexico's very visible Americanization did not escape the barbed tongue of the Mexican left's traditional patron saint, Fidel Castro. "Ask a number of Mexican children, for example, who were the founding fathers of their country, and many of them probably won't know the answer," Castro told a conference in Havana during a tirade against NAFTA in 1998. "But they sure know who is Mickey Mouse and other cartoon characters that come from the United States."[6]

Changing consumer tastes were among the more tangible legacies of the NAFTA era. Another could be heard in the growing importance and penetration of the English language. The classified ad sections of Mexico City newspapers were littered with entries from employers seeking job applicants with advanced fluency in English. An advertising flyer for a Mexico City foreign language school declared: "Knowing English can save your life."

The global language had become embedded in the daily discourse of modern Mexicans, from the president on down. When an indigenous street vendor tried to sell Ernesto Zedillo a wooden statue of Mexico's patron saint, the Virgin of Guadalupe, during a presidential tour of the countryside, the chief of state famously apologized, "*No tengo* [I don't have] cash." Instead of saying "*adios*" or "*hasta luego*" in the manner of their parents, young *chilangos* ended their phone conversations with a terse "bye," and the newspaper columns of young Mexicans like Katia D'Artigues and Carlos Mota were peppered with colloquial English terms such as "wannabes" and "groupies" and even the odd profanity like "bullshit." When I phoned a crime reporter for the Mexico City tabloid *La Prensa* for help in tracking down the identity of a recent murder victim, he began by saying, "*te voy a dar un* [I'm going to give you a] tip"—and then directed me to the website of the Mexico City attorney general's office. The linguistic bastard child known as Spanglish that my father had ridiculed over the family dinner table decades ago had become not just acceptable but downright trendy.

All of this marked a radical departure from Mexico's past. Signs of creeping Americanization have been consistently resisted in a country that throughout its history has often defined itself in terms of how it differed from the United States. The term "Americanization" was appearing in print by the late nineteenth century in magazine articles warning about the threat that U.S. influences posed to Mexico's national identity.

The negative stigma associated with the word was undoubtedly fostered by U.S. writers who hailed the American way of life in the early years of the twentieth century as a panacea for the assorted ills of their supposedly backward southern neighbor. That patronizing attitude imbued a 1909 magazine article written by Edward Conley, who hailed the positive effects of what he called the "American invasion" of Mexico that had occurred during the long reign of the dictator Porfirio Díaz. "We have taught the Mexicans banking and the use of banks," enthused Conley. "We have built hydraulic power plants and taught the Mexicans how to utilize the enormous amount of energy which was going to waste in their waterfalls. We have, by our example and our commercial products, taught the peon to wear shoes and a hat, and have increased the wages all over his republic." Quoted by the Chicano academic Gilbert G. Rodríguez in his book *Culture of Empire: American Writers, Mexico, and Mexican Immigrants, 1880–1930*, Conley predicted that the structure of the Mexican family would be eventually recast "on the American basis" and declared confidently, "each year the American way of living is taking a deeper hold on the Mexican people."[7]

The outbreak of the Mexican Revolution one year later exposed how premature Conley's vision was at the time. But over the ensuing decades American culture did make significant inroads inside Mexico. The country soon became one of Hollywood's most important foreign markets: by the 1930s, three of every four new movies screening in Mexico City were U.S.-made films. The rise of rock and roll in the 1950s spawned copycat bands like Los Teen Tops and Los Rebeldes de Roc (The Rebels of Rock), who grafted Spanish-language lyrics onto hit songs from the United States. A Mexican version of the emerging counterculture movement in the States arrived in the mid-1960s in the form of the cultural movement *la onda* (the wave), and some of its leading writers spiced up their iconoclastic prose with rock music lyrics.[8] The sense of encroaching Americanization was lampooned in the work of the famous Mexican political cartoonist Eduardo del Río, who signed his drawings with the nom de plume "Rius." A cartoon dated 1966 showed the map of Mexico covered with twenty-nine placards all of which included the word "*Yanqui,*" as in "*Yanqui* hotels," "*Yanqui* music," "*Yanqui* tourism," "*Yanqui* snacks," "*Yanqui*-style army," etc. At the top of the map a smirking President Lyndon B. Johnson was shown asking his Mexican counterpart Gustavo Díaz Ordaz, "Do you still speak Spanish?"

The relentless invasion of American culture triggered a backlash at various junctures. In the 1920s, Mexico's highly respected minister of education José Vasconcelos refused to subsidize the country's fledgling film industry on the grounds that movies were "typically North American"[9] and his boss, President Álvaro Obregón, banned the screening of all Paramount-produced movies until that Hollywood film studio suspended the global distribution of the 1922 motion picture *Her Husband's Trademark*, which supposedly depicted Mexicans unfairly.[10] In the 1930s the staunchly nationalistic president Lázaro Cárdenas ordered the censoring of U.S. movies that ridiculed the image of Mexicans and even lobbied other Latin American chiefs of state in support of a regional ban.[11] Successive governments later reversed Vasconcelos's edict and established a national cinematographic bank to help promote the nation's film industry as an alternative to the latest crop of Hollywood movies. By the 1950s the bank financed over half of all movies made inside Mexico, a figure that would rise to 70 percent by the late 1960s. Cinema, concluded the film scholar Paulo Antonio Paranagua, "had become a State industry."[12]

In more recent times, a production of the Broadway hit musical *Hair* was abruptly closed down in the resort city of Acapulco in 1969 when the actors inserted references to the infamous massacre of students in the Tlatelolco district of Mexico City on the eve of the previous year's Summer Olympics in the capital. The sporadic efforts to contain Americanization achieved perhaps their most ludicrous expression in 1982, when the Mexican government established a Commission for the Defense of the Spanish Language as part of a doomed bid to halt the infiltration of English terms and, in particular, the apostrophe—a punctuation mark foreign to the orthography of the Castilian tongue.[13]

But in an era of U.S.-led globalization, those past efforts to stem the tide of Americanizing influences seem almost quaint. Under NAFTA, annual flows of direct American investment became a deluge, increasing from $1.3 billion in 1992 to $15 billion in 2001.[14] U.S. companies were responsible for 86 percent of all the foreign capital that entered the country in 2000. The thickening economic ties binding Mexico to the United States are not limited to the area of direct foreign investment. Two of the country's three largest sources of foreign exchange come directly from the United States— one from the remittances sent home by Mexican workers living in *El Norte* (nearly $24 billion in 2007 according to Mexico's central bank), the other from the 17 million Americans who visit Mexico each year and make up over 80 percent of the country's total foreign tourist trade.[15]

Symptoms of Americanization in modern Mexico can pop up at the strangest times. My Argentine wife Olga Wornat and I walked into a Holiday Inn in the northern city of Monterrey one afternoon with two Mexican friends and ordered drinks. When I returned from the rest room I saw Olga sipping Mexico's greatest gift to the world of cocktails, a classic margarita served on the rocks with just the right dash of triple sec and lime juice. Our friends by contrast had opted for frozen margaritas, a mound of crushed ice sitting in a puddle of tequila with protruding plastic drinking straws. To my mind and taste in tippling, that icy concoction is to a real margarita what a Miller Lite is to a Sam Adams Boston Lager—an ersatz version of the genuine article—and when I asked our friends why on earth they were drinking *that*, they shrugged their shoulders and smiled sheepishly. The next evening Olga and I wandered into a restaurant in the Polanco district of Mexico City called La Buena Tierra. I ordered a round of drinks and made a point of explaining to a waiter with a name tag that said Ray that we wanted a proper margarita, not one "*al estilo norteamericano* [in the American style]." In hindsight, the restaurant's health-food format and the baseball cap on Ray's head should have set my alarm bells ringing. And sure enough, when the waiter came back to our table, there perched on his tray was the dreaded frozen drink, an Americanized travesty of a national treasure if ever there was one.

It's not just tipplers who are copying American tastes and trends. So too are Mexican politicians. When Fox hired Francisco Ortiz, a former marketing executive for the Ohio-based corporation Procter and Gamble, to run his broadcast media campaign, he told the aide, "Look at me as a product and figure out how to sell me." Both he and Labastida quietly hired leading Washington political consultants with close ties to President Bill Clinton to share their expertise. Fox brought in Dick Morris while his PRI rival employed the services of James Carville.

Mexico's subsequent presidential vote in 2006 was eerily reminiscent of the controversial election George W. Bush won six years previously. When the ballots were tallied in July 2006, less than 240,000 votes separated the National Action Party's winning candidate, Felipe Calderón, from the left-wing runner-up Andrés Manuel López Obrador. And just as Bush's razor-thin margin of victory over Al Gore in Florida's popular vote ushered in weeks of legal wrangling until the U.S. Supreme Court finally upheld the Republican nominee's election, López Obrador demanded a complete recount of all 41 million ballots cast and took his case to the nation's supreme electoral tribunal.

The former Mexico City mayor also took to the streets of the national capital to press claims that the election had been stolen and deployed thousands of his supporters in makeshift camps along two of the city's major thoroughfares for several weeks. In the end, the electoral tribunal judges rejected López Obrador's claims of vote fraud and the left-wing politician also lost in the court of public opinion as millions of commuters in Mexico City fumed over the traffic jams caused by his followers' extended sit-in along the Paseo de la Reforma boulevard. But as was the case when Bush was finally inaugurated the forty-third president of the United States in the winter of 2001, Calderón took office in December 2006 in a deeply polarized political environment in which millions of his compatriots continued to reject his election as illegitimate.

During the recently concluded 2008 U.S. presidential campaign, the term *lobbyist* became a kind of epithet, as candidates took turns accusing their rivals of accepting donations from such Washington insiders. But the word hadn't yet entered Mexico's political lexicon when I moved there in 1984. If a major foreign or Mexican company wanted to change an existing law or derail a pending piece of legislation it deemed inimical to its interests, its executives made a beeline for the presidential residence of Los Pinos as the final, incontrovertible arbiter. But Washington-style lobbying has become a salient fact of life in Mexican politics in an era when the congress is no longer a rubber-stamp body at the beck and call of the sitting chief of state. With political power now more evenly divided between the executive and legislative branches of the federal government, corporations see it in their interests to hire the services of full-time lobbyists like Gustavo Almaraz Montaño, a former senator from the state of Baja California who practically invented the industry when he founded a political consulting firm with two partners in 1996.

Some Mexicans don't view the rise of access merchants like Almaraz as necessarily a good thing. The veteran left-wing politician Pablo Gómez of the Party of the Democratic Revolution once compared those lobbyists to the ladies of the night who ply their wares on Sullivan Street in Mexico City's Cuauhtémoc district. But for better or worse, lobbyists have inserted themselves into the body politic as well-connected players that major foreign and domestic corporations can ill afford to do without. "The power and influence of political parties have noticeably diminished, and this shift gives us a chance to continue our work," says María Emilia Farías, a former congresswoman turned lobbyist. "We will have a market."[16]

Toward a Strategic Relationship with Uncle Sam

From the outset of his presidency, Fox staked a huge chunk of his political capital on achieving better ties with Washington than any of his predecessors in modern Mexican history. The Holy Grail of this bold foreign policy initiative was a comprehensive immigration accord with the incoming Bush administration that would legalize the status of millions of undocumented Mexican immigrants in the United States. The rationale behind the quest for a new, "strategic" relationship with the United States

was laid out by Fox's foreign minister, Jorge G. Castañeda, in the monthly magazine *Nexos* a year after he took office. "Mexico wants to establish
a relation with the United States that will be, by necessity, more broad,"
wrote Castañeda. "But contrary to what a certain intellectual conventional
wisdom tends to think, that does not signify that it will be more subordinate. In the current context of our interdependence, the mutual interests of
Mexico and the United States require us to consolidate a firm, long-term
relationship."[17]

The new era in U.S.-Mexican relations could not have begun under
more auspicious circumstances. As a teenager growing up in the state of
Guanajuato, Vicente Fox had sported the Levi's blue jeans and tight T-shirts
adorned with NFL team logos that were popular among his American
peers, and throughout his adult life he had always been favorably predis-
posed toward El Norte. "I save a special place in my heart for the United
States," wrote Fox in his 2007 memoirs after leaving office, "where every
child is raised to achieve anything he or she will earn."[18]

For his part, George W. Bush broke with a longstanding tradition that
required a newly inaugurated American president to make Canada his
first foreign port of call and instead flew to Fox's ranch in Guanajuato
state in February 2001. Aides to both men played up the good personal
chemistry between the folksy chiefs of state. In the early months of his
administration, Bush proclaimed the dawn of what he called the Century
of the Americas and characterized his country's ties with Mexico as the
single most important bilateral relationship for the United States.

Amid the smoke and ruins of the September 11 terrorist attacks, all that
Century of the Americas rhetoric vanished quicker than a bottle of
Cuervo Gold tequila at a twenty-first birthday party for President Bush's
twin daughters. A collateral casualty of al Qaeda's assault on New York and
Washington was Castañeda's hopes for a comprehensive immigration
agreement with the United States. But even before the suicidal foot sol-
diers of Osama bin Laden would steer George Bush's attention away from
Latin America for the rest of his presidency, the Texan's honeymoon with
Fox was showing signs of coming to an end. The Mexican president

irritated Bush administration officials during a visit to Chicago in July 2001 when he affirmed the right of illegal Mexican workers in the United States to obtain driver's licenses and gain more access to American universities. Fox's official state visit to Washington on the eve of 9/11 got off on the wrong foot when the Mexican president arrived on the South Lawn of the White House and publicly gave his host a deadline for clinching the immigration deal Fox so ardently wanted. "We must, and we can, reach an agreement on migration before the end of this year," Fox said. The Americans' reaction was later described by a former White House speechwriter named David Frum in rather pointed language. "The objectionable tone of Fox's opening comments foreshadowed the entire disastrous visit," Frum wrote. "At the staff and cabinet meetings, Mexicans made blunt demands on their American counterparts for concessions on immigration, while refusing to discuss even the opening of their energy market [to private U.S. oil companies]."[19]

Mexico's demotion as a foreign policy priority for the Bush administration did not immediately alter the new, decidedly pro-U.S. tilt of the Fox government's foreign policy. Cuba provided the most conspicuous example of this sea change. Under Fox's leadership, Mexico completely broke with a tradition of cultivating warm ties with Havana and instead backed U.S.-sponsored resolutions condemning Cuba's poor human rights record at the annual meetings of the United Nations Commission on Human Rights in Geneva. In the early months of the Fox presidency Castañeda, a member of the Mexican Communist Party in his youth, announced that the doors of the Mexican embassy in Havana would be open to any Cuban citizen interested in visiting Mexico, and the foreign minister chose to make that pronouncement in Miami, of all places. The statement was widely interpreted as a standing invitation to any Cuban interested in obtaining political asylum, and within hours the embassy was invaded by hundreds of unemployed youths.

Fidel Castro would take his revenge in due course. When Fox foresaw the possibility of an embarrassing showdown between Bush and Castro at a U.N.-sponsored summit in Monterrey in 2002, he phoned the Cuban leader and offered Castro a tasty dinner of roast goat in exchange for his agreement to leave the country a day ahead of the American president's arrival. An apoplectic Castro later embarrassed Fox at a Havana press conference by playing tape recordings of what the Mexican president had thought was a private phone conversation. Two years later the Cuban dictator boycotted a meeting of European, Latin American, and Caribbean leaders in Guadalajara and explained his decision in a harshly worded eight-page letter that condemned the Fox government's "shameless obedience of U.S. orders."[20] The sniping from Havana was relentless: when a Cuban exile suspected of plotting to assassinate Castro suddenly turned up on American soil in the spring of 2005, Fidel accused the Fox government of allowing the alleged assassin to pass through Mexican territory with impunity on his way into the United States. "The man has been putting his foot in it time after time," sneered Castro, referring to the Mexican president.[21]

Castañeda defends the fundamental shift in Mexican foreign policy toward the Castro regime as the product of a broadly based consensus inside the government that he was serving. "Fox and I and [Interior Minister Santiago] Creel and [national security adviser Adolfo] Aguilar Zinser honestly felt that we had been freed from the PRI's complicity with the Cuban dictatorship," he says. "We didn't feel bound by it, we basically jettisoned that understanding, and it really wasn't that much to do with the United States."[22]

But Castañeda dismisses criticism that he turned Mexico into a willing accomplice of Washington on foreign policy matters during his tenure in the Fox cabinet. As evidence that the Fox government adopted positions at variance with the Bush administration on a number of issues, Castañeda mentions the decision to withdraw Mexico from the Washington-backed Inter-American Mutual Assistance defense treaty, the aggressive lobbying campaign that the Fox government mounted in favor of the rights of illegal Mexican workers inside the United States, and the ultimately successful lawsuit brought against the U.S government at the International Court of Justice on behalf of over fifty Mexican citizens who were accused of committing violent crimes north of the border that carried the death penalty.[23] That said, Castañeda acknowledges the widespread impression inside Mexico that the Fox administration, particularly in its early years, tried to placate the Bush administration. "Fox's policies toward the U.S. are seen as having failed, that he caved into the U.S. and got nothing out of it," he notes. "Neither of the two things is true, but that's the perception in Mexico. Certainly we were jilted by the Bush Administration [after 9/11], and certainly we were let down."[24]

On other fronts, the Fox government took unprecedented measures to solidify its relationship with Washington. The drug trafficking problem that was such a recurring source of friction between the Reagan administration and the de la Madrid government in the 1980s became an example of how well the two countries could work together on an issue of mutual concern. During the first half of Fox's six-year presidency, two of the country's biggest drug lords, Tijuana kingpin Benjamín Arellano Félix and Gulf of Mexico cartel boss Osiel Cárdenas Guillén, were captured, and the Mexican Navy stepped up its antidrug operations in close coordination with the U.S. Navy and Coast Guard. "[Fox] knew that PRI administrations had often rationalized their hesitation to work more fully with the United States by making the bogus argument that cooperation meant a loss of national sovereignty," former U.S. ambassador to Mexico Jeffrey Davidow later wrote. "Fox's leadership won him deep admiration in the United States. At the beginning of 2003, the White House declared that the two countries had achieved unparalleled levels of cooperation in the anti-narcotics effort."[25]

Under Fox, Mexico relaxed a longstanding policy of refusing certain kinds of U.S. government training and assistance. In the fall of 2003—more than forty years after President John F. Kennedy unveiled the highly successful Peace Corps program—the Fox government announced it had given Washington permission to send its first ever delegation of American volunteers to Mexico under that program's auspices. Previous governments had denied entry to the Peace Corps out of fear of appearing too pro-Washington. In a nod to Mexican sensitivities about being perceived as a backward Third World country, the initial group of fifteen volunteers shunned traditional Peace Corps tasks like the training of farmers or the building of health clinics in favor of information technology and business development projects that were implemented jointly with the Mexican Environment Secretariat and the Mexican Council for Science and Technology. "The Mexicans didn't want a bunch of hippies digging latrines," quipped one senior U.S. official. By the summer of 2007, the number of in-country American volunteers had swollen to forty-five who were deployed in four Mexican states, and U.S. ambassador to Mexico Tony Garza publicly hailed the successful establishment of a Peace Corps program as one more example of a thriving bilateral relationship based on "cooperation."[26]

A lesser-known U.S. government agency also commenced operations in Mexico during the Fox presidency after encountering resistance for many years. When the Nixon administration set up the Overseas Private Investment Corporation (OPIC) in 1971, one of its stated aims was to protect U.S. companies against expropriation of their assets in foreign countries. Successive Mexican governments vetoed OPIC requests for permission to offer political risk insurance to American companies with operations south of the border, arguing that Mexico had compiled an impressive track record of political stability over several decades and that U.S. firms therefore had no reason to fear for the security of their investments. But Fox finally relented in 2002 and signed an agreement that okayed the provision of such insurance coverage.

THE SERVILITY SYNDROME

Is there a danger that Americanization may be going too far? Many Mexicans think so, as evidenced by the hundreds of demonstrators who streamed into the world-famous archaeological site of Teotihuacán in 2004 to protest the construction of a nearby store belonging to Wal-Mart's Mexican subsidiary. Mexico City's cozier ties with Washington in recent times have certainly become a recurring grievance of the left. The cover of the January 11, 2004, issue of *Proceso* magazine featured a mocking cartoon of Fox dressed in a top hat adorned with the stars and stripes of the American flag and standing next to the words, "The Servility." Inside the magazine were grainy black-and-white photos of U.S. agents from the FBI and the Transportation Security Agency who had been recently deployed at Mexico City's international airport to review passports and assist their Mexican colleagues in antiterrorism procedures. "With the pretext of fighting drugs and terrorism," observed the *Proceso* article, "the government of Vicente Fox opened its doors to the security agencies of the United States like no other predecessor had ever done."[27]

Critics of Fox and Castañeda echo Fidel Castro's harsh criticism of their approach to U.S.-Mexican relations. De la Madrid described their approach to relations with the United States as that of a "sellout," and a former foreign relations secretary issued a similar verdict. "During Jorge's stint the Mexican government became exceedingly obsequious in its behavior toward the U.S.," said the ex-minister. "It did not approach Latin America or the European Union, it was not interested in Asia. It bet everything on achieving a special relationship with Bush and the United States."[28]

The late Adolfo Aguilar Zinser shared that critique. A left-leaning academic by training, he was one of Fox's more surprising appointments when Aguilar Zinser was named national security adviser to the president, and he was later posted to New York as Mexico's ambassador to the U.N. During the run-up to the U.S. invasion of Iraq, Aguilar Zinser was an enthusiastic mouthpiece for Fox's rejection of Bush's saber-rattling. But he ran afoul of the Mexican president's keen desire to repair post-invasion ties with the United States when he told a university audience in Mexico City in November 2003 that Washington was only interested in a "close relationship of convenience and subordination" with Mexico. To ram the point home, Aguilar Zinser accused the United States of treating its southern neighbor as a "backyard" rather than a partner. He was removed as Mexico's ambassador to the U.N. within a matter of days. "There is a growing sense among Mexican political elites that the most realistic option for Mexico is to obey U.S. commands and reap benefits from that," says Aguilar Zinser, who died in a traffic accident in 2005. "Our destiny is to show the United States not just friendship but allegiance and subordination."[29]

Toward a More Mature Nationalism

Old habits and ways of thinking about the United States die hard. That should come as no surprise: year in and year out, in schools stretching from the city of Tijuana south of San Diego to the town of Tapachula on the southern border with Guatemala, the disastrous outcome of the mid-nineteenth-century war with the United States and the naked land grab it represented are drilled into the minds of successive generations of Mexican children. "In the school textbooks, there is the constant theme of the American invasion and the Boy Heroes, which are at the heart of Mexican nationalism," says the historian Héctor Aguilar Camín. "It is a nationalism of martyrdom which asserts its eternal right to seek redress from its persecutor, which is the United States. It is a very old and profound trait of Mexican nationalism, and it is nurtured every day in school classrooms. So from the standpoint of politically correct thinking, Mexico has to be an anti-American country."[30]

That enduring rule of Mexican politics caught the eye of one controversial American academic. Harvard professor Samuel Huntington recounted a conversation he once had with a top adviser of Carlos Salinas de Gortari, who was touting the neoliberal economic policies the then Mexican president was aggressively pursuing. "That's most impressive," Huntington told the senior aide. "It seems to me that basically you want to change Mexico from a Latin American country into a North American country." The Salinas adviser replied, "Exactly! That's precisely what we are trying to do, but of course we could never say so publicly."[31]

The reluctance to appear even mildly pro-American in public may be fading. Influential opinion makers no longer shrink from calling for more mature attitudes toward the United States. In a column that took Aguilar Zinser to task for his "backyard" remark about U.S. views of the country, Mexican political scientist Denise Dresser wrote: "He displayed a

long-held and deeply felt anti-American stance typical of Mexico's nationalistic elites. . . . Should Mexico behave as a wounded civilization and fight
the United States at every turn, as Aguilar Zinser has suggested? Or should
it leave its pride and prejudices behind while pursuing concrete bilateral
interests?" A professor at the Autonomous Technological Institute of
Mexico, she urged the country's leaders to, in effect, grow up in its dealings with their northern neighbor. "Mexico should be less histrionic and
more strategic in its relations with the United States," concluded Dresser.[32]

That was certainly the thinking of Jorge Castañeda when he took over
the foreign relations portfolio in the Fox cabinet. In his judgment, the
time had come for Mexico to drop its passive-aggressive behavior and
turn to its advantage the geopolitical realities of sitting on the doorstep of
the world's reigning economic superpower. "The Mexican economy today
is more closely linked to the American economy than ever before in history, and Mexican society is more closely linked to American society than
ever before," he told me over coffee one Saturday morning at a Starbucks
cafe opposite his Mexico City apartment building. "That's the way it is. We
abandoned the anti-American rhetoric totally, and we tried to transform
it into a rhetoric of cooperation but at the same time really pursue an
agenda based on Mexican interests."[33]

Self-serving as it may sound, Castañeda's portrayal of this particular
aspect of foreign policy in the Fox era is not inaccurate. Mexico proved to
be anything but a reliable lackey of the United States in the weeks preced-
ing Bush's invasion of Iraq in the winter of 2003. Faced with relentless
pressure from Washington to endorse the Bush administration's war plans
as a temporary member of the United Nations Security Council, Mexico
simply refused to buckle. Domestic political factors may have swayed
the Fox government: with midterm congressional elections scheduled for
July of that year, opinion polls showed that an overwhelming number of
Mexicans opposed the invasion. Whether it was for principle or expediency,
history will show that Fox stuck to his guns all the same.

In other respects, the Fox government displayed a refreshing readiness
to side with the United States on some issues and resolutely oppose it on

others whenever the interests of the two countries clashed. When U.S. ambassador Tony Garza issued a series of travel advisories warning American citizens about the lawlessness of some Mexican border towns and temporarily shuttered the U.S. consulate in Nuevo Laredo opposite the town of Laredo, Texas, Fox cried foul. But when Venezuelan president Hugo Chávez sought to bury a U.S.-sponsored proposal to reopen talks on a Free Trade of the Americas Area treaty encompassing the entire Western Hemisphere at a summit in Argentina in November 2005, Fox supported the Bush administration to the hilt. That position prompted a revealing outburst from the self-proclaimed socialist leader of Venezuela. "It is saddening to see President Fox's sellout ways," Chavez fumed during a live TV broadcast in Venezuela. "How sad it is to see the president of a people like the Mexicans allow himself to become a cub of the [U.S.] empire." The harsh attack on the Mexican president by a foreign leader rallied millions of his countrymen to Fox's defense at a time when his approval ratings were sagging. It even elicited a declaration of solidarity from a ranking member of the opposition, Roberto Madrazo, the PRI's nominee for president in the then upcoming 2006 election.

Is Americanization Only Skin-Deep?

There remain formidable limits to the Americanizing of Mexico. Heads still turn in Mexico City elevators when strangers speak in English. Baseball has a fervent following among millions of Mexicans, but soccer remains the undisputed king among spectator sports. (That said, the NFL's first ever regular-season game on foreign soil sold out Mexico City's huge Azteca Stadium in September 2005, and on the morning after Peyton Manning led the Indianapolis Colts to victory in the 2007 Super Bowl, many newspapers in the Mexican capital led their front pages with photos of the quarterback celebrating his team's triumph.)

Anti-Americanism lives on as a powerful strain in Mexican politics and society and can surface in very public and even puerile ways. During a soccer game in the city of Guadalajara that pitted Mexico against its U.S.

archrivals for a berth in the 2004 Olympic Games, fans in the stadium could be heard on TV chanting, "O-sa-ma, O-sa-ma" in honor of the al Qaeda leader. When Mexico City hosted the Miss Universe beauty pageant in May 2007 the American contestant, Tennessee native Rachel Smith, got the full Bronx cheer treatment. During a parade of national costumes in the Mexican capital's downtown, Smith's Elvis Presley–styled suit drew hearty boos from onlookers, and some of the answers she gave to a panel of judges during a live interview were drowned out by booing and chants of "Mé-xi-co, Mé-xi-co" from the audience. The journalism graduate crowned her star-crossed visit to the country by slipping at one point during the evening gown competition and landing directly on her derriere. The daughter of an African American father and a white mother, Smith still managed to finish among the top five finalists in the pageant, an undeserved outcome in the eyes of local fans rooting for Mexico's beauty queen, according to the newspaper *El Universal*.[34]

In the pecking order of Mexican society, the absorption of American values is strongest among the business and political elites. But among those movers and shakers, argues one of the country's most incisive social commentators, American influences are little more than a thin veneer of university diplomas and media consumption habits that leaves their Mexican roots untouched. "They certainly go to the American universities, the Ivy League, or the University of California system or even the Amarillo, Texas, high school," says Carlos Monsiváis. "But they don't know anything about American culture. They don't read Walt Whitman or Edgar Allan Poe or Ralph Waldo Emerson or F. Scott Fitzgerald. For instance, [President Ernesto] Zedillo went to Yale, but he doesn't know about American culture. They saw all the new American movies. They read *Time* magazine or *Newsweek*. Occasionally the highest politicians read the *New York Times* and watch CNN. That is Americanization for them."[35]

A leading political analyst points out that Americanization has failed to cure such quintessentially Mexican ills as corruption and inefficiency. "Technocrats today can hardly utter a single sentence without using a word like software, and some stores and even neighborhoods may look more like the United States," says Luis Rubio of the Center for Development Research. "[But] the quality of [public] services is Mexican, and the cop on the corner is as stupid and lacking in training as any Mexican politician. You don't have to dig very deeply to realize you're not in the United States."

At the same time, the country's traditionally robust brand of patriotism has been undermined by the series of severe economic crises that has buffeted the country at regular intervals since 1976. "That sense of deep nationalism that stamped all Mexicans thirty years ago has been eroded by crisis and misgovernment," concedes Rubio. "For younger generations, those values of being Mexican are much less strong than those taught to my generation."[36] A prominent European journalist made a similar observation five years into the NAFTA era but drew a somewhat different conclusion. "What I have found in Mexico is a revolutionary sense of disillusionment that I approve of," said Jean Daniel, the founder and director of the Parisian newspaper *Le Nouvel Observateur*. "A diminished nationalism which was self-parodying, and the almost complete disappearance of anti-U.S. sentiment."[37]

Some Mexican intellectuals who spent their youth railing against Yankee imperialism concur that perceptions of the United States are changing. As editor of the monthly journal of opinion and literature called *Nexos*, Héctor Aguilar Camín carved out an intellectual and cultural niche that placed him squarely in the camp of the Mexican left in the 1980s. Now in his late fifties, Aguilar Camín recognizes a more nuanced, less emotive view of the United States on the part of many Mexicans. "I don't believe the American way of life has invaded Mexico," says the historian. "But there is today a much more balanced and pragmatic vision of the United States. There is greater knowledge and naturalness for coexistence. Attitudes toward the United States have changed a lot in the sense that there is a high percentage of the population that has a favorable opinion of the institutions of American society. That resentful, victimized nationalism is something that the Mexicans should cure themselves of."[38]

And slowly but surely, that self-healing process is now underway. Reflexive anti-Americanism is still alive and well in newsrooms throughout the country, and every utterance of the American ambassador continues to be scrutinized for hidden content and meaning. Another four years of George W. Bush in the White House kept the embers of anti-gringo sentiment smoldering. But the abyss separating the distant neighbors at the time Alan Riding published his acclaimed book in 1985 has narrowed substantially over the intervening two decades. The signature slogan of a $40 million advertising campaign that the Fox government aimed at the U.S. tourism market captured that reality in four simple words: "Mexico, closer than ever."[39] That growing sense of proximity represents the latest swing in the pendulum of changing Mexican attitudes toward the Colossus of the North.

CHAPTER 3

Looking Northward

The ambivalence that Mexicans harbor toward the United States is a familiar cliché. But when you think about it, the mere fact that Mexicans have mixed emotions about their American neighbors, as opposed to the unadulterated hatred that most Palestinians feel toward Israel, is remarkable by itself. Some might argue that, with the passage of time, the Palestinians will one day come around to a more nuanced view of their neighbors. As a journalist who has worked in the Middle East, I rather doubt it. There are in any case other corners of the planet where the wounds inflicted by conflicts predate the U.S.-Mexican War by centuries, yet the mutual animosities remain as fierce as ever. Witness the case of Serbia and the ethnic Albanian population of Kosovo, where differences over land and culture go back to the Middle Ages. In the case of Mexico, however, attitudes toward the United States have swung back and forth violently throughout the country's nearly 200 years of national sovereignty—and in the new century, the positive elements in the love-hate prism show signs of gaining new ascendancy.

Prevailing views of the United States were by and large favorable when Mexico finally won its independence from Spain in 1821 after a bloody rebellion that lasted over a decade. The profound influence that America's Founding Fathers exerted over their Mexican counterparts could be readily seen in the fledgling nation's first constitution of 1824. From its federalist framework and the formal separation of powers among the executive, legislative, and judicial branches to its very name, the Federal Constitution of the United Mexican States, Mexico's first magna carta bore the unmistakable imprint of U.S. political values. Its authors were mostly self-styled liberals who wanted to adopt their American neighbors' decentralized system of government and separation of church and state and actively opposed the designs of their conservative countrymen to concentrate power in the hands of a reconstituted monarchy. "In the main, liberals of the . . . era were mesmerized by the ideal society to the north, and by the spectacular material progress of the United States under republican federal institutions," wrote the historian Charles A. Hale. "They talked openly of imitating the United States in reforming Mexico."[1]

Yet even at that very early juncture, years before the government of President Andrew Jackson would quietly encourage American settlers in Texas to secede from Mexico and Washington's duplicity would be magnified by President James Polk's deliberate provocation of the Mexican War in 1846, a leading liberal thinker like José María Luis Mora had misgivings about taking the American model too far. "For [the liberals], the United States could serve as a model for goals but not for methods," noted Hale. "The two societies and their respective histories were too different. . . . Mora's problem was how to modernize a traditional Hispanic society without Americanizing it and thereby sacrificing its national identity. The problem is yet to be solved."[2]

AN ARDENT ADMIRER OF THE UNITED STATES

One of Mora's liberal colleagues entertained no such reservations about embracing the American model. In many ways Lorenzo de Zavala was the first Americanized Mexican in history, and his seemingly boundless admiration for the United States ultimately led him to side with Mexico's enemies. A native of the Yucatán Peninsula, de Zavala was one of the principal drafters and signatories of Mexico's 1824 constitution, and he held a series of prominent posts under the country's first two liberal presidents, Guadalupe Victoria and Vicente Guerrero. De Zavala left Mexico in 1830 after a conservative coup toppled the Guerrero government in which he was serving as treasury secretary, and during a two-year exile he took a New York native named Emily West as his second wife.

In 1834 he was serving as Mexico's minister to France when President Antonio López de Santa Anna disbanded the congress and gave himself dictatorial powers. That prompted de Zavala to resign his diplomatic post in protest and move from Paris to New York City. De Zavala eventually resettled in Texas, where he owned land and which at the time formed part of the northern Mexican state of Coahuila and Tejas. In 1835 he made common cause with the American settlers who took up arms to gain their independence from the Santa Anna regime in Mexico City. De Zavala helped write the constitution of the newly independent Republic of Texas, and in the spring of 1836 he was elected its first vice president. But De Zavala did not meet a happy end: he bickered frequently with the republic's first president, David G. Burnet, and after two unsuccessful attempts to leave the government, de Zavala's resignation as vice president was finally accepted in October 1836. He died of pneumonia barely a month later at the age of forty-eight, a bitter and disillusioned man.

De Zavala showered Mexico's northern neighbor with paeans of praise in his 1834 book *Journey to the United States of North America*. The book recounts de Zavala's odyssey through the United States after he fled Mexico in the spring of 1830, and the author's high esteem for the country and its people leaps from the printed page. "The people of the United States are wise, economical and fond of accumulating capital for the future," he wrote. Speaking of Mexico, de Zavala averred that "there is not a more seductive example for a nation that does not enjoy complete liberty than that of a neighbor where are found in all public acts, in all writings, lessons and practices of an unlimited liberty."[3] De Zavala likened President Andrew Jackson, who received the Mexican on two occasions during his travels, to "one of those ancient heroes of Homer"[4] and voiced the frank hope that "the influence of the United States upon Mexico will with time be a power of opinion, of teaching by guidance, all the stronger because it is purely moral, founded upon its doctrines and lessons."[5]

De Zavala has gone down in Mexican history as a traitor to his country, and not only on account of his unabashed enthusiasm for Americans and their values. In a remarkable passage in the opening pages of the book, he drew a most unflattering comparison between his compatriots and his American hosts. "The Mexican is easy going," asserted de Zavala:

> lazy, intolerant, generous almost to prodigality, vain, belligerent, superstitious, ignorant, and an enemy of all restraint. The North American works, the Mexican has a good time; the first spends less than he has, the second [spends] even that which he does not have; the former carries out the most arduous enterprises to their conclusion, the latter abandons them in the early stages; the one lives in his house, decorates it, furnishes it, preserves it against the inclement weather; the other spends his time in the street, flees from his home, and in a land where there are no seasons he worries little about a place to rest. In the United States all men are property owners and tend to increase their fortune; in Mexico the few who have anything are careless with it and fritter it away.[6]

THE POST-1847 BACKLASH

Such views became political heresy in Mexico after the loss of Texas and the calamitous outcome of the 1846–1847 war with the United States. Anti-Americanism became deeply entrenched in the political culture during the U.S. Army's ten-month occupation of the country after the fall of Mexico City in September 1847, and its most eloquent spokesman was Lucas Alamán, the influential historian and former cabinet minister who led the country's conservatives for over three decades. Anticipating the likely debacle that armed conflict with the United States would visit upon his country, Alamán had actually opposed the Mexican government's decision to go to war over the Polk administration's annexation of Texas. He blamed that decision largely on Mexico's liberal leaders, whose indignation and disenchantment with the United States had led most of them to back a reckless military confrontation and who, in Alamán's view, "have brought us nothing but one appalling disaster after another." But Alamán also vented his outrage at the perfidious gringos. The recently concluded military conflict was "the most unjust war in history," declared Alamán, "provoked by the ambition not of an absolute monarch but of a republic that claims to be at the forefront of nineteenth-century civilization."[7]

The conservative revisionism of Alamán introduced the first in a series of oscillating perspectives toward the United States. As the U.S. Army made its way from the Gulf Coast port of Veracruz to Mexico City in 1847, the so-called War of the Castes erupted in the Yucatán Peninsula between the region's small white elite and the Mayan Indian majority. So great was the carnage wrought by the indigenous uprising—women were gang-raped, captives were burned and skinned alive—that a prominent local liberal named Justo Sierra O'Reilly journeyed to Washington in September 1847 to urge U.S. officials to annex the semi-autonomous peninsula and thereby save the white minority population.[8]

During the War of the Reform of 1858–61 that pitted Alamán's ideological heirs and the Catholic Church against the liberal forces led by the nation's deposed constitutional President Benito Juárez, several prominent allies of Juárez sought refuge in New Orleans and New York. The full-blooded Indian politician from the southern state of Oaxaca gladly accepted economic and military aid from across the border that would ultimately prove instrumental in securing the liberals' victory over their conservative foes.[9] But a fresh round of disillusionment with the gringos lay in store for Mexican liberals after the defeat of the Confederacy in 1865 and Juárez's overthrow of the French-backed Austrian emperor Maximilian two years later. Post–Civil War governments in Washington did little to help Juárez rebuild a Mexican economy that had been shattered by nine years of nearly uninterrupted warfare against the conservatives and Napoleon III's invading army.[10]

AMBIVALENCE

The early years of the *Porfiriato* mirrored the deep divide in the sentiments of Mexicans about the United States. On one side of the aisle stood the apostles of Lucas Alamán's conservative gospel, who looked to Spain for inspiration from abroad and warned darkly about the pernicious influence of Mexico's predominantly Protestant, Anglo-Saxon neighbor to the north. As in past decades, anti-Americanism in late-nineteenth-century Mexico was in large part stoked by the Catholic right.[11] It was a conservative Catholic opposition newspaper called *El Tiempo* that coined one of the signature phrases of the era, "Mexico, mother of foreigners, stepmother to Mexicans," to censure the dictator Porfirio Díaz's eager embrace of foreign, and particularly Yankee, capital.[12]

But secular voices also joined the anti-gringo clamor. The most prominent of these belonged to Justo Sierra Méndez, a congressman and future public education minister who would later emerge as the premier intellectual figure of the *Porfiriato*. Though he remained loyal to the dictator Díaz until he was finally toppled by the Mexican Revolution in 1911, Sierra warned about the risks of untrammeled U.S. investment in Mexico that was ushering in an era of "economic Americanism" and could eventually transform the country into "a protectorate." Of even greater danger in Sierra's eyes was "perhaps the most dangerous form" of U.S. influence, the "attempt at moral and intellectual annexation." An educator and historian by profession whose father had tried to coax the Americans into seizing the Yucatán Peninsula in 1847, Sierra was especially worried over Governor Evaristo Madero's plans to permit the opening of three teacher training schools run by U.S. Baptist missionaries in the northern border state of Coahuila. Turning over "the most delicate part of our education [i.e., the preparation of teachers] to a Protestant sect" posed a direct threat to Mexico's culture, heritage, and even language, he argued in an 1883 newspaper column.[13] Leading newspapers echoed Sierra's anxieties, warning that a proposed treaty of alliance between the two countries in the 1880s in reality "aimed at establishing an American protectorate over Mexico with the ultimate aim of annexation."[14]

At the opposite end of the spectrum was José María Vigil, a liberal journalist and politician who wrote editorials for the quasi-official newspaper *La Patria* in the 1880s. Some of his published work evokes the gushing encomiums that Lorenzo de Zavala had addressed to the United States fifty years earlier. If Mexico wants to fulfill its destiny, Vigil maintained, "it must follow resolutely the example before its eyes; at hand is the model it must imitate in everything." He pooh-poohed concerns that a flood of American capital and immigrants might jeopardize Mexico's "supposed character as a Latin nation." To the contrary, said Vigil, the United States had preserved its "moral identity" amid the "heterogeneous" waves of immigrants who had landed on her shores. The Guadalajara native took the gringophile argument one step further: Vigil foresaw a "radical evolution . . . which might end up by absorbing [Mexico's] present inhabitants into a superior entity," language that sounded to some ears like a call for Washington's annexation of Mexico's remaining national territory.[15]

Vigil stood in a direct line of descent from Mexico's pro-U.S. founding fathers and the liberal thinker José María Luis Mora. But over time, the United States's ever deeper economic penetration of Mexico—ex-president Ulysses S. Grant once likened the country to a "magnificent mine" during a visit in 1880[16]—aroused opposition from Mexican liberals as well. Francisco Madero's landmark 1908 book *La sucesión presidencial en 1910* helped lay the groundwork for the revolution that erupted against the Díaz regime two years later. Madero cited excessive concessions to the United States as one of the old dictator's major errors, along with the repression of labor strikes, widespread illiteracy, and the centralization of political power.[17]

Not surprisingly, those areas of the country where American investment was especially prominent were often more susceptible to waves of anti-Yankee sentiment. On the eve of the revolution's outbreak in 1910 the U.S. consul in the state of Chihuahua, where American mining companies had extensive interests and where newspaper tycoon William Randolph Hearst owned a huge hacienda, warned State Department officials in the terse telegraphese of the era about "anti American feeling general over state particularly cities and along railways."[18] The army of rebel warlord Pascual Orozco repeatedly raided large, U.S.-owned cattle and farming estates in Chihuahua and the neighboring state of Durango, and the homes of Mormon settlers in Chihuahua and the border state of Sonora were looted and, in some cases, expropriated. Several decades later, the Mexican novelist Carlos Fuentes would write an essay describing the Mexican Revolution as essentially "a war of national liberation against the United States."[19]

THE RESURGENCE OF ANTI-AMERICANISM

Three traumatic episodes at the height of the revolution fanned the embers of residual anti-Americanism into an all-out inferno. The first took place against the turbulent backdrop of a bloody coup that killed Madero in February 1913. When the democratically elected Mexican president was toppled by his own army commander-in-chief, General Victoriano Huerta, the U.S. ambassador Henry Lane Wilson not only backed the coup but proceeded to ignore the pleas of Madero's wife to prevail upon Huerta to spare her husband's life. Fourteen months later, President Woodrow Wilson sent U.S. sailors and Marines to occupy the Mexican gulf port of Veracruz to prevent a German ship from delivering arms and ammunition to the Huerta regime. Although the dispatch of American forces in April 1914 was meant to send a strong signal of Wilson's displeasure to the military strongman, this latest landing of foreign soldiers on Mexican soil understandably triggered an outpouring of patriotism that Huerta briefly tried to milk for his own political survival before he was ousted from power in July of that year.

For many Mexicans, the final straw came in March 1916 when a "punitive expedition" of U.S. soldiers under the command of Gen. John J. Pershing entered the northern state of Chihuahua in pursuit of Pancho Villa after the bandit-turned-revolutionary staged a bloody raid on the border town of Columbus, New Mexico, that killed seventeen Americans. Pershing and his men roamed the arid Chihuahua desert in search of Villa for eleven months before leaving Mexico empty-handed in February 1917. But the damage to American prestige and credibility had been done. "The United States lost something much more important and more permanent than the expansion of its economic interests and its political influence," wrote the eminent historian Daniel Cosío Villegas. "It lost the admiration and trust of the Mexicans. . . . [The United States obtained] economic preponderance at the price of losing esteem and admiration."[20]

Not for the first time had history repeated itself, and a whole new generation of Mexicans would invoke the memories of Madero, Veracruz, and Villa as rallying cries just as their grandfathers and great-grandfathers had paid tribute to the Boy Heroes who perished defending Chapultepec Castle on the final day of the Mexican War. Ironically, the revolutionary leader whom President Wilson eventually settled on to replace the disgraced Huerta as chief of state, former Coahuila state governor Venustiano Carranza, wasted no time in distancing Mexico from the United States when he consolidated his presidential powers in 1915. Carranza even briefly courted Imperial Germany during World War I as a possible counterweight to the Great Colossus of the North.[21] On this issue and only this issue did Carranza enjoy the support of the legendary peasant revolutionary leader Emiliano Zapata (whose assassination Carranza would later order) and his peasant followers. "It doesn't matter if [the gringos] send millions of soldiers," declared Zapata's brother Eufemio. "[If we're outnumbered] 200 to one, we'll fight them. Even if we don't have arms or ammunition, we'll still have chests to absorb their bullets."[22]

The bitter aftertaste left by the Wilson administration's twin military interventions lingered for many years. The nationalist generals Álvaro Obregón and Plutarco Elías Calles, who eventually succeeded Carranza and ruled Mexico throughout the 1920s, adopted their predecessor's patriotic rhetoric and ratified economic nationalism as a fundamental pillar of the 1917 constitution. When Calles sought to renegotiate the concessions awarded to American oil companies, U.S. ambassador James Sheffield issued stern warnings that Mexico might be on its way toward becoming the second Bolshevik country on earth. Talk of a nascent "Soviet Mexico" on America's doorstep was encouraged by Moscow's new envoy, who declared upon her arrival in the Mexican capital that "no two countries in the world [are] more alike than modern Mexico and the new Russia."

The ensuing confrontation between the Calles government and the oil firms appeared to culminate in January 1927 when the Mexican president unilaterally canceled the permits of all companies unwilling to comply with newly issued regulations governing the industry. President Calvin Coolidge declared that Mexico could end up receiving the same treatment that had recently befallen Nicaragua, where the marines had landed the previous year to prop up an unpopular right-wing dictator. Calles responded by threatening to set ablaze Mexico's oil fields along its Gulf Coast, which would cause a conflagration that "would light up the sky all the way to New Orleans." The diplomatic fireworks only ended after Mexican spies smuggled out of the American embassy documents that discussed contingency plans for a future U.S. military incursion. When Coolidge's secretary of state learned that the politically sensitive documents had fallen into the Calles government's hands, he prudently decided to turn down the volume a few decibels and withdraw the commie-baiting Sheffield as U.S. ambassador.[23]

ANOTHER SWING OF THE PENDULUM

The showdown over oil did not prevent a few more swings of the pendulum. The arrival of the New York investment banker Dwight Morrow as U.S. ambassador in 1927 heralded the dawn of a new era in bilateral relations. The same deft blend of courtesy, shrewdness, and respect that had served Morrow so well at J. P. Morgan became his calling card in the Mexican capital, and within months of his arrival he was working closely with Calles's new finance minister Luis Montes de Oca to restructure Mexico's foreign debt. Morrow helped hammer out a new deal with Calles under which judgments that were favorable to the oil companies would be treated as legal precedents. He displayed his formidable public relations skills by donning the fancy duds of a Mexican *charro* (cowboy) and bringing down his son-in-law, the celebrity aviator Charles Lindbergh, to pay a goodwill visit to Mexico City.[24]

Morrow laid the groundwork for the Good Neighbor policy toward Latin America that Franklin D. Roosevelt introduced after he became president in 1933. Relations between Mexico and the United States had improved markedly by the time Lázaro Cárdenas was elected president a year later, and if the two countries had been any less friendly the relationship might not have withstood the shocks it underwent during the retired Mexican general's six-year tenure in office. It was Cárdenas who took the unprecedented step of expropriating the entire oil industry in 1938 on the grounds that the foreign companies operating in Mexico were not benefiting the nation, and the Roosevelt administration elected not to intervene in the matter—much to the dismay of the U.S. firms that dominated the sector.

The strength of the bilateral relationship was demonstrated anew under Cárdenas's successor, President Manuel Ávila Camacho. In 1941 the two countries signed an agreement that settled all outstanding claims between the United States and Mexico dating back to the Mexican Revolution. That was followed by a 1942 trade treaty that lowered import duties on both certain U.S.-manufactured items headed for Mexico as well as Mexican goods bound for the American market. Trade between the two neighbors soared as a result, but that was not all. Washington and Mexico City negotiated a pioneering guest-worker program to supply the United States with labor at a time when millions of able-bodied Americans were serving their country overseas in World War II.[25] The benign atmospherics extended to the world of culture, as government-funded Mexican films toned down their anti-gringo rhetoric and downplayed class-conflict themes.[26]

The heady heights attained by the bilateral relationship were acknowledged in forthright language by Ávila Camacho's successor, Miguel Alemán. In his first state of the union address, Alemán alluded to the recent stay of his American counterpart Harry Truman in the Mexican capital when he declared that "never have our relations with the North American union reached the broad cordiality of which the presidential visits were public testimony."[27] Truman had scored a major public relations coup in March 1947 when he wrapped up a three-day visit to Mexico City by laying a wreath at the foot of the Monument to the Boy Heroes in Chapultepec Park. Occurring in the centennial year of the young cadets' celebrated deaths, Truman's masterly gesture aptly captured the robust state of relations between the two neighbors. "One hundred years of misunderstanding and bitterness wiped out by one man in one minute," gushed a Mexican engineer named Ramón Ayala in a contemporary news account of the episode. "That is the best neighbor policy."[28] An American historian concurred years later. "Mexico and the United States are interacting more vigorously, more extensively, and more intensely than at any earlier time," asserted the historian Howard Cline in assessing the bilateral zeitgeist of the years immediately following the Second World War. "The deep reservoir of good will that has been thus accumulated displaces many of the hidden resentments, which formerly poked above the surface to founder the unwary."[29]

THE BILATERAL RELATIONSHIP COOLS

The advent of the cold war brought a gradual end to the era of good feelings between the two countries. In this, Mexico was hardly alone: as the Eisenhower administration flexed its political, diplomatic, and military muscles in the mid- and late 1950s, a resurgence of anti-Americanism swept across much of Latin America, triggered in part by the CIA-backed coup that toppled a democratically elected left-of-center government in Guatemala in 1954. A mob attack on the motorcade of then Vice President Richard Nixon during a 1958 visit to Caracas symbolized in very graphic terms the groundswell of Yankee-go-home sentiment in much of America's so-called backyard. With tensions between Washington and Moscow at an all-time high in the 1950s, Mexico refused to sign a military assistance program with the United States, and the trade treaty signed in 1942 died a quiet death. The steadfast refusal of President Adolfo López Mateos and his successors to sever diplomatic ties with Cuba in the aftermath of Fidel Castro's seizure of power epitomized the renewed spirit of independence on foreign policy matters then prevailing in Mexico City, even though López Mateos publicly professed interest in bolstering his country's "special relationship" with the United States.[30] At the same time, Mexico under López Mateos and Gustavo Díaz Ordaz refrained from openly siding with the communist regime in Havana and instead charted a sometimes ambiguous course, often serving as a valuable conduit for exchanging messages between two governments that were literally not on speaking terms.[31]

The self-conscious distancing of the country from its northern neighbor in the international arena peaked in the 1970s under President Luis Echeverría, who introduced a new "Mexicanization" law that required 51 percent national ownership of new companies and created a new government body to okay or reject new foreign investment. Echeverría further tweaked Uncle Sam's nose by spearheading calls for a New International Economic Order that would have privileged Third World producers of raw materials, and he openly questioned "the suitability of concentrating on the bilateral relationship with the United States."[32]

MEXICO'S ELITES AND ANTI-AMERICANISM

Anti-Americanism has traditionally been more the preserve of Mexico's elites than its lower classes. When the country's newly minted national anthem made its debut in 1854 during Antonio López de Santa Anna's last stint in power, everyone in the audience understood which country the lyricist had in mind when they heard the words, "But if a foreign enemy should dare/To profane your soil with his steps." (Those lines were apparently lifted directly from one of the aging general's many manifestos.)

In his magisterial biography of Pancho Villa, the historian Friedrich Katz states that hostility to Americans was far less widespread in the countryside than in the cities during the Mexican Revolution.[33] Villa himself positively admired the United States until President Wilson threw Washington's support behind Villa's arch-nemesis Venustiano Carranza in 1915.[34] Once in power, Carranza ironically put Mexican foreign policy on a far less friendly footing toward the Wilson administration, in part to placate his strongest constituency, Mexico's nationalist, urban middle class.[35] But even as relations were cooling between Mexico City and Washington, thousands of ordinary Mexicans were pouring across the border to land jobs in a booming American economy fueled by the material demands of World War I.[36]

The usefulness of the United States as leading national bogeyman was demonstrated time and time again during the decades following the Mexican Revolution. With the creation of the National Revolutionary

Party (PNR)—the forerunner to the PRI—in 1929 under strongman Plutarco Elías Calles, Mexico's political elites found it convenient to portray the United States as an ever present menace in order to perpetuate themselves in power. According to the political scientist Stephen Morris, the adoption of a corporatist system under the PNR/PRI that united the state with big business and organized labor and the consolidation of a one-party pseudo-democracy in the 1950s can only be fully understood as products of "the forced unity derived from or justified by the perception of an external [U.S.] threat." Morris describes anti-Americanism as a crucial element "in mobilizing support for one's cause or demobilizing one's opponents." In his view, the recurring depiction of the United States as a threat throughout the long reign of the PNR/PRI helped justify "a host of policy outcomes, ranging from Mexico's struggle to maintain an independent and at times anti-imperialist foreign policy, to its post-Revolutionary policy casting the State as the supreme arbiter and sole embodiment of the national interest."[37]

That message from the country's political establishment was reinforced by Mexico's motion picture industry during its Golden Age of the 1940s and early 1950s. The 1951 film *Una gringuita en México* (A Little American Woman in Mexico) condemned U.S. influence over the country. It opened with scenes of Mexico City and a voice-over noting how much the Mexican capital has changed, as evidenced by the signs in a modern restaurant touting the eatery's "waffles" and "hot cakes." "Little by little," the unseen narrator intones, "the physiognomy of a magical, customary, romantic Mexico is being lost." In a similar vein, the 1950 movie *Primero soy mexicano* (First I'm a Mexican) told the tale of a young Mexican who comes home after studying in the United States for a decade. The film recounts the young man's acquired preference for American cuisine and distinctively gringo mannerisms (upon his return to Mexico, he addresses his father as "Daddy" and shakes his hand instead of hugging him). But the Americanized veneer wanes over time, and by the end of the movie the youth has embraced anew the culture and customs of his native land. Yet another feature film of the era entitled *Acá las tortas* (1951) provided moviegoers with a like-minded parable: children returning from their studies north of the border openly disdained Mexican cuisine in favor of "more refined food" and spoke the bastard tongue of Spanglish, a development that their parents found to be most "embarassamente" (the correct term in Spanish would have been "vergonzoso"). Only after the death of a brother do the Americanized youngsters return to their roots and take their places in the family-owned business making *tortas* (sandwiches).[38]

Mexico's Lower Classes and the Lure of *El Norte*

During the PRI's long hegemony, the orthodox gospel preached by Mexico's political and cultural establishments championed the country's lower classes as the purest repository of national character. "The lower the station," wrote one film scholar, "the more genuine the Mexicanness."[39] But as market research firms would later discover, the country's lower classes have never fully shared the elites' penchant for anti-Americanism—and over time, the chest-pounding nationalism that typified PRI politicians throughout most of the party's reign became increasingly out of step with the evolving viewpoints of ordinary Mexicans.

That was documented by a series of opinion surveys that uncovered surprisingly benign views of the United States among the population at large. A poll published in the magazine *Este País* in 1991 asked people whether they would support a political union of the United States and Mexico if that would improve their living standards, and fully 59 percent answered yes.[40] Nine years later an almost identical percentage of Mexican respondents answered the same question in the affirmative. During the decade that witnessed the beginning of the NAFTA era, the percentage of Mexicans who endorsed greater economic ties with the United States rose significantly, from 57 percent in 1990 to 63 percent ten years later.

In the aftermath of another collapse in the value of the Mexican peso in 1994, the firm Market and Opinion Research International (MORI) asked respondents whom they blamed for the country's latest financial debacle. Nearly half held their government responsible, 18 percent pointed a finger at the leader of the recent Zapatista uprising in Chiapas, another 7 percent mentioned unspecified "foreign investors"—and only one in twenty blamed the United States.[41] When a third poll asked people which country would they most like Mexico to resemble, the United States topped the list. "The idea of a fervent nationalism and anti-Americanism has been exploited by the Mexican government [in the past] to enhance its negotiating position," said MORI pollster Miguel Basañez. "It's a myth. . . . It has been a weapon used by Mexican governments time and again, but is not supported by the facts."[42]

THE LEGACY OF SALINAS DE GORTARI

It was President Carlos Salinas de Gortari who fully registered the gap between the PRI's anti-gringo gospel and grassroots perceptions of the United States. Six months into his presidential term, the U.S.-educated economist was still mouthing the traditional PRI doctrine that Mexico had no interest in joining a free trade zone.[43] But in the view of Robert Pastor, a former Latin America affairs advisor to Jimmy Carter who met Salinas de Gortari when they were both graduate students at Harvard in the 1970s, Salinas's conversion to the free-trade faith was a response in part to the findings of a comprehensive government poll he commissioned as president. The opinion survey uncovered surprisingly positive attitudes toward the United States among the respondents. "When Salinas went for free trade, it was an extraordinary, 180-degree turn for Mexico, and he changed his mind for very practical, concrete reasons," says Pastor, who is now director of the Center for North American Studies at American University in Washington. "Mexico needed more foreign investment, and Salinas began to realize that the old anti-U.S. rhetoric was barely tolerated by the population. Salinas recognized that Mexico had changed in ways that the PRI didn't realize, and anti-Americanism just wouldn't cut it."[44]

Salinas de Gortari didn't understand those changes merely in intellectual terms, he made important policy choices based upon them. As president, he abolished quotas on the importation of books in Spanish and eliminated a long-standing requirement that movie theaters set aside 50 percent of all screen time for Mexican-made films. Salinas de Gortari eased restrictions on foreign participation in electronic media and amended an intellectual property protection law to make way for an invasion of established U.S. franchise retail chains like Home Depot and Starbucks.[45]

As we shall see in subsequent pages of this book, not all Mexicans view these policies as a positive development. But the implications of Salinas de Gortari's policy shifts for official and unofficial perceptions of the United States were vast and are still being felt years later. "Nationalism and sovereignty were redefined so that the United States became an ally rather than the enemy," wrote the Mexican American political scientist Rodolfo O. de la Garza.[46] The sociologist María García Castro agreed, stating that "in the last few years the State has begun erasing the nationalist discourse."[47] In the process, Morris writes, the Mexican government has redefined its role as one "of a far less activist State, relieved in a sense of the burden of having to mobilize to defend the nation against U.S. influence or to create and assert nationalist identity."[48]

Recent polling data have revealed some striking similarities between American and Mexican views of democracy and foreign policy issues. A 2004 binational opinion survey sponsored by the Chicago Council on Foreign Relations and two Mexican nongovernmental organizations found that an overwhelming majority of Mexicans (81 percent) and Americans (75 percent) regarded international terrorism as a critical threat to their vital interests. Nearly two-thirds of both Americans and Mexicans disagreed with the notion that rich countries play fair in trade negotiations with poor nations. A majority of Americans and Mexicans agreed that the United States should not play the role of world policeman and believed the United Nations should be strengthened, in part by giving the U.N. Security Council the right to authorize the use of force in the face of various security, political, and humanitarian crises. Mexican and American participants said they had generally favorable opinions of each other and also held positive opinions of Canada and friendly European countries. Solid majorities among both nationalities expressed support for a quid pro quo agreement that would give Mexicans more opportunities to work and live in the United States in exchange for a greater effort by Mexico to reduce illegal immigration and drug smuggling across the border.[49]

A September 2000 survey of nearly 3,000 people in the two countries funded by the Hewlett Foundation found that both Americans and Mexicans overwhelmingly preferred democracy over an authoritarian system of government. But the poll also revealed that the neighbors can have very different notions about what "democracy" signifies. A strong consensus (64 percent) existed among Americans of non-Mexican ancestry that the term "liberty" best captured the meaning of democracy. No such broad agreement was found among Mexican respondents: only one in four agreed with the selection of "liberty," while a similar number (26 percent) said that "equality" represented the essence of democracy. Only 8 percent of the Americans of non-Mexican descent chose "equality." (Interestingly, Mexican Americans like myself fell somewhere between those two groups, with about 42 percent agreeing that liberty equals democracy and 16 percent opting for equality as the true meaning of a democratic system.)

The American political scientist Roderic Ai Camp attributed the differing perspectives on democracy to most Mexicans' checkered experience with elections, which at least prior to 2000, had served mainly to keep the PRI in power through fair or foul means. "Mexicans have had little experience with democracy, and that democracy has functioned as a means to change a long-standing, authoritarian political model," noted Camp, writing two years after National Action Party presidential candidate Vicente Fox finally ended the PRI's seventy-one-year reign. "For Mexicans and many Latin Americans, democracy has more to do with equality, a social concept, than with freedom or liberty, traditional, political definitions."[50]

THE LAST WORD: CARLOS MONISVÁIS

Since the death of Octavio Paz in 1998, no Mexican intellectual has written more thoughtfully and knowledgeably about the impact of the

United States on Mexican society and culture than Carlos Monsiváis. In his published works, the writer and social critic has displayed a nuanced understanding and appreciation of American culture and consistently resisted any recourse to facile stereotypes about the Great Colossus of the North and its people. Now in his seventies, the Mexico City native has seen how the steady penetration of Americanizing influences has picked up in pace. But unlike some knee-jerk Mexican commentators, Monsiváis does not see this as necessarily a bad thing: as a young man he was in fact a "great fan" of the counterculture that burst upon the United States—and by extension, the entire world—in the 1960s.[51]

On the dichotomy of attitudes toward the United States that separates the country's elites from its lower classes, Monsiváis at first glance appears to buy into the prevailing PRI-era orthodoxy that true Mexican identity can only be found on the lower rungs of the social ladder. He contrasts the urge to imitate all things foreign among his more affluent countrymen with his less fortunate compatriots' loyalty to national values and customs. "[The elites] are obsessed daily with being less Mexican," he observed, "[while] the dominated are interested in re-appropriating the national, since this is all they can feel, their Mexicanness."[52]

Born in 1938, Monsiváis traces the former tendency back to the decade when he came of age, the 1950s, a time when a Mexican middle class hungry for glamour and "international status" also came into its own. This urbanized petty bourgeoisie was fed up with national films and Diego Rivera's murals, says Monsiváis; it was "indifferent to tradition, unable to fabricate coherent versions of the national past and future" and began to desert "the practice of Mexicanness." This emerging Mexican middle class embraced what he calls "the rampant North-Americanization of the country," and its sons and daughters soon became a captive market for the music of Elvis Presley and the latest blockbuster films fresh off the Hollywood studio assembly line.[53]

But Monsiváis parts company with the PRI-era political and cultural establishment in rejecting its idealized image of a pristine Mexican nation and culture once unsullied by American influence. Such a Mexico never existed for this worldly observer, and in his view it is pointless to speak of what Mexico might have been like without such a powerful, self-imposing neighbor to its north or how its remaining national essence should be shielded from further Americanization. "The process is global, irreversible and should be examined from perspectives that do not see everything as 'cultural penetration,' or imagine societies as perennially virginal," Monsiváis wrote in 1992. "If Americanization affects the culture, social vitality promotes resistances and 'Mexicanizes' in some way the Americanization."[54] Mexicanness in this view is a dynamic identity that affects the agent of change—Americanization—at the same time as it is being altered by that agent. It is, in other words, a two-way street, and Mexican identity is not threatened with extinction in the process. "The Mexican is no longer an existential and cultural problem," argued Monsiváis in language that seems at odds with some of Octavio Paz's musings in *The Labyrinth of Solitude*. "And despite the abundant discussions, national identity is not at risk. It is a changing identity, continually enriched with the talk of the poor, the contributions of the mass media, the academic renovations, the ideological discussions, Americanization, and resistance to the widening of misery."[55]

Monsiváis revisited the topic nine years later. In an article written for Harvard University's Latin American affairs quarterly *ReVista* about Mexico in transition, he addressed the rhetorical question "What is Mexico?" with a series of answers, many of which were done with tongue firmly in cheek. But in a more reflective passage, Monsiváis looked back on what he called "a century of Americanization obligating imitation, suppressing imagination, increasing tolerance, and taking classes in the contemporary world through vigilant observation of *lo gringo*."

There is, however, an upside as well as a downside to Americanization in his view. In a 2002 speech given in San Diego, California, the Mexican writer credited U.S. influence for pushing his country in the direction of democratic reform and greater respect for the rights of women and minorities.[56] But in assessing the overall impact of the United States on his nation, Monsiváis has also employed his sardonic wit to good effect.

"In 1847 the largest half of the national territory was lost, and since then the historical traumas have gotten worse," he wrote in 1995. "We once were a nation and now we are the spoils of the [U.S.] franchises."[57] Those words were penned barely a year after the NAFTA era had dawned, and nothing has accelerated the Americanization of modern Mexico more than that landmark trade agreement.

Part II

CHAPTER 4

NAFTA

THE DOUBLE-EDGED SWORD OF FREE TRADE

When Malcolm Lowry moved to Cuernavaca in 1938 to work on the manuscript of what eventually became his classic novel *Under the Volcano*, the Hotel Casino de la Selva was *the* gathering place for foreigners living in the picturesque city south of the Mexican capital. The resort hotel appears in the opening pages of the book, and Lowry is unsparing in his description of its already dilapidated state. "Palatial, a certain air of desolate splendor pervades it," the English author wrote. "For it is no longer a casino. You may not even dice for drinks in the bar. The ghosts of ruined gamblers haunt it. No one ever seems to swim in the magnificent Olympic pool. The springboards stand empty and mournful. Its jai-alai courts are grass-grown and deserted. Two tennis courts only are kept up in the season."[1]

Built in 1932 by a consortium of Mexican businessmen who enjoyed the backing of then President Abelardo Rodríguez, the hotel had passed into the hands of a Spanish immigrant named Manuel Suárez by the time Lowry turned up in Cuernavaca. A self-made millionaire, Suárez was a patron of the arts who hired Mexican and Spanish muralists like José Reyes Meza and Josep Renau to decorate the walls with colorful paintings depicting the history of Mexico from pre-Columbian times to the modern era. The Casino de la Selva soon emerged as the cultural epicenter of Cuernavaca, where visiting artists, writers, and political activists could rent bungalows on the luxuriantly foliaged twenty-four-acre site that had been carved out of the Amanalco Forest.

Suárez died in 1987, and his heavily indebted heirs later sold the Casino de la Selva to a hotel chain based in the city of Guadalajara. In 1996 the hotel's new owners defaulted on $63.7 million in back taxes they owed to the Mexican government; the property was then seized by the finance ministry. That spelled the beginning of the end for the storied Casino de la Selva. In 2001 a government agency in charge of selling off confiscated properties put the hotel on the auction block, and a winning bid in the amount of $10.4 million was submitted jointly by the U.S. discount store chain Costco and the Mexican retail store company Comercial Mexicana.[2] By most accounts, the grounds of the old hotel had fallen on even harder times than those described by Malcolm Lowry: bat guano covered the interior walls of some buildings, some of the old frescoes were crumbling from years of neglect, and the floor of the mural salon housing some of the finest art works was strewn with trash and human excrement. The two companies announced plans to build a pair of megastores on the hotel site, and within a matter of weeks the bulldozers had arrived, uprooting hundreds of trees and demolishing many of the old buildings erected by the late Manuel Suárez.

The suddenly endangered status of the murals galvanized environmentalists and political activists into forming a grassroots organization to halt the wholesale razing of the complex. In short order the future of the old hotel became a cause célèbre in Mexico, generating headlines in the national news media and drawing the attention of foreign correspondents based in the national capital. Lawsuits were filed, a boycott of Costco's existing network of stores in Mexico was launched, and a series of public demonstrations was held outside the entrance to the construction site.

The protest campaign culminated in August 2002 with an extended sit-in by demonstrators who wanted access to the hotel grounds in order to count the number of trees that were still standing. On the evening of August 21, hundreds of state and municipal policemen descended on the site and arrested thirty-three protesters on criminal charges ranging from sabotage and armed assault to vandalism and resisting arrest. The heavy-handed tactics used in the police crackdown triggered a protest march six days later that drew 15,000 onto the streets of downtown Cuernavaca.[3] But the drive to save the Casino from the wrecking ball failed in the end. A year after the sit-in was quashed, two massive, air-conditioned concrete blocks housing Costco's newest branch outlets and a Mega supermarket opened their doors to the buying public.

Where lush trees, shaded walkways, and quiet cabanas once stood, a vast sea of asphalt has been neatly partitioned into parking spots for shoppers lured by the bargain prices for soft drinks, breakfast cereal, automobile tires, and sporting goods. Customers wanting to grab a quick bite can choose between an outdoor snack bar adjacent to the Costco store that has tables festooned with Coca-Cola umbrellas or an unsightly coffee shop supposedly modeled on one of the Casino's old buildings that is fittingly called California. The sole concession to local culture is a small museum, housing one of the country's outstanding private collections of Mexican contemporary art, that sits on the edge of the premises. The only thing missing from this sad tableau of modern Mexico was a Muzak version of Joni Mitchell's famous song "Big Yellow Taxi" being piped in over the public address system of the Costco warehouse store. As I wandered down its aisles and past its well-stocked shelves, I could hear in my mind the signature lyric from the tune: "They paved paradise/and put up a parking lot."

THE INVASION OF THE MEGASTORES

The sacrifice of the old hotel complex upon the altar of American-style consumerism infuriates Flor Guerrero Goff. A self-taught artist who has devoted much of her adult life to political causes ranging from environmental issues to supporting the Zapatista guerrilla movement in Chiapas, Guerrero grew up in a household rich in culture. Her father Jesús Guerrero Galván was a successful painter from the state of Michoacán who married the daughter of a Spanish immigrant, and Flor's aunt was Elena Garro, the first wife of Mexican philosopher Octavio Paz and a respected author in her own right. Flor Guerrero is a quietly elegant woman whose slender figure belies her middle age, and her politics are decidedly left of center. But it would be misleading to describe Guerrero as anti-American. Her husband of twenty-four years is a U.S. citizen whom she met when they were both teenagers, and Charlie Goff runs one of the oldest English-language instruction schools in Cuernavaca. The couple were among the demonstrators who were jailed in August 2002, and in Charlie's case his bail was set at an exorbitant $10,000 as part of a clumsy effort by local authorities to portray the anti-Costco campaign as a plot hatched by meddlesome foreigners to deny Cuernavaca a sorely needed source of new jobs.

Flor Guerrero sees the ultimate failure to protect the Casino de la Selva from the designs of Costco/Comercial Mexicana as a parable for modern Mexico's embrace of the U.S. free-trade gospel. "Our struggle to defend the Casino de la Selva was basically a struggle against neo-liberalism," she explains in the living room of her painting-filled Cuernavaca home. "We see neo-liberalism here in our country as an economic, cultural, and political penetration at every level. In Latin America today, it isn't armies that are conquering us, it's megastores, transnational corporations. The Casino de la Selva is a dramatic case that should be held up as an example on a global scale. It was a devastating attack against our culture, our art and our environment."[4]

The residents of Oaxaca city felt the same way when McDonald's unveiled plans to open a fast-food restaurant under the stone arcades of the city's sixteenth-century main plaza known as the *zócalo*. The prospect of seeing the golden arches on a storefront in the heart of the city spurred many longtime Oaxaca residents to take action. Led by Francisco Toledo, Mexico's best-known living artist, protesters collected thousands of signatures from residents for an anti-McDonald's petition and covered the chosen site with banners that read, "No McZócalo" and "We don't want McDollars." To bolster national pride in Oaxaca's homegrown cooking, community activists started to hand out free servings of *atole*, a cornstarch-based beverage served hot, and traditional tamales stuffed with shrimp and pumpkin seeds to passersby in the city's main square. The clever ploy generated widespread sympathy among many city residents and highlighted the culinary heritage of a state that has contributed seven different varieties of mole sauce and two dozen kinds of chili peppers to Mexico's national cuisine.[5]

Toledo and his fellow *oaxaqueños* actually won their battle in the losing war against American-flavored globalization in Mexico when McDonald's shelved its plans to bring Big Macs and Quarter-Pounders to the city's *zócalo*. But Oaxaca is the exception that proves the rule: a similar bid to prevent Wal-Mart from opening a new store belonging to its Mexican subsidiary Bodega Aurrerá near the famous pyramids of Teotihuacán was abandoned after months of street protests, legal motions, and hunger strikes. (To be fair, the case against Wal-Mart was nowhere near as compelling as the arguments invoked against Costco in Cuernavaca and McDonald's in Oaxaca. The new store is over a mile away from the site of the ancient city that was built by an unknown indigenous civilization, and from the summit of the Pyramid of the Sun it is almost impossible to spot the Bodega Aurrerá amid the cluster of tacky commercial buildings in the nearby town of San Juan Teotihuacán.)

A Gigantic Steamroller

Big American companies did not figure prominently in most of the major privatizations of state-owned firms and banks carried out in the 1990s under President Carlos Salinas de Gortari. But even before the NAFTA treaty was signed by the United States, Canadian, and Mexican governments, Wal-Mart had identified Mexico as the first foreign market it would enter. In 1991 the Arkansas-based retail giant formed a partnership with Cifra, the holding company of the Bodega Aurrerá chain, and Wal-Mart has never looked back. Its growth has been extraordinary, and today Wal-Mart ranks as Mexico's single largest private-sector employer, with more than 150,000 workers on the payroll. It operates over 1,000 retail outlets nationwide, including 338 Aurrerá stores, 141 Wal-Mart Supercenter stores, 85 Sam's Club discount stores, 80 Suburbia department stores, 64 Superama supermarkets, and 360 Vips restaurants. In 2006 Wal-Mart de México racked up annual sales of over $18.3 billion, a figure that exceeded the total revenues of Mexico's entire tourism industry, and reported net profits over $1.148 billion for the year. Its revenue flows are equivalent to roughly 1 percent of Mexico's annual gross domestic product and account for almost 30 percent of all supermarket food sales nationwide. Wal-Mart has also acquired a loyal clientele: in a single year, customers visited its cash registers 565 million times.[6]

Only in Britain does Wal-Mart employ more people outside the United States, and Mexico's depressed wage scales enable the company to pay its Mexican workers a fraction of the salaries earned by its American employees. While the average Wal-Mart employee in the United States earns around $9 an hour, a newly hired Mexican cashier makes about $1.50 an hour. (And they're well remunerated compared to the teenaged volunteers who bag groceries and merchandise for free at Wal-Mart Supercenters and Superama supermarkets and depend entirely for their income on customers' tips.)

Small wonder that Mexican critics like Flor Guerrero challenge the claims by big American retail companies that they are doing the country a great service. "Who really benefits from these megastores?" she asks. "Perhaps the only good thing about these companies coming to Mexico is the jobs they create. But what kinds of jobs do we see? The salaries are terribly low, but the unemployment rate forces people to take those jobs."

Not all Mexicans share her point of view. Hundreds of residents in the town of San Juan Teotihuacán were lined up outside the new Bodega Aurrerá store when it opened its doors in the fall of 2004, and the taxi driver who brought me to Flor Guerrero's doorstep in Cuernavaca dismissed the naysayers who tried to block the arrival of Costco and Comercial Mexicana. "They said we were all against those stores, but the stores may bring more benefits than harm," shrugged Daniel Nieto Silva. "New jobs and investment were created, and there's a greater variety of products to choose from in those stores. Besides, the Casino de la Selva hotel never belonged to the people."

Guerrero acknowledges those rebuttals with an air of resignation. "The vast majority of the population is happy with these megastores," she concedes. "They're like a gigantic steamroller, and that's why we will be unable to stop them. There is a stretch of five street blocks in Cuernavaca where you feel as though you're in the United States. There's McDonald's, Burger King, Blockbuster, and that's what the people like. Among human beings there is an enormous, spiritual vacuum, and one way of filling that hole is to go shopping at these megastores."

The Mixed Legacy of NAFTA

The Home Depots, Pizza Huts, and Wal-Marts constitute some of the most visible signs of the Mexican economy's relentless Americanization. Not even at the height of Porfirio Díaz's long reign was the country ever so economically dependent on the Great Colossus of the North as it is today, partly because Díaz himself understood the perils of economic colonization. In a letter written to the governor of Sonora state in 1889, Díaz warned, "I would recommend you to favor European capital in order to balance it with American capital, since there is already a good deal of the latter in Mexico."[7] The dictator later made a point of awarding key railroad and oil-drilling concessions to British interests as a counterweight to the rapidly expanding presence of major American companies in the Mexico he ruled for three decades.

In the NAFTA era there is no such felt need to diversify the country's partners in trade and investment because Mexico's leadership sees no viable alternative to the United States. The free trade treaty that took effect on January 1, 1994, paved the way for an explosion in U.S. investment and trade with Mexico. Over the ensuing eight years the total amount of U.S. capital invested in the country rose by 58 percent, and U.S. exports to Mexico increased fourfold during the 1990s, from $28 billion to $111 billion.[8] Prior to the introduction of NAFTA, Mexico's exports to the United States represented only about 10 percent of its annual gross domestic product (GDP). Today that figure is closer to 32 percent. Add in the amounts of goods and services that Mexico imports from its northern neighbor, and two-way trade with the United States accounts for an estimated two-thirds of Mexico's annual GDP.[9]

The implications for Mexico's economic independence are sweeping. "In reality, NAFTA was much more than a trade treaty for Mexico," wrote the historian Lorenzo Meyer in 2003. "It was the beginning of a profound change in its historic relationship with the great neighbor to the north. Mexico ceased to define its national interest in terms of the degree of its independence relative to the United States and identified it instead with its closeness to and integration with that country."[10]

But the benefits of NAFTA for Mexico's future prosperity never fully lived up to its proponents' hype. Greater trade ties with the United States were supposed to boost wages and employment inside Mexico and reduce the pull factor drawing its citizens across the border in search of work. That demonstrably did not happen: the numbers of Mexicans entering the United States as illegal immigrants are greater today than was the case in 1994, in part because real wages in Mexico are actually lower now than they were at the time the treaty took effect. In all fairness, NAFTA was not entirely nor perhaps primarily at fault. The devastating peso crisis of the mid-1990s slashed real wages by 20 percent, and only now are salaries beginning to approach the levels prevailing in 1994. Advocates of the trade accords point to the estimated 700,000 new jobs that were created inside the in-bond assembly plants known as *maquiladoras* during the first seven years of the NAFTA era. But Mexico saw the competitive advantage afforded by its cheap labor gravely undermined by the rise of China as a global exporting behemoth, and, by the tenth anniversary of the NAFTA agreement, 300,000 of those new jobs had been eliminated as scores of American companies shuttered their Mexican operations and relocated to China and other countries with even lower wage scales.[11] In that same year, China replaced Mexico as the second largest supplier of imported goods to the United States.

The expansion of the *maquiladora* sector in the age of NAFTA has not necessarily bettered working conditions for its Mexican employees.

A report issued by the Washington-based Council on Hemispheric Affairs in the summer of 2007 noted that some Mexican companies that supply U.S. firms on a subcontractor basis pay their teenage employees less than 40 cents an hour, and worker protection provisions that were put in place under NAFTA are often ignored in practice inside the workplace. "Sweatshop workers possess almost no leverage to negotiate improved labor rights," the report concluded. "Refusing to work overtime, taking breaks (in spite of the fact that they are required by unenforced law), illness, visits to the doctor, and pregnancy tests have all been recorded as reasons for job terminations in the *maquiladora* sector."[12]

The unequal distribution of the fruits yielded by NAFTA has exacerbated existing inequalities of economic development within Mexico. An estimated 90 percent of new foreign investment under the treaty has gone to only four of Mexico's thirty-two states, and three of them are located along the U.S. border. In recent years those border states have grown at rates ten times greater than states like Oaxaca and Chiapas in Mexico's impoverished south.[13] "NAFTA has caused the gap to grow wider apart between the haves and the have-nots, between the north and the south, and between the exporting sectors of the economy and the sectors of manufacturing that cater to the domestic market," argues Carlos Heredia Zubieta, an economist and former congressman from the left-wing Party of the Democratic Revolution (PRD). "The mirage that exports have exponentially grown hides the fact that over two-thirds of them come from U.S. companies already established in Mexico. Mexican-operated and -owned companies have been displaced to a large extent, and we haven't looked after our national interests. We've gone from being a closed, protected economy to one that highly depends on foreign investment and free trade as engines of growth."[14]

That said, even some of NAFTA's harshest critics do not believe that Mexico might have been better off without the treaty. Stiffer competition from American companies and products forced Mexican workers and their employers to become more efficient, and a 2003 World Bank study concluded that the income gap between Mexico and the United States was smaller than would have been the case in the absence of NAFTA.[15] A more critical report issued by the Washington-based Carnegie Endowment for International Peace rendered a similar verdict about NAFTA's positive effects on the productivity of Mexican workers.

But that report also found that rising U.S. food exports to Mexico had devastated much of the economy in the hinterland. "The agricultural sector, where almost a fifth of Mexicans still work, has lost 1.3 million jobs since 1994," stated the report, entitled *NAFTA's Promise and Reality: Lessons from Mexico for the Hemisphere.* "U.S. exports of subsidized crops, such as corn, have depressed agricultural prices in Mexico. The rural poor have borne the brunt of adjustment to NAFTA and have been forced to adapt without government support."[16]

The View from Nopalucan de la Granja

The corn farmers of Nopalucan de la Granja consider themselves an endangered species in the age of NAFTA. Located ninety miles east of Mexico City, the town of 17,000 sits in the heart of a fertile agricultural valley where *campesinos* have been cultivating corn, beans, and barley for hundreds of years. Nopalucan's main claim to fame is based on a fluke of history. In 1851, a Spanish immigrant named Juan de la Granja transmitted the country's first ever telegram from the hitherto obscure farming town to Mexico City, an event that later inspired its residents to proclaim Nopalucan the national cradle of the telegraph and rename their community in the Spaniard's honor. A century and a half later, the residents of Nopalucan fear their town may soon make history of a different order. Like thousands of other rural communities scattered across Mexico, Nopalucan is seeing its economic lifeline directly threatened by the changes wrought by NAFTA—and the lifting of all tariffs and other restrictions on imported American corn and other crops in 2008 could eventually wipe out a long-established way of life in the Mexican countryside.

The cultivation of corn in what is now Mexico dates back five millennia, and the crop is grown on 60 percent of the country's farmland. Prior to the signing of the NAFTA accords, the nation's three million corn farmers were protected under a longstanding government policy of paying a guaranteed price for their annual harvests. Under the state-run National Company for Popular Subsistence (CONASUPO), these farmers benefited from an elaborate program of government subsidies and distribution networks that provided a safety net in the event of droughts or collapsing market prices. The program was hardly a success story: Mexico had become a net corn importer by the 1970s, and it was clear by the time Salinas de Gortari became president in 1988 that the system had manifestly failed to increase production sufficiently to meet rising demand for the food staple.

The CONASUPO program was earmarked for elimination under the terms of NAFTA, and since the treaty took effect the farmers of Nopalucan have seen the cost of fertilizer, fuel, and insecticides rise steadily while prices for their crops have remained flat. By their own admission, these farmers have no hope of ever competing with cheaper corn from Iowa and other farm belt states in the United States. Big multinational agribusiness companies like Cargill and Mexico's own Minsa and Maseca firms understandably prefer to buy a ton of imported U.S. corn that typically costs anywhere from 25 to 30 percent less than the same quantity of Mexican maize.

Not surprisingly, imports of Mexico's most basic foodstuff have soared in the NAFTA era. During the three years prior to the signing of the trade treaty, Mexico was importing about a million tons of maize on an annual basis. By 2001 that figure had surpassed the six-million-ton benchmark. It didn't take long for Felipe Calderón to feel the adverse effects of the country's rising dependence on imported U.S. corn. Corn tortilla prices skyrocketed within weeks of his inauguration in December 2006 as demand for corn-based ethanol fuel north of the border drove prices in the United States to their highest levels in a decade, and the ensuing "tortilla crisis" of that winter presented Calderón with the first major challenge of his fledgling administration.[17]

The consequences of enhanced competition from north of the border were not long in coming to Nopalucan. Stripped of their guaranteed price floor, many farmers in the town have been forced to seek part-time employment as construction workers in the nearby city of Puebla during the idle summer months to supplement their declining incomes. About one of every ten people in Nopalucan has voted with his feet and moved to either Puebla or Mexico City or immigrated to the United States. Some of the more fortunate farmers of Nopalucan have alleviated their plight by building corn flour plants to add market value to their harvests. Bertín Torres García is the president of an association of thirty-three farmers who pooled their resources to open such a processing plant in 2003 at a cost of $250,000. The plant produces 4,000 kilos of corn flour each day, and a portion of the output is set aside for a tortilla retail store that Torres and his colleagues established in the town to create an additional stream of revenue.

But the long-term prospects aren't rosy. Torres's three eldest children left Nopalucan and now live in the city of Puebla, and the fifty-year-old *campesino* has no idea who will take over his twenty-five-acre farm when the time comes for him to retire. "We still believe we have the strength to continue farming the land," says Torres. "But the outlook is bleak."

The farmers of Nopalucan believe the Mexican government is deliberately trying to drive them into extinction. Under the state-run PROCAMPO program, these farmers receive a subsidy of around $40 per acre, and that rural support scheme was scheduled to be phased out at the end of 2008. Yet the same U.S. government that champions the virtues of free trade at international summits still provides its farmers with huge subsidies that dwarf the PROCAMPO subsidy. The perceived double standard adds insult to injury. "The Mexican government should be more conscientious about giving small producers incentives to compete with our neighbors," complains Sergio Contreras Castillo, a father of five who belongs to the association headed by Bertín Torres. "When the border becomes completely open we don't know how we're going to survive, and that's why we are for the renegotiation of the free trade treaty."

When I visited Nopalucan in the fall of 2005, the PRD's presidential candidate, Andrés Manuel López Obrador, was the front-runner in the polls, and in his stump speech he repeatedly vowed to review those clauses of NAFTA that threaten to wipe out millions of Mexico's farmers in the coming years. But the *campesinos* of Nopalucan remained unconvinced that such pledges would ever be fulfilled by López Obrador or any other politician. "Right now they are campaign promises, and who knows if they'll remember having made them," sniffed Contreras. "Not a single president has been interested in making the country self-sufficient in grain production. That's just the way it is, unfortunately."[18]

Having Your Cake and Eating It, Too

In general terms, the NAFTA era has been hard on the little guy in the United States and Mexico, whether he be a corn farmer in the countryside of Puebla state or a unionized auto worker on a Michigan assembly line. But the trade treaty has been a big boon for big business in both countries. The steady elimination of trade barriers under the treaty has opened up the world's biggest economy to modern Mexican corporations like the cement producer CEMEX and the corn flour manufacturer Maseca that think globally and have outgrown their domestic markets. These companies are experienced hands at raising capital on Wall Street, and each spring they can have their pick of the brightest Mexican graduates of top U.S. business schools to replenish their managerial and executive staffs.

But the treaty has done almost nothing to open up some of Mexico's most oligopolistic industries to greater competition. More than a decade has elapsed since NAFTA became a reality, and the country's two leading breweries have maintained their iron grip over the national beer market. Just try ordering a bottle of Budweiser or Heineken the next time you visit Mexico City or Guadalajara. The barriers erected by a company with marketing and political clout can even apply to the products of a Mexican competitor from out of town. I've walked into dozens of bars and eateries in the national capital that offer the full range of beers distributed by the Mexico City–based Modelo brewery but refuse to stock my favorite Mexican lager, Bohemia, presumably because it's made by Modelo's Monterrey-based rival Cuauhtémoc. Imagine being unable to order a pitcher of Miller Genuine Draft in a St. Louis tavern simply because Anheuser-Busch happens to be based in that city!

The pattern is repeated in other major sectors of the Mexican economy. CEMEX controls between 45 and 50 percent of the domestic cement market. Telmex, the formerly state-owned telecommunications giant that was sold to a consortium headed by the Mexico City millionaire Carlos Slim in 1990, owns about 95 percent of the country's telephone land lines and has no real competitors in the data transmission industry. Owing to a single company's domination of a key industry like telecommunications, the cheaper prices for goods and services that privatization of government-owned corporations is supposed to deliver have yet to materialize for the Mexican consumer in many instances. A recent report issued by the Organisation for Economic Co-operation and Development found that Mexican business clients pay the highest long-distance phone rates among its thirty member countries.[19]

Not surprisingly, Carlos Slim has ranked as the richest man in Latin America for some time now, and he broke new ground in 2007 when he overtook Warren Buffet as the tycoon with the second highest net worth on *Forbes* magazine's annual list of the world's billionaires.[20] The octopus-like reach of his business empire makes it easy for middle-class Mexicans to spend a fair portion of their normal day padding the industrialist's bulging profit margins. A Mexico City white-collar worker can eat lunch at one of Slim's Sanborns chain restaurants, call his wife on a mobile phone supplied by Slim's Telcel company, buy a CD for his daughter's sixteenth birthday at one of Slim's record stores, pick up a chocolate cake on the way home from work at one of Slim's El Globo bakeries, and consult his account balance at Slim's bank online via Slim's internet service provider before going to bed.[21] The flagship of Slim's business empire will never be mistaken for a consumer-friendly operation. Telmex is notorious for cutting off phone service to a customer who hasn't paid his bill within a few days after the due date, and American and European expatriates frequently complain about the lousy reception furnished by the Telcel cellular phone network.

This state of affairs is unlikely to change any time soon. The country's two dominant television networks joined forces midway through Vicente Fox's term in office to lobby his government against proposals to license a third television network that would have substantially boosted competition in the broadcasting industry. Televisa and TV Azteca have the power to make or break politicians through their nightly newscasts and commercial airtime, and even left-wing politicians have occasionally expressed reluctance to challenge their stranglehold on the airwaves. During an hour-long interview that Andrés Manuel López Obrador gave me in the spring of 2005, the then Mexico City mayor comfortably fielded nearly every question I hurled at him about his presidential ambitions. But when I asked him whether a López Obrador government would revive the idea of breaking the Televisa/TV Azteca duopoly with a third television network, the candidate suddenly turned timid. "We're not going to stick our noses in that," he said with a nervous laugh, presumably mindful of how the television networks' coverage could torpedo his prospects in the then upcoming 2006 election. "Look, it's a very thorny subject." I followed that up with a question about Carlos Slim's quasi-monopoly in the telecommunications sector, and López Obrador went from being cautious to being downright disingenuous. "There already is competition [in that industry], there are other companies," he spluttered. "I think that Telmex has shown itself to be an efficient company."[22]

As a chronically dissatisfied customer of the company, I would have begged to differ. But his answers sent a very clear message to me at the time: the fattest cats of Mexico's private sector wouldn't have much to fear even if this so-called populist were to be elected president. López Obrador fell short of that goal in the end, and with yet another Harvard-educated technocrat in the presidential chair through the fall of 2012, the big corporations on the top rungs of the Mexican private sector can bank on healthy bottom lines and scant competition in their domestic markets for the foreseeable future.

The advent of NAFTA opened up many sectors of the national economy to U.S. companies. The results were a mixed bag: middle-class consumers benefited from the cheaper prices and wider product availability on offer at the megastores, but for Mexicans like Flor Guerrero it came at the price of an eroding cultural identity. NAFTA also put large numbers of rural Mexicans at grave risk while leaving unscathed a relative handful of tycoons who retained their grip on telecommunications, broadcasting, building materials, and other key industries. The challenges and opportunities posed by NAFTA also helped spawn a new breed of Mexican entrepreneur who welcomed Americanization with open arms.

CHAPTER 5

The New Breed of Mexican Businessmen

Emilio Azcárraga Jean doesn't make much of an impression when he enters a room. I was chatting with his lifelong friend Bernardo Gómez in Azcárraga's private office at one of Televisa's Mexico City studio complexes when the boyish-looking scion of the country's top broadcasting dynasty walked in. Gómez, who heads up the television network's news division, kept his gaze fixed on me and never so much as turned around to greet his putative boss. Azcárraga Jean wrested control of Latin America's biggest media company from a cousin after his father Emilio Azcárraga Milmo died in 1997, and it would have been unthinkable for a subordinate to behave in the presence of the elder Azcárraga like Gómez did that morning. An imperious, larger-than-life captain of industry, Azcárraga Milmo built Mexico's most profitable broadcasting company into a globe-spanning giant whose maudlin soap operas known as *telenovelas* have become popular prime-time fare for viewers in far-flung world capitals like Nairobi, Jerusalem, and Kuala Lumpur.

The elder Azcárraga had vision. He was one of the first Mexican businessmen to see in the millions of Spanish-speaking residents of the United States a huge mother lode of future profits. It was Azcárraga Milmo who founded the twelve-station Spanish International Network television company in the early 1960s that later evolved into the Univisión network that today dominates Spanish-language TV screens in the United States.

Azcárraga Milmo wore his patriotism on his sleeve and went to great lengths to conceal the inconvenient fact of his birth in San Antonio, Texas.[1] Yet by the winter of 2003, his Mexico City–born son said he was prepared to become a naturalized American citizen if that would help expand Televisa's business operations inside the United States. It struck me as a concession to expediency that would have appalled his red-white-and-green father, who succumbed to cancer at the age of sixty-six. "The most important market for us is the American, and at the end of the day it's also the safest," Azcárraga Jean told me in an exclusive interview in February 2003. "I am very proud of my country. [But] we need to grow in the United States by whatever means necessary. So if getting U.S. citizenship is the way to go, then we'll go that route."[2]

The Azcárraga family has no reason to harbor any feelings of warmth or gratitude toward the United States government bureaucracy. In 1986 Azcárraga Milmo was ordered to sell off most of his shares in the Univisión network by a judge with the Federal Communications Commission (FCC). The judge ruled that the elder Azcárraga's interests in the Los Angeles–based network violated a fifty-year-old law that placed a ceiling on the percentage of shares a foreigner can own in an American radio or television company. That FCC ruling indirectly led to one of Azcárraga Milmo's worst business decisions. If the Televisa magnate couldn't invest in the U.S. broadcasting industry to the degree he wished, then he'd try his hand at print media—and in 1990 the elder Azcárraga launched a daily sports newspaper called *The National*. The new publication piled up losses of $100 million and folded in less than eighteen months.

Hence my astonishment over his son's expressed interest in acquiring a second passport from the same government that had sabotaged Azcárraga Milmo's expansion plans in the U.S. television industry. If one of Mexico's richest tycoons in the young century was willing to pledge his allegiance to the United States of America in exchange for better access to that country's Hispanic market, that surely was compelling evidence that Mexicans' perspectives toward their northern neighbor were undergoing a transformation of historic proportions.

Azcárraga Jean subsequently shelved the U.S. citizenship project when tax lawyers advised him that his naturalization would make the worldwide earnings of the Televisa empire fair game for the Internal Revenue Service. But Azcárraga Jean is not a man who gives up easily. When his second wife, Sharon Fastlicht, was about to deliver their first child in February 2005, the Televisa chief packed her off to a hospital in San Diego to give birth—thereby ensuring that Azcárraga Jean's heir would forever be entitled to a U.S. passport.

Azcárraga Jean and the thirtysomething executives who run Televisa expressed their admiration for the United States in frank terms that their fathers and grandfathers would have been reluctant to utter to a fellow Mexican, let alone an American reporter. "All the executives of Televisa identify with American culture," allowed the company's vice president for finances, Alfonso de Angoitia. "I studied at the American College here. Some of my colleagues lived over there, some studied there and others have had a relationship with the United States for many years." When I asked Azcárraga Jean how he feels on the other side of the border, he contrasted his own experiences as a university student in San Diego in the late 1980s with the vogue that Latino celebrities and culture enjoy in the United States today. "The Hispanic was not well thought of, and speaking Spanish was bad," he noted. "Today you go to New York and speak Spanish, and people understand you. In Miami practically nobody speaks only English. Either an American learns to speak Spanish or he won't be understood. It's not like being at home in Mexico, but you do feel comfortable there."

The younger Azcárraga has done good business in the United States throughout most of his tenure as head of the family's media conglomerate. In 2003 Televisa and the Univisión network formed a partnership to launch five pay-TV cable channels aimed at U.S. Hispanic and Latin American audiences, and in 2004 Televisa collected nearly $100 million in royalties on original programming it sold to the U.S. broadcasting company. (Such healthy earnings did not prevent a bitter dispute from erupting between the two media giants in 2005 over a relatively meager $1.5 million in royalties that Univisión allegedly still owed the Mexican broadcaster from the previous year, and that row triggered a flurry of lawsuits that eventually ended in Televisa's decision to sell off all its shares in the U.S. company by the winter of 2007.)[3] According to Televisa executives, the estimated 44.3 million Hispanics and Latin Americans living in the United States now command disposable income that is at least equal to if not greater than Mexico's $1.2 trillion dollar annual gross domestic product. Against the backdrop of the Mexican economy's sluggish rate of growth in the new century, the Spanish-language market in the United States beckons like a modern-day version of the mythical El Dorado that Spain's *conquistadores* obsessively sought but never found. "The Mexican economy will grow at a much slower rate than will the Hispanic population on the other side of the border," says Bernardo Gómez. "It's the most important minority population in the United States."

THE LURE OF THE WORLD'S BIGGEST EMPORIUM

Televisa heads a select group of top Mexican corporations that are shedding old insecurities as they dive headlong into the U.S. economy. Economist Octavio Palacios of the Monterrey Institute for Technological and Higher Studies reckons there are no more than fifty companies in this adventurous class, yet the amount of Mexican direct investment in the United States has more than tripled in the ten years since NAFTA took effect, from $2.07 billion in 1994 to $7.9 billion in 2004.[4] The purchasing power of U.S.-born Hispanics in general and Mexican immigrants in particular are the big draw, and from corn tortillas to compact disc recordings of *norteña* music bands, Mexican companies are ideally positioned to satisfy their needs.

But Mexican immigrants and Hispanic Americans weren't always the main objectives for some Mexican companies that competed successfully in the United States before the dawn of NAFTA. José Cuervo tequila has been on the shelves of American liquor stores for decades, but as recently as the late 1990s the company didn't have an advertising campaign aimed specifically at the U.S. Latino community.[5] The Mexico City brewery Modelo enlisted the Florida Keys pop crooner Jimmy Buffet in the 1990s

to push its Corona Extra beer, and the hugely successful advertising campaign catapulted the bland-tasting lager past Heineken to become the
biggest-selling imported beer in the United States. But the tipplers target-
ed by the Jimmy Buffet ads weren't Latinos so much as college students
and non-Hispanic white yuppies. For Mexican companies operating
north of the border, the strategic decision to either promote a product to
the widest possible market or hone in on its traditional consumers may be
a function of the product's potential crossover appeal. You don't have to
be Mexican to enjoy a margarita or a plate of guacamole dip, but it sure
helps to fully appreciate the twists and turns in a *telenovela's plot*.

The experiences of Mexican companies that have invested in American
firms have not been universally happy ones. The Grupo México conglomerate acquired the U.S. mining company Asarco and its subsidiary
Southern Peru Copper Co. in 1999—just as world prices for commodities
started to tank. Carlos Slim's legendary Midas touch failed him when he
bought the money-losing CompUSA computer products retail chain and
watched it bleed even more red ink. Azcárraga Jean's ambitious plans for
the U.S. Hispanic market were dealt a severe blow in the summer of 2006
when the Univisión network's aging principal shareholder Jerry Perenchio
spurned a buyout bid from Televisa in favor of a $12.3 billion cash offer
from a consortium of investors led by the Israeli media mogul Haim
Saban. Within days of that setback, the Televisa Group announced plans
to unload the 11.4 percent stake of Univisión shares it owned.[6] CEMEX
chief Lorenzo Zambrano drew up ambitious plans for moving into the
U.S. cement industry soon after he took over as the company's CEO in
1993. But those plans hit a snag when the U.S. Commerce Department
slapped steep anti-dumping duties on Mexican cement exports, and
Zambrano refocused his sights on Spain for his first significant overseas
acquisitions.

NAFTA changed the rules of the game by making it much easier for
Mexican companies to enter the U.S. market. In 2000 Zambrano finalized
the $2.8 billion purchase of the largest cement company in the United
States, Houston-based Southdown. Other companies have had happier

experiences on The Other Side after NAFTA took effect. The Mexico City–based fruit drink company JUMEX has tripled sales to American consumers since 1993, and its top executives look forward to the day when its popular line of nectars and tropical juices can be bottled entirely inside the United States in order to save on shipping costs. "NAFTA had a very positive effect in every sense of the word," says JUMEX director-general Marcelo Rivero. "It promoted greater acceptance of Mexican products and made it easier to market them."[7]

As Azcárraga and his colleagues at Televisa demonstrate, attitudes toward the United States among younger generations of Mexican businessmen mark a significant departure from their predecessors. A retired American diplomat was struck by that change during his four-year stint in Mexico City. "Many of them are U.S.-educated and operate their business in a globalized environment, and they've internalized that," says former U.S. ambassador to Mexico Jeffrey Davidow. "Whereas their fathers had the stuffing knocked out of them by NAFTA and free trade, the younger people are a lot more switched on and willing to make the changes necessary to be seen as good partners."[8]

This new breed of Mexican businessmen faithfully reflects the times in which they have matured and taken charge, and how that environment differs from the one their self-made fathers knew. "Mexico's global or baby boomer capitalist is typically a child or a grandchild of the bootstrap capitalist," wrote the American political scientist Roderic Ai Camp. "This new generation recognized the globalization of the economy and capitalized on their linkages with North American and European firms."[9]

THE HEIRESS AND THE AMBASSADOR

The Mexican business elite's attraction to the United States has never been stronger. It achieved perhaps its ultimate expression in January 2005 when the U.S. embassy in Mexico City announced the engagement of the Mexican American envoy Tony Garza to Modelo brewery heiress María Asunción Aramburuzabala. In another era, that announcement might have triggered an outpouring of negative news stories questioning the patriotic loyalties of Mexico's richest woman. Not so in the early twenty-first century: while a cover story in *Proceso* did scorn news of their engagement as "a marriage of convenience," other Mexico City media outlets crowned Garza and Aramburuzabala "the golden couple" and hailed their forthcoming nuptials as "the wedding of the year." "At last some good news," gushed high society columnist Guadalupe Loaeza in the opinion pages of the newspaper *Reforma*. "At last something pleasant, beautiful, but above all romantic. Hallelujah, hallelujah! Do you realize what this signifies, what this symbolizes and the transcendental importance this can have for two friendly peoples, two neighbors who at times have their quarrels but adore each other deep down?"[10] One of the country's most respected analysts of international affairs used less florid language to characterize the broader significance of the matrimony. "It reflects the new reality of U.S.-Mexico relations," said Rafael Fernández de Castro, editor of the quarterly journal *Foreign Affairs en Español*. "We're so intertwined, I don't see any conflict of interest."[11]

The three-day wedding party that the heiress and the ambassador threw for themselves in the resort region of Valle de Bravo west of Mexico City was awash in American style and symbolism. First Lady Laura Bush flew in for the festivities and guests were treated to a Texas-style, open-air barbecue. Male guests were invited to play a round of golf with the bride-groom while their wives and girlfriends could go hiking in the hills above the valley with the blushing bride.

Marketing to Mexico's Middle Class

During the PRI's seventy-one consecutive years of rule in the twentieth century, there was one time-honored way to make a lot of money in Mexico: leverage your connections in the country's political establishment to snare fat government contracts. But as the bloated state sold off hundreds of public-sector companies and curtailed its role in the national economy in the 1990s, many Mexican businessmen placed renewed emphasis on courting the country's expanding middle-income families. Like Henry Ford, who designed the Model T in the early years of the twentieth century with the United States's burgeoning middle classes uppermost in mind, Ricardo Salinas Pliego has his gaze fixed squarely on their Mexican counterparts today. When the U.S.-educated entrepreneur became CEO of his family's Elektra appliance store chain in 1987, the business was on the verge of bankruptcy. But under his stewardship the company has grown from fifty-nine outlets to over a thousand in Mexico and three other Latin American countries, thanks in good measure to the success of a bank Salinas Pliego opened in 2002 to give Mexico's working and lower-middle classes easier access to consumer credit. Within five years of its inception, Banco Azteca had assembled the third largest network of branches in the industry, and its impressive track record encouraged Salinas Pliego to launch operations in Honduras, Guatemala, El Salvador, Peru, and Brazil in 2007.

Described by *Forbes* magazine as the country's third-richest citizen, with a personal fortune estimated at $4.6 billion, Salinas Pliego is a literally high-flying businessman who commutes to work via helicopter to avoid Mexico City's notorious traffic jams. He answers his own e-mail and doesn't see himself in the mold of the country's traditional capitalists. "The businessmen of 20, 30, or 40 years ago were part of the government and depended on the favors and contracts of the government,'" he told me in a rare interview in 2007. "That is no longer the case today, and we have been focused on the Mexican middle class."[12]

To be fair, much of Salinas Pliego's ten-figure wealth has come from his ownership of the country's second-largest television network TV Azteca, which he acquired through the government privatization program of President Carlos Salinas de Gortari (who is no relation) and with the help of a loan from the latter's scandal-smeared brother Raúl. And Salinas Pliego is no saint. He drew the attention of U.S. and Mexican regulators in 2003 when he made a $109 million profit off the purchase and resale of discounted debt owed by his Unefon cellphone company. The Securities and Exchange Commission (SEC) filed a landmark lawsuit accusing

Salinas Pliego of fraud, and under the terms of a settlement reached in September 2006 he agreed to cough up $7.5 million in penalties and compensation.[13] In 2005 the Mexican equivalent of the SEC ordered Salinas Pliego, TV Azteca, and one of his top executives to pay $2.3 million in fines in connection with the Unefon transaction.[14] That ruling is on appeal.

Over the years he has also used the bully pulpit of his television network to attack an array of political enemies and ex-employees, ranging from the disgraced Mexican pop diva Gloria Trevi to the country's then finance minister Francisco Gil Díaz. But in an era when the Bangladeshi microcredit banker Muhammad Yunus has been honored with the Nobel Peace Prize for making loans more accessible to his less advantaged customers, Salinas Pliego's pioneering efforts in that field have also won him high praise. "Maybe he's not the most scrupulous person in the world," says Jerry Haar, a Florida International University professor who uses Banco Azteca as an example of good business practice in a graduate management course. "But he wants to stimulate a consumer class among urban, working-class Mexicans, and I salute him for that."[15]

ITAM and the Mexican Technocracy

The evolution of economic policy in Mexico has charted a distinctly Americanized course in recent decades. The rise of the private Autonomous Technological Institute of Mexico (ITAM) as the country's leading incubator of neoliberal ideology was a watershed in that process. Founded by private business groups in 1946 as an alternative to the economics faculty at the publicly funded National Autonomous University of Mexico (UNAM), the ITAM had rather modest beginnings as an obscure night school. Its profile started to rise after the ITAM launched a new economics school in 1965 modeled on similar departments at foreign universities. The director of the ITAM's School of Economics was Gustavo Petricioli, a Yale-educated official at the country's central bank who would later become finance minister under President Miguel de la Madrid. Under Petricioli's stewardship, economics students at the ITAM acquired a thorough steeping in orthodox economic theory and were required to take two full years of English-language courses. As the political climate of the UNAM became more radicalized in the 1960s and less stringent admission standards inflated the number of enrolled students, the ITAM found its niche as an elitist institution that charged tuition fees beyond the reach of lower-class families and required full-time commitment by its students. The ITAM economics school specialized in monetarist theory grounded in the writings of the conservative American economist Milton Friedman, and outstanding pupils were recommended for graduate study at Friedman's school, the University of Chicago.

The transformation of the ITAM had the full backing of the central bank, the Banco de México. Within the Mexican government the central bank acquired a significant degree of autonomy throughout the late 1950s and 1960s, and its senior echelons included a number of officials who had studied at American universities on scholarships provided by the Banco de México starting in the 1940s. Perhaps the most influential official in this context was Leopoldo Solís, a product of the UNAM who obtained a graduate degree in economics from Yale in 1959 on a Banco de México scholarship and later became director of the central bank's department of economic studies. Solís chose to teach economics at the ITAM and the state-funded university Colegio de México instead of the leftist-dominated UNAM, and among his protégés were Francisco Gil Díaz (who went on to become finance minister under Vicente Fox), future Banco de México chief Miguel Mancera, and the young Ernesto Zedillo. "During the 1960s and 70s, the ITAM economics program became thoroughly Americanized," wrote the American sociologist Sarah Babb. "The source of this Americanization was not the businessmen who financed the ITAM and sat on its governing board but rather the Mexican central bank. It was principally through the Banco de México that new foreign models were transmitted to the ITAM in the 1960s and 70s."[16]

This Americanizing trend was not universally applauded by older Mexican economists. Their generation had been schooled in protectionist models of economic development that advocated government spending as a healthy stimulus for growth. "It is easy to send people to study in the United States," Consuelo Meyer L'Epee told Babb in a 1996 interview. "The problem is that they come back thinking that Mexico is the United States. I studied to be an economist in the service of my country." Similar words of caution were expressed by Jesús Silva-Herzog Flores, who served as finance minister in de la Madrid's first cabinet but later resigned in protest in 1986 over the president's belt-tightening austerity policies. In a 1967 book entitled *To a Young Mexican Economist*, Silva-Herzog issued a caustic warning to future generations of Mexican policymakers: "The native economist of a peripheral country . . . who follows the writings of a foreign author to the very letter . . . resembles the servant who grotesquely imitates the fine manners of his master."[17]

THE IMPORTANCE OF THE AMERICAN MBA DEGREE

A parallel process of Americanization has occurred at the highest echelons of the Mexican private sector. For an aspiring corporate executive, a master's degree in business administration from a top-drawer American university has become the equivalent of a Ph.D. in economics from Yale or Chicago for a future functionary of the country's finance ministry. The tradition of sending children across the border to complete their university education dates at least as far back as the late nineteenth century, when the parents of future president Francisco I. Madero packed him off to the Berkeley campus of the University of California for a year to polish his English and study agronomy.[18]

The wealthiest families of Monterrey did the same in the early years of the twentieth century. The Massachusetts Institute of Technology (MIT) was a particular magnet for the city's leading capitalists like Andrés Marcelo Sada, who enrolled at MIT in 1947 and later became president of the Grupo Cydsa textiles and chemicals conglomerate. A more contemporary example is Dionisio Garza Medina, the chairman and chief executive officer of the Monterrey-based automobile parts and petrochemicals company Alfa, who obtained graduate degrees from both Stanford and

Harvard. "Unlike many self-made Mexican capitalists, this younger global capitalist is well-educated, with advanced degrees in business and engineering," noted professor Roderic Ai Camp in 2002. "Many of these younger capitalists, similar to the technocratic prototype in the political power elite, have studied at American universities, typically at Ivy League schools. Their graduate studies in these academic programs, and their residence in the United States, contributed to some shared networking and socialization experiences."[19]

There are of course a few conspicuous exceptions to this general rule. Emilio Azcárraga Jean doesn't have a single university degree to his name, having flunked out of a series of academic institutions before entering the executive ranks of the family's Televisa group. TV Azteca chief Ricardo Salinas Pliego does have an MBA on his resumé from Tulane University, but he is rather scornful of the degree as a qualification for job applicants. "It is of zero importance because [business schools] teach them to think like bureaucrats," says Salinas Pliego. "I and the world at large need people with initiative and creativity, people who don't belong to a conformity. I don't regard [the MBA] as a requirement, quite the contrary, I see it as a negative."

But for most employers, an MBA from a prestigious American university remains an almost indispensable credential for any young Mexican who wants to land a well-paying managerial position fresh out of school. Rodrigo Becerra Mizuno was a first-year student at Dartmouth's Amos Tuck School of Business Administration when I asked him for advice about his alma mater, Boston University (BU), where my elder daughter Claire wanted to attend. When Becerra began applying to universities in the fall of 1993, the NAFTA accords were only months away from taking effect under then President Carlos Salinas de Gortari, and that was a key factor behind his decision to enroll at a U.S. college for his undergraduate studies. "I chose BU because Mexico was undergoing a lot of changes with Salinas, and all these guys in his government were American-educated people like him from top schools in the northeastern United States," he explained. "I felt there would be a lot of opportunities opening up, that we were going to be closer to the U.S., and if American firms started to settle in Mexico they would prefer to have Mexicans who've been educated in the U.S."[20]

Becerra thought he had good connections as the son of a lawyer who had worked at Televisa under Azcárraga Jean's father. But as he discovered when he graduated from BU in 1998, a bachelor's degree from an American university does not automatically translate into the kind of attractive position in government service that Becerra wanted. "When I went back to Mexico I didn't know anybody, and there wasn't that much of a difference in the salaries paid to somebody with a bachelor's degree from the United States and someone with a bachelor's degree from Mexico," he recalled. "The value I placed on my degree from BU was perhaps not as high as I had thought."

Becerra spent two years working in the Mexican private sector before finally landing a government job in 2000 as deputy chief of staff under President Fox's finance minister Gil Díaz. During his nearly four years at the ministry, Becerra noticed that most of the senior staff aides had attended the ITAM and a number had gone on to obtain their master's degrees from exclusive U.S. universities. He drew the obvious conclusion. "I found that the degrees that were most highly valued were master's degrees and doctorates, and I was starting to feel the pressure that I was the only one without an advanced degree," recalled Becerra. "In order for you to get promoted, you have to prove you could get an advanced degree from an elite school. The selection process is very stringent compared to a Mexican program, and they really like people who get through that process. It's like proving you're good enough to work with the team."

Becerra applied to ten business schools in the United States and chose Dartmouth's Tuck School. It didn't take him long to discover how attractive a young Mexican with an MBA degree from a top American university has become for his own country's private sector. The Mexican office of the international consulting group McKinsey sends recruiters to New York each year in search of such prospects, and CEMEX will pick up the tuition expenses of a promising employee who gains admission to a business school like Stanford or Harvard. "The networking problem I had after getting my bachelor's degree won't be a problem after getting a master's from Tuck," predicts Becerra.

The recent passage of corporate governance laws in the United States like the Sarbanes-Oxley Act will further enhance the appeal of a freshly minted MBA graduate like the thirtyish Becerra. One of the provisions in that legislation requires foreign companies listed on American stock exchanges to tighten up their internal fraud controls or face possible legal sanction by U.S. government regulators. The importance of complying with those new requirements was underscored by the SEC's investigation of Salinas Pliego's lucrative purchase of discounted debt from his own cellphone company, and the civil suit brought by the feds against his media empire spurred Becerra to learn more about corporate governance issues. He spent the summer between his first and second years at business school working as an intern at the Washington offices of the International Business Ethics Institute. "As Mexican companies develop and new corporations emerge, they'll have to learn the rules of the game in the U.S. and comply with those regulations," notes Becerra. "Those who don't will lose access to the world's biggest capital market, the New York Stock Exchange." The investment in time and tuition money was well worth it. Within weeks of getting his diploma from Dartmouth in the spring of 2006, Becerra had moved to Seattle to work for Microsoft as a manager marketing the company's new Windows Vista software to government sector clients.

The United States looms larger today for young Mexican entrepreneurs and executives than it did for their forerunners of thirty years ago. A select number of globally oriented Mexican corporations have shed old insecurities and plunged head-first into the world's biggest emporium. Some have done extremely well, like the Modelo brewery and its trademark Corona Extra beer; others have fared poorly, like Carlos Slim and his ill-fated acquisition of the CompUSA retail chain. An MBA from a prestigious American business school has become the *sine qua non* degree for an aspiring corporate vice president. At home, this new breed of Mexican businessmen sees their fortunes intertwined with those of their country's expanding middle class in ways that evoke American captains of industry in the first half of the twentieth century. A revealing microcosm of Americanization in the Mexican private sector is a newspaper that made its debut just weeks before the start of the NAFTA era and showed the rest of the media industry that quality journalism in modern Mexico was not only possible, it could also be quite profitable.

CHAPTER 6

The Modern Mexican News Media

My return to Mexico in June 2000 after an absence of twelve years was full of eye-opening episodes. Owing to my professional background, perhaps the most palpable revelation of all occurred on the morning I picked up a copy of the newspaper *Reforma* for the first time. In visual terms, the broadsheet was a far cry from the stodgy, black-and-white dailies I read in Mexico City during my stint there in the 1980s. The splashy use of color and attractive layouts brought to mind the front page of *USA Today*, the impressive stable of influential columnists evoked the editorial pages of the *New York Times*, and the expanse of sections covering everything from financial news and show business to fashion and food reminded me of the bulky contents of my hometown newspaper, the *Los Angeles Times*. Everything about *Reforma* betokened a state-of-the-art, big-city newspaper from the United States.

The rise of *Reforma* represented a major milestone in the history of the Mexico City press in ways that transcended the cosmetic. It was the brain-child of Alejandro Junco de la Vega, the University of Texas–educated scion of a newspaper publishing family who owned the Monterrey daily *El Norte*, and Ramón Alberto Garza, the *El Norte* editor who began his distinguished career in journalism as a copy boy at the age of seventeen. *Reforma* was originally conceived as a joint venture between the Junco family and Dow Jones, the parent company of the *Wall Street Journal*, that would combine the authoritative business news coverage of the American partner with the reputation for independent political journalism that had become a hallmark of *El Norte* ever since Alejandro and his brother Rodolfo inherited the paper in 1973. The proposed partnership with Dow Jones was later downgraded to the introduction of a news service, and *Reforma* made its debut on Mexico City newsstands as the exclusive property of the Junco family on November 20, 1993.

Junco and Garza had established an impressive track record of profitability and editorial excellence at *El Norte*. When he became publisher of the newspaper at twenty-four, Junco took over a morning daily of modest journalistic repute with a circulation of around 40,000. In the early 1980s *El Norte* became the first provincial paper from outside Mexico City to open a news bureau in the capital, and that far-sighted decision was amply rewarded when it became the only Mexican newspaper to garner major awards for its coverage of the September 1985 earthquake that killed an estimated 20,000 people. Under the joint direction of Junco and Garza, who was appointed editor-in-chief in 1982, *El Norte* achieved a 90 percent penetration of Monterrey's newspaper market and boosted its subscriber base to over 150,000.

Yet there were many in Mexico City who wondered whether the formula that had worked so well for the Juncos on their home turf would succeed in the nation's capital. One was Rossana Fuentes-Berain, the finance editor for the respected tabloid *El Financiero* who initially declined Garza's invitation to join *Reforma* during its first six months of operations. Another was Lorenzo Meyer, the widely quoted historian from the state-funded Colegio de México university, who later became one of several respected columnists raided by Garza from *Excélsior, La Jornada*, and other rivals to bolster the prestige of *Reforma* in the early going. "I was actually in meetings where people from Mexico City openly asked us why we were going there since we were going to fail," recalls Lázaro Rios, a native of Monterrey who worked closely with Garza to launch the newspaper and later replaced him as editor-in-chief. "For which we were very thankful, because the other newspapers stayed put where they were and did not change."[1]

SHOWDOWN

The episode that convinced the Mexico City skeptics of the upstart out-siders' resolve to produce a truly independent newspaper began on the first anniversary of its founding. On November 20, 1994, the PRI-controlled union of newspaper vendors ordered its members to stop selling *Reforma* on the streets of Mexico City, a move widely interpreted as a punishment by the outgoing government of President Carlos Salinas de Gortari for the negative coverage it had received in the newspaper. The announced boycott did not represent Junco's first showdown with a vengeful Mexican presi-dent. In 1974, barely a year after he took over the reins at *El Norte*, the gov-ernment-run newsprint monopoly Pipsa cut off the paper's supply as a sign of Luis Echeverría's displeasure with the Juncos. In 1982 *El Norte* ran a headline that criticized President José López Portillo, and armed federal police were stationed outside *El Norte's* building in downtown Monterrey and the school where Junco's children attended classes.

Twelve years later the *Reforma* publisher responded to this latest round of government intimidation by deploying his wife, the newspaper's reporters, and even high-profile columnists like Germán Dehesa on the streets of the Mexican capital to sell papers. Junco then hired his own army of vendors, but when some of them were beaten up by thugs, he assigned photography students to accompany the vendors and take pic-tures of fresh assaults, which got prominent play in the newspaper. The orchestrated boycott eventually failed, and *Reforma's* credibility as a news-paper that would stand up to the powers that be was firmly established in the public's mind.[2] "The fact that *Reforma* had resisted a veiled govern-ment attempt to blackmail it through distribution became a marketing device in and of itself," recalls Fuentes-Berain, who joined *Reforma* in 1994 and spent six years on its staff as a senior editor in charge of special investigative projects and opinion surveys. "After that distribution fight, it was clear to me that it would become a newspaper that could portray the kind of openness that Mexican society was already engaged in and committed to."[3]

On its front page *Reforma* calls itself the *Corazón de México* (The Heart of Mexico). But from the outset Garza and Junco intended to create a newspaper patterned after leading American dailies in style, substance, and even personnel policies. *Reforma* adopted the broadsheet format of major U.S. newspapers and offered young journalists wages that were among the highest in the industry. The competitive salary structure had a dual purpose—to lure top talent and also deter reporters from accepting *embutes*, the cash payments in sealed envelopes that had long been distributed by government spokesmen to underpaid journalists in exchange for positive coverage. Junco and Garza had no interest in putting out a paper that read like a government mouthpiece, such as *Excélsior*, or that copied the stridently ideological stance of the left-wing tabloid *La Jornada*. "The newspapers in Mexico City had always been Europeanized and sided with a political agenda," explained Garza. "We wanted a journalism based on facts. That is the American school, and that's what people liked."[4]

Like his boss, Garza had studied journalism at the University of Texas on a scholarship provided by the company, and both he and Junco had been strongly influenced by a professor at its journalism school named Mary Gardner. After Junco became publisher of *El Norte*, he started bringing Gardner down to Monterrey on her summer breaks from teaching to train his young staff members in the finer points of reporting, writing, and ethics. "*El Norte* was her summer school, and Mary Gardner was a kind of moral accountant for the newspaper," Garza said. "What Gardner and the Juncos inculcated in us were very important techniques like investigative journalism, a pragmatic idealism and, perhaps most important of all, the need to work in a newsroom as a team. We blended the best aspects of the U.S. news media."

Changing the Face of the Mexican Press

Junco and Garza also appreciated the importance of a newspaper's design. And they knew just the right man for the job: Eduardo Danilo Ruiz, a gifted, Stanford-educated native of Monterrey who was hired as the art director for *El Norte* in 1982 even before he received his bachelor's degree in fine arts. Influenced by *USA Today* and other American newspapers, Danilo introduced extensive use of color at *El Norte*. The final results caught the eye of Roger Black, the renowned American design guru who had updated the look of *Newsweek* when he was the magazine's art director in the early 1980s. Danilo later left *El Norte* in 1989 to form a joint venture with Black with offices in New York and Monterrey.

As they made preparations for the launch of *Reforma*, Junco and Garza recruited Danilo to develop a fresh design that would instantly set apart the new publication from its competitors in the Mexico City market. He leapt at the opportunity. "Junco and Ramón value design as a strategic process and a practice for making a newspaper look more competitive and easier to read," Danilo told me during an interview at his Monterrey office. "When I began working at *El Norte*, the newspaper was already forty-five years old and I had to respect that lineage of style. But *Reforma* gave us the opportunity to reinterpret *El Norte*, and it was a moment in the history of newspaper design to offer the industry a new interpretation of what a newspaper should look like in the 1990s."[5] He devised a finer serif typeface than that of *El Norte*, giving *Reforma* a more sophisticated appearance, and the newspaper's green logo in Egiziano font bore a faint resemblance to the distinctive red letters of the *Newsweek* magazine brand.

The design of *Reforma* was an instant hit, both at home and abroad. When it debuted on newsstands alongside the dull, anachronistic front pages of *Excélsior* and *El Universal*, *Reforma* looked like a peacock in a display case full of gray pigeons. The fledgling publication won awards from the prestigious Society of Newspaper Design in 1995 and again in 1998. "There is definitely an American influence," says Danilo. "The whole revolution in newspaper design occurred in the United States during the 1970s, and in my work with Roger Black we have evolved a philosophy and design style that is American as opposed to European. We were the first paper [in Mexico City] to launch weekly feature sections, Sunday magazines, and suburban supplements, and that is clearly an American way of organizing a newspaper. It was totally different from any newspaper in Mexico City."

"More Than a Newspaper, *Reforma* Is a Brand"

Reforma has its share of critics, and some former employees believe the newspaper has lost the spark and dynamism of its early years. Its center-right editorial slant and the Monterrey background of its owners leave the newspaper open to suspicions that it has a secret pro-U.S. agenda, a charge that *Reforma* editors emphatically deny. There certainly were days during the heated 2006 presidential election when the editors seemed to have abandoned all pretense of objectivity in their single-minded quest to bolster the conservative Felipe Calderón's prospects at the expense of Andrés Manuel López Obrador.

In some respects, *Reforma* can be rather parochial for a publication widely regarded as the premier newspaper in one of the world's great capital cities. International news was buried at the end of the first section for the first ten years of *Reforma*'s existence, and only on rare occasions does a foreign news story with no obvious Mexican angle lead the front page. Its coverage of U.S. news is by all accounts pedestrian and almost entirely done out of Washington and New York. (When the newspaper introduced an updated design on the twelfth anniversary of its founding on November 20, 2005, the Sunday edition carried a new, sixteen-page section devoted primarily to international news, but its content was still mostly wire service copy.) The veteran journalist Raymundo Riva Palacio minces no words about the newspaper where he once worked as a columnist and head of its investigative reporting team. "They focused best on their marketing strategy with a very questionable criterion, which was to subordinate information to publicity," wrote Riva Palacio. "More than a newspaper, *Reforma* is a marketing brand."[6]

A fellow ex-employee of *Reforma* also sees the newspaper as very much a commercially driven enterprise. "It's fair to say it's a yuppie newspaper," says Rossana Fuentes-Berain. "It will become more so as the Mexican population is more and more divided into different consuming sectors, and advertisers are looking for those sectors with the most disposable income rather than the general public." *Reforma* editor-in-chief Lázaro Rios acknowledges that the newspaper is principally aimed at highly educated readers on the top rungs of Mexico City's socioeconomic ladder, and Riva Palacio notes that *Reforma* isn't the only major newspaper in town to succumb to commercial considerations. He faults *El Universal*, where he was recently named editor-in-chief, for also caving in to those dictates. "These two newspapers seem to have fallen prey to one of the great paradoxes of the press, whereby financial dependence on private advertisers undermines its political and economic coverage," argued Riva Palacio. "The bulk of their content is dedicated to the entertainment [of their readers]."[7]

That said, Riva Palacio salutes the great strides that *Reforma* and a select group of other print media have made toward creating a genuinely free press in Mexico. "*Reforma*," he wrote, "joined a handful of publications in Mexico City like *La Jornada*, *El Financiero*, and *Proceso* that maintained an independent and persistent editorial line during the 1980s and 1990s, which made an enormous contribution to changing perceptions among voters." Junco has become a role model for an entire generation of Mexican news media executives: the publishers of the Hermosillo newspaper *El Imparcial* and the León daily A.M. have cited their colleague from Monterrey as someone who inspired them to adopt more independent and assertive standards of journalistic coverage.

Reforma's formula has clearly delivered the goods in commercial terms, judging from the enormous number of ads that are packed into the various sections of each day's paper. Its demonstrated success was instrumental in convincing Junco's counterpart at *El Universal*, Juan Francisco Ealy Ortiz, to transform what one American scholar called a lapdog of a newspaper into more of a watchdog.[8] When it comes to the bottom line, the Junco family appears to have fulfilled the vision of William Orme, Jr., a former executive director of the Committee to Protect Journalists and a foreign correspondent based in Mexico City in the 1980s. In the foreword to a book he edited about the Mexican press in 1997, Orme wrote: "Several leading publishers and broadcasters have discovered that editorial independence is not only possible but often profitable. And that is potentially revolutionary."[9]

That conceptual breakthrough also took hold to a limited degree inside the news division of Televisa. When I lived in Mexico in the mid-1980s, the broadcasting behemoth blatantly favored the PRI in its coverage of elections and other political news. The campaigns of opposition party candidates either received short shrift on anchorman Jacobo Zabludovsky's nightly newscasts or were completely ignored. Its owner, Emilio Azcárraga Milmo, personally reviewed story lists for Zabludovsky's *24 Horas* program and issued directives on how sensitive topics should be covered. Televisa's unconditional loyalty to the PRI was openly acknowledged by the network's information director, Félix Cortés Camarillo, in 1986. The allegiance of Azcárraga Milmo and top executives of Televisa to the PRI gives "our communications policy a partisan line," declared Cortés. "Our commentators interpret and place news items with the confidence of the company in accordance with our political tendency."[10] His boss put matters more bluntly. "We are of the PRI, members of the PRI," Azcárraga Milmo told a gathering of prominent politicians in 1988. "We do not believe in any other option. And as members of our party, we will do everything possible so that our candidate triumphs."[11]

When Azcárraga Milmo died of cancer in 1997, his son realized that a change in news coverage policies was long overdue. At the age of twenty-nine Emilio Azcárraga Jean inherited a company in debt to the tune of $1.3 billion, and the once sky-high ratings of Zabludovsky's newscast had fallen behind those of *Hechos de la Noche* (Events of the Night), the flagship news program of Mexico's second major network, TV Azteca. On the print side of the news industry, *Reforma* had raised the bar for fairness and credibility in ways that resembled the U.S. news media, and its achievements had made an impression on Azcárraga Jean. The new Televisa chief knew it was no longer viable for the network to serve as a thinly disguised mouthpiece for the Mexican government and ruling party. "In news, the credibility issue was very sensitive," he later admitted in an interview. "We had a very grave problem here."[12]

Within a matter of months, Zabludovsky had been removed from *24 Horas* and outspoken critics of the PRI were brought in as guest commentators. Azcárraga Jean's managers hired an American consultant, and Televisa technicians were dispatched to CNN's headquarters in Atlanta to study state-of-the-art broadcast news practices. Televisa's coverage of the 2000 presidential election campaign that finally broke the PRI's long grip on power was the most even-handed in its history. But six years later the network was being accused once again of bias, in this instance for Felipe Calderón of President Vicente Fox's National Action Party, and supporters of losing candidate Andrés Manuel López Obrador jeered and threatened Televisa camera crews at a number of outdoor rallies in the summer of 2006.

Is There Mexican Content Beneath an Americanized Look?

The American influence on Mexico's fourth estate dates back to the early years of the twentieth century. The founding of *El Universal* and *Excélsior* in 1916 and 1917, respectively, is widely regarded as the dawn of the modern era in Mexican journalism, and both newspapers broke new ground when they began carrying wire service stories from the Associated Press. The new Mexico City dailies borrowed the inverted pyramid structure of news articles favored by American papers and copied many visual aspects of the *New York Times*, from its trademark typeface to layouts that routinely packed the front page with upward of twenty stories. Rodrigo de Llano, the longtime publisher of *Excélsior*, spent six months out of every year living in New York, and under his leadership the newspaper reproduced foreign news stories supplied by the New York Times News Service.

The author and journalist Jenaro Villamil writes frequently about the Mexican news media for the respected weekly newsmagazine *Proceso*, and he cites *El Financiero* as the best example of a modern newspaper that was successfully modeled on American publications. In its heyday in the early

1990s, *El Financiero* combined authoritative reporting of financial and business news with a nonpartisan approach to its political coverage.

But Villamil also notes that some publications bear little resemblance to their American counterparts. His present employer *Proceso* is unabashedly left-wing in its editorial slant, and the same holds true for the daily tabloid *La Jornada*. In other instances, the parallels with U.S. newspapers and magazines have more to do with design and business organization than with editorial content. "The notion of an Americanized media consists of copying the technological advances, the designs, the layouts, the brief articles, and the high quality of printing," says Villamil. In that sense, the modern Mexican press may mirror the dynamics of Americanization in the society at large: it may increasingly *look* American, but its defining essence remains intact. "The Americanization of society has taken place in terms of form and taste, but the hard core of Mexican identity continues to be a very special identity," he notes. "Mexico's media reflect that tension. In formal terms they are very similar to American media, but in terms of content they continue to be very Mexican. *Reforma* may be inspired by the *Miami Herald* as a newspaper of good image and printing quality. But it's still a metropolitan daily with a focus on the city that publishes stories on sewage, chaotic traffic and potholes in the streets."[13]

THE ANTI-GRINGO IMPULSE

Much of Mexico's mainstream press continues to function as a vehicle for lingering anti-American sentiment. Its favorite lightning rod for such resentment is, ex officio, the serving U.S. ambassador. That is in good measure the legacy of Henry Lane Wilson, the ruthless American ambassador who secretly backed Victoriano Huerta's bloody coup against the country's democratically elected president, Francisco I. Madero, in 1913. In more recent times, most U.S. envoys have tried to conduct themselves with greater discretion and, well, diplomacy. But there have been notable exceptions, like the actor-turned-ambassador John Gavin, who was appointed to the post by Ronald Reagan and behaved like a strutting pro-consul throughout much of his five-year tour in Mexico City.

The nation's news media had a field day with Gavin, but even career diplomats with a more nuanced sense of the way things work in Mexico have been treated roughly in the national press. Former ambassador Jeffrey Davidow recalled a photo that appeared in Mexico City newspapers on the morning after he presented his credentials to President Ernesto Zedillo in 1998. "One sour note was the delight the photo editors took in using a photo of a smiling President Zedillo grabbing on to my arm," wrote the tall, burly, and now retired diplomat. "Though it was nothing more than a friendly gesture, the disparity in our heights made it look as if the towering new American ambassador was about to lift the president off the ground like a child—or better yet, like a puppet. . . . There was no need for interpretation. It was a warning that Mexico's president might be getting too close to this new heavyweight representative of the colossus of the north."[14]

In time Davidow would learn that any utterance of Washington's man in Mexico City was considered fair game for publication by local newshounds. On the night of the traditional independence celebrations held in front of the National Palace in September 1998, Davidow heard the huge crowd in the *Zócalo* square erupt into hearty cries of "Viva!" during President Zedillo's address to the nation. Turning to one of his colleagues in the diplomatic corps, Davidow joked that the president's remarks had the makings of one of the year's most successful speeches. A reporter overheard him and turned a deaf ear to the ambassador's remonstrations that the quip was a harmless piece of off-the-record humor. The journalist filed a story that accused Davidow of insulting the president, the country's gallant fight for independence, and every other national icon on display that evening. A commentator in the left-wing newspaper *La Jornada* later chided the envoy for "the lack of respect that the U.S. gives a traditional speech by the weak president of a subordinate nation."

Davidow blamed the episode in part on his own carelessness. But even his most meticulously phrased answers to reporters' questions were liable to be distorted or misquoted. "I was a target for malicious reporters, hostile editors, and editorial cartoonists who greeted the advent of a six-foot, six-inch overweight gringo ambassador as a gift equal to a lifetime's supply of free crayons," noted Davidow in his memoirs.[15]

And the special treatment didn't end when he completed his tour as ambassador and left the State Department's employ. In his new role as president of the San Diego–based Institute of the Americas, Davidow was invited to chair a high-profile discussion with the country's top three presidential candidates at the annual convention of the American Chamber of Commerce of Mexico in November 2005. The front page of the following day's edition of *El Universal* featured a picture of the corpulent American gesturing with an extended hand that covered the mouth and right cheek of Felipe Calderón—as if Davidow were about to smack the diminutive Mexican. The photo caption read, "Encounter."[16]

Se Habla Inglés

The first time I read the daily column of Marcela Gómez Zalce in the tabloid daily *Milenio*, I assumed she was either a Chicano like myself or a Mexican citizen who had spent a large chunk of her life in the United States. The column, "A Puertas Cerradas" (Behind Closed Doors), is sprinkled with English-language phrases and terms that can only be fully grasped with a thorough fluency in the foreign tongue. A typical example appeared in the November 22, 2005, issue of *Milenio*, which carried Marcela's musings about a series of scandals then engulfing the wife and stepsons of lame-duck President Vicente Fox. The column ended with the following sentence in English: "This blue story will have a black and white stripes ending . . . so wake up girl!" The stripes were a veiled suggestion that members of Mexico's First Family could wind up behind bars one day, dressed in the distinctive uniforms issued to prison inmates. But since it took me a while to figure out what exactly Gómez was driving at, I couldn't help but wonder how many of her Mexican readers understood the code language references.

A founding partner of the Mexican concert and entertainment promotion company CIE, Marcela had never worked in the news business when she approached a friend at the Milenio media company in 2003 with the idea of penning a column for the company's weekly magazine of the same name. "A Puertas Cerradas" ended up in the corporation's daily newspaper instead, and it has little in common with more traditional punditry practiced by journalistic institutions like *Reforma* columnist Miguel Ángel Granados Chapa. Written in a breezy, self-consciously hip style, Marcela's columns dart from one topic to another with no particular pattern or logic, and its signature mix of Spanish and English echoes the bilingual parlance of jet-setting Mexico City yuppies.

I was therefore quite surprised to learn that the Mexico City native has never lived north of the border for any extended period of time. She did grow up speaking English in her parents' polyglot household, and during her student days at the Ibero-American University in the 1980s, Gómez took summer courses at Texas A&M and the University of California at Los Angeles. But apart from having a mother who spent the first eight years of her life in New York City where Marcela's grandfather had trained as an oncologist, there was nothing in her past that could account for the thoroughly bilingual and bicultural content of "A Puertas Cerradas."

She stays abreast of the latest trends and buzzwords in the United States through the wonders of twenty-first-century technology. "I have my satellite dish and I'm in constant contact with what is happening in the United States," says Gómez as she recounts her daily work routine. "I see all the news and television programs in English, and I read all the American newspapers on the internet—the *New York Times*, the *Wall Street Journal*, the *Washington Post*." Marcela says she has never encountered any resistance from her editors over the column's rather liberal use of English. Reaction among her readers divides along mainly generational lines. "You do have the reader who complains about the use of English, and he tends to be older," she says. "But the younger reader loves it, and there is a large number of college students and people between the ages of thirty and forty who understand my slang well."[17]

Those contrasting responses to Marcela's column speak to a basic change in outlook among younger Mexicans. "These new, up-and-coming generations have been born with a different chip, and for them the universal language is English," says the forty-two-year-old mother of two small children. "We are very near the United States, we find ourselves amid an enormous globalization that doesn't allow you to be alienated from this process of Americanization. It isn't possible to shut yourself out."

Ana María Salazar has traveled a different path to arrive at a similar conclusion. The daughter of an American mother and a Mexican father who was born in Tucson but grew up in the border state of Sonora, Salazar is about as binational as you can get. The Harvard-trained lawyer held a series of important posts in the White House, the State Department, and the Pentagon under the Clinton administration, and when she moved south of the border with her Mexican husband in 2001 Ana María was struck by the almost total absence of any English-language news media in Mexico City. The country's only English-language daily newspaper *The News* was on its last legs and finally went out of business at the end of 2002. There was no English-language radio or TV news program available for American expatriates who wanted to monitor current affairs in their native tongue. In 2003 Salazar approached a fellow Sonoran at the Grupo Imagen media company with the idea of doing a radio newscast in English. "My argument was that Mexico is way too important now in terms of its economy and its role in the international arena for there not to be information about Mexico in English," says Salazar. "Secondly, there is a relatively large community of Mexicans who speak English who wouldn't mind listening to news in English on the radio."[18]

Her proposal encountered opposition at first. "The idea was not easy to sell because there were fears they [the executives] would be accused of being anti-Mexican," recalls Salazar. But the executives at Grupo Imagen eventually warmed to the idea of becoming the only station in the country broadcasting news in English, and the program *Living in Mexico* made its debut on the airwaves in October 2003 as a weekend show. In February 2005 the twenty-four-minute-long program was renamed *Imagen News* and started airing on a daily basis in Mexico City at the ungodly hour of 5:30 in the morning. It now broadcasts in over a dozen urban markets nationwide. Like Marcela Gómez Zalce, Salazar has discovered an especially receptive audience among younger Mexicans. "I get e-mails from high school and college students and yuppies, and English is clearly not their first language," says the UC Berkeley graduate. "They listen to the show either because their English teacher uses it to assign homework or because it's their daily medicine for practicing their English."

Under Mexican law, Salazar must include some Spanish-language content in the program, and she saves that portion for the concluding minutes of each day's broadcast. But the regulation strikes her as being out of sync with evolving attitudes in today's Mexico. "That shows you what kind of perceptions and fears there still are about American culture taking over," Salazar notes. But times are nonetheless changing. "There isn't the taboo there used to be about speaking English and somehow not being patriotic." The folks in charge of the Mexican presidency's official website would seem to agree, judging from its fully bilingual format. And by the early fall of 2007, the same English-language Mexico City *News* daily that shuttered a year after Salazar's arrival was publishing again after a five-year hiatus. At a time when print media companies in the United States are going through their industry's worst ever economic crisis, the resurrected *News* has at least one thing going for it: the swelling ranks of *norteamericanos* who are pulling up stakes to find their place in the Mexican sun.

Part III

CHAPTER 7

The Mexican Dream

On Sunday mornings the courtyard of the public library in the colonial town of San Miguel de Allende fills up with Americans. The drawing card is a weekly house-and-garden tour that spotlights some of the splendid homes purchased by American expatriates in the historic city center and on the hillsides overlooking San Miguel, and on a typical weekend in the fall of 2005 I am one of 176 tourists who have filed into the library building for the start of the two-hour-long sightseeing excursion. Eleven Mexican musicians resplendently dressed in burgundy-and-gold tunics and velvet breeches stand to one side of the cobblestone courtyard, playing a mix of familiar home-grown staples like "La Bamba" and classic Spanish folk songs dating back to the days of the celebrated author of *Don Quixote*, Miguel de Cervantes.

By the time the buses roll up outside the library's street entrance to ferry the visitors to the first stop on the tour, the courtyard is a sea of gringos chatting amiably in English. They sport the typical garb and accessories of vacationing *norteamericanos*—baseball caps, walking shorts, white sneakers, sunglasses, T-shirts, and sandals. They wear name tags bearing their first names and the cities and states from whence they have come—Tucson and Tulsa, Maryland and Montana, San Antonio and Santa Cruz, New Mexico and New York. Apart from the musicians, the only Mexicans on hand for the tour are a young, middle-class family of five from the nearby city of Querétaro who look a tad bewildered by the tableau unfolding before them.

The mood is festive, and it's all for a good cause. Proceeds from the weekend tour are donated to the library, which houses one of the largest collections of English-language books in the country, and at $15 a head the weekly excursion generates a tidy stream of revenue. Doing good works is one of the main pastimes for the town's burgeoning American community, who makes up an estimated one-tenth of San Miguel's 63,000 inhabitants. A walking tour of the historic center on weekdays helps raise money to provide dental and medical care to the needy children of San Miguel, which is a three-hour drive from Mexico City. One group of American residents called Amigos del Parque (Friends of the Park) is working on the renovation of the town's long-neglected Juárez Park, and yet another organization of expats donates money to the Hospital de la Fe.

In one corner of the library courtyard that morning stands a forty-four-year-old ex-banker named Chris Doolin. He is telling tourists about a photography project he runs that has raised thousands of dollars in scholarships for over fifty underprivileged high school students in San Miguel. It is his way of saying thank you to the town to which he moved from Arizona four years ago. "It's a privilege to be living here in more ways than you can imagine," says Doolin, handing me a business card that bears the e-mail address, ex_gringo@hotmail.com. My chuckling over the inscription on his business card lights up the eyes of Doolin, an athletically built man dressed in gray jeans, a tight-fitting white T-shirt, brown cowboy boots, and a straw hat he wears on his shaved head. "I don't think I'll ever live in the United States again," says Doolin, who gave up an $80,000-a-year white-collar job in Phoenix to try his hand at freelance tourism photography in Mexico. "Once I got finished living my American dream, I paid off my credit cards, sold off everything I had and moved down here with two suitcases. Everything that's happened in the country since Mr. Bush took power has been going against my whole values structure. I am never going to pay taxes to those fuckheads anymore."[1]

Doolin belongs to a growing number of Americans who are fleeing the Fruited Plain to pursue their own Mexican dream. They represent the flipside of the exodus of Mexicans pouring across the southern border of the United States each day in search of a better life, though admittedly on a much smaller scale. Many of these Americans are pensioners lured by the cheaper cost of living in towns like San Miguel de Allende and Ajijic. Others are aging baby boomers who want to relive the adventurous days of their fast receding youth. And there is a small but vocal minority of folks like Chris Doolin who no longer want any part of the polarized political and moral climate of the United States.

Mexico has played host to an American expatriate community since the early years of its independence. The first group of gringos to put down roots in Mexican soil was the nearly 300 families led by Stephen F. Austin who arrived in what was then the state of Coahuila and Tejas in the mid-1820s. The ranks of those pioneers grew fast, and by 1830 the 7,000 Americans living in Texas were more than double its Mexican population.[2] Many of these settlers later rebelled against Antonio López de Santa Anna after he disbanded the national congress and suspended the federalist constitution in 1834. The number of Americans living in the national capital grew exponentially during the *Porfiriato*. In the early years of Díaz's rule, the American population of Mexico City and nearby villages was estimated at 360. But the flood of U.S. investment in the late nineteenth and early twentieth centuries helped swell its numbers: in 1898 an estimated 1,200 Americans lived in Mexico City and environs, and by the eve of the Mexican Revolution in 1910 that figure had climbed to 10,000.[3]

The trend was not limited to the capital. Between 1900 and 1910, approximately 3,000 American immigrants entered Mexico each year, boosting the nationwide expatriate community to nearly 40,000 by the time Díaz was finally driven from power. Many of the new arrivals chose to live in the northern region of the country in the belief that it would eventually be acquired by the United States, as had occurred decades previously in Texas.[4] The burgeoning industrial city of Torreón in the northern state of Coahuila has been described as "arguably the most North American city in Mexico" in 1907, with a resident U.S. population of 1,500.[5] Members of the Church of Jesus Christ of Latter-Day Saints started moving into

Mexico in 1885, and by 1910 they had established nine prosperous settlements in the border states of Chihuahua and Sonora.[6]

This immigration pattern was temporarily reversed by the chaos of the Mexican Revolution and isolated outbursts of anti-gringo violence and looting, which triggered the flight of thousands of Americans from Mexico. But a small community of bohemian American intellectuals emerged in Mexico City by the 1920s, and the numbers of gringos moving south of the border rose sharply with the onset of the Great Depression under President Herbert Hoover. Some bypassed the capital in favor of Cuernavaca, Guadalajara, San Miguel de Allende, and the Lake Chapala district of Jalisco state.[7]

The American expatriate community has grown by leaps and bounds in the young century. According to the U.S. State Department, the number of Americans living in Mexico has soared from an estimated 200,000 in the mid-1990s to between 600,000 and one million a decade later.[8] Their expanding numbers have caught the eyes of political strategists back home. In 2004, the campaign staffs of both George Bush and John Kerry decided there were enough votes at stake in Mexico to warrant visits by trusted members of the candidates' inner circle, who spoke on their behalf. The Massachusetts senator's sister Diana stumped all over Mexico and helped sign up more than 800 registered Democrats over a twelve-month period. The Republican incumbent dispatched his strikingly handsome nephew George Prescott Bush to press American flesh in Mexico City, Guadalajara, and San Miguel de Allende.[9] That represented a major shift from the 2000 election, when Mexico's population of U.S. expatriates was almost completely ignored by the campaigns of Bush and Al Gore.

THE GREAT MEXICAN LAND RUSH

And it's not just political consultants who are taking notice. Jorge Pérez made a fortune building luxury condominiums at the height of south Florida's real estate boom in the late 1990s, and with a development portfolio valued in excess of $10 billion his Miami-based company The

Related Group bills itself as the largest builder of condos and apartment buildings in the United States and the biggest Hispanic-owned company in the country. But by 2005, the son of Cuban exiles could foresee the end of the property bonanza in the United States that had made Pérez a billionaire—these days he's also setting his sights south of the border. In the winter of 2007, The Related Group unveiled plans to develop three major condominium and luxury hotel projects in the Mexican beach resorts of Puerto Vallarta, Acapulco, and Zihuatanejo, with a combined estimated value of over $1 billion.

This certainly isn't what the authors of Mexico's 1917 constitution had in mind. Article 27 actually prohibits foreigners from owning property within 30 miles of the country's coastlines. But governments subsequently created a loophole in the constitutional ban that allows foreigners to acquire seafront property provided that the legal title to the land be held in trust by a Mexican bank. Under this arrangement, large numbers of Americans have snapped up prime real estate in Baja California, the Yucatán Peninsula, and the mainland Pacific Coast. With oceanfront condos priced at anywhere from one-third to one-half the going rate for comparable housing in Miami Beach, Pérez sees Mexico's seacoasts as the next El Dorado for his company. And the prospective buyers he is targeting will be first and foremost affluent Americans who are already familiar with the country or are interested in acquiring a second home, followed by rich Mexicans. "The progression of that second home buyer and tourist goes most logically to Mexico," says Pérez. "It's on the border of the United States, it's got great climate, great beaches, great mountains, great culture, great food, and it's got a population that generally likes the United States and Americans."[10]

The setting chosen by Pérez to roll out the 343-unit ICON Vallarta high-rise condominium project in March 2007 was most appropriate for the occasion. The W Hotel in Mexico City sits along one of the toniest avenues in the capital: a Cadillac and Hummer dealership is just down the street from the hotel's lobby entrance, and within a couple of blocks in either direction are a Hard Rock Café, a couple of Starbuckses, and a five-star Marriott. On a balmy spring evening, black-clad waiters served trays of canapés and cocktails to a crowd of well-heeled Mexican yuppies and businessmen on the hotel's second-floor terrace while searchlights lit up the darkened skies overhead. A giant screen at one end of the terrace displayed a promotional video for the $200 million condo development, and all the text blocks accompanying the photos and artist's renderings of the towers were written exclusively in English. "Everything will be exceptional, everything will be special with Jorge Pérez," gushed ICON Vallarta's renowned French designer Philippe Starck in one frame. "Exclusive beachfront residences," beckoned another slide. "Become an icon, be the first to know all the details."

Pérez knows a great business opportunity when he sees one. The U.S. State Department estimates that up to 400,000 Americans and Canadians have purchased second homes and vacation properties in Mexico, and three U.S. banking institutions started offering mortgage financing to American citizens interested in buying real estate in Mexico for the first time in 2004. One of them is Collateral International, an Alabama-based bank that launched an innovative program in 2004 called Mexico—My Dream that reduces closing costs for prospective buyers by working with Mexican attorneys, notaries public, and title agencies. Collateral International has been offering financing to foreign clients with interest rates between 6 and 8 percent, well below the 10 to 12 percent rates usually provided by property developers in Mexico. The Mexico—My Dream program has been a success story from its inception: the initial loan portfolio of $5 million had grown to more than $13 million through the first quarter of 2005.

Another yardstick of the booming real estate industry in Mexico comes from Houston-based Stewart Title Guaranty Company, a pioneer in the field that started insuring property title deeds in Mexico in the mid-1990s. A title insurance policy protects the property owner or, in the case of a mortgage, the bank holding the deed, against fraudulent claims of ownership by other parties, liens that have been placed on the property by creditors, forged documentation, or any other irregularities. It is an indispensable instrument for banking institutions that provide mortgage financing, and Stewart Title's Mexican operations took off in 2004 when the company insured over 700 titles on residential properties, double the figure for the previous year. During that same twelve-month period, Stewart Title tripled the number of escrow orders it serviced in comparison to 2003. The company's Mexico division manager says that the number of U.S. citizens who now own property south of the border has surpassed the one million mark and will continue to rise as more and more Americans find themselves priced out of popular real estate markets at home.[11]

The big draws in Mexico are the country's popular beachfront resorts like Cabo San Lucas in Baja California, Puerto Vallarta and Punta Mita along the mainland's Pacific Coast, along with the Maya Riviera stretching south of Cancún to the town of Tulum on the Yucatán Peninsula's eastern shoreline. The signs decorating the construction site of the Residencial Bay View Grand condominium complex in Cancún's hotel zone leave little to the imagination about the market coveted by its developers: they prominently feature a blue-eyed family of Nordic appearance frolicking in the sands of the world-famous resort. Before construction began on the Las Olas apartment complex in Cancún in 2004, two-bedroom units were being advertised at $600,000. Within fourteen months, all but one of the units had been sold, and prices had climbed to $820,000 in the interim. "This is an American market," says R. J. Thoman, a real estate agent from east Texas who moved from the central state of Guanajuato to Cancún with his Mexican wife in 2002. "Americans are coming down to invest their money here instead of the stock market because it's more secure."[12]

There was a time not so long ago when the notion that Mexican real estate could represent a safer bet than Wall Street might have seemed laughable. The recurring peso devaluations and economic crises of the 1970s and 1980s deterred American banks from lending money for property purchases south of the border, and the well-deserved reputation of corrupt Mexican officialdom posed another formidable hurdle. But laws governing investment and real estate property ownership by foreigners have changed since NAFTA took effect in 1994, and the Mexican government's introduction of a guaranteed trust law has encouraged U.S. lenders to offer mortgage financing in the Mexican market.

Since the lion's share of real estate transactions in Mexico is done in cash, the subprime mortgage crisis that rocked the U.S. banking industry in 2007 had only a mild ripple effect south of the border. Realtors in a prime real estate market like Puerto Vallarta did report a 5 to 10 percent fall in the number of American clients in the early months of 2008, as prospective buyers who were planning to refinance their existing homes in the United States to raise money for an investment in Mexico dropped out of the market. But wealthy baby boomers who didn't need to get a line of credit or take out a second mortgage continued to snap up seafront condos in the high six figures and 15,000-square-feet houses valued in the millions. Some Mexican immigrants in the United States who faced foreclosure on account of their soaring adjustable-rate mortgage payments also turned southward, purchasing cheaper residential property in states like Coahuila and Jalisco.[13]

THE INVASION OF THE BABY BOOMERS

The long-term implications for the Mexican real estate industry could be far-reaching if the giants of the U.S. banking sector ever engage in large-scale mortgage financing south of the border. But the 2007 mortgage meltdown has put that possibility on indefinite hold, and for the foreseeable future the vast majority of Americans wanting to acquire property in Mexico will still have to pay cash up front. Happily for realtors, there seems to be no shortage of gringos willing to invest a big chunk of their life's savings in such a proposition. Becky and Julian Palinski did just that after they made a $200,000 profit on the sale of their house in Fort Washington, Maryland, in 2004. The Arkansas couple had moved to the Washington, D.C., area three years previously after Julian accepted a job administering a grants program at the Smithsonian Institution and Becky retired at full pay from her twenty-five-year career as a kindergarten teacher.

Becky especially hated life in the nation's capital, and as they considered their options the Palinskis harked back to a trip they made in 1998 to Guadalajara, where their elder daughter was spending a semester abroad studying Spanish. During that visit they stopped by a kiosk in one of the city's shopping malls where a real estate developer named Jaime Hernández was promoting property in Ajijic, a picturesque town of 13,000 on the shores of nearby Lake Chapala. Hundreds of American and Canadian expatriates have established year-round residences in that region of Jalisco state, and Hernández offered to take the Palinskis on a guided tour of the homes he was building. The couple accepted his invitation and Ajijic left a lasting impression on the visitors. "We always thought we'd go back," recalls Becky.[14]

Prior to putting their Fort Washington house on the market, the Palinskis made a foray to the Baja California towns of Rosarito and Ensenada near the U.S. border in the summer of 2004. Becky had seen a couple of ads on television touting that corner of the country, but the noise and heavy traffic of the densely populated area south of Tijuana put them off. After returning to the United States, they booked a trip to the Lake Chapala district over the long Thanksgiving Day weekend to see what was available. They moved into a rental house a month later and eventually found a comfortable, two-story condominium about 600 feet from the edge of the lake in a residential neighborhood called Riberas del Pilar that they purchased with the proceeds from the sale of the Fort Washington house.

The Palinskis were approaching the first anniversary of their move to Mexico when I met them, and the region's mild year-round climate had already done wonders for Julian's health. His blood pressure and cholesterol levels had gone down in the twelve months since the couple's arrival, and his arthritis no longer troubled him. To keep busy, Becky teaches English to Mexican children two days a week and Julian does volunteer work at the offices of the Lake Chapala Society, an organization of mostly American expatriates that performs charitable work and schedules a steady diet of social events for its 3,500 dues-paying members. There seemed to be very little the couple missed about living in the United States, apart from a few hard-to-find food items like Velveeta cheese and black-eyed peas and the more efficient service they were accustomed to getting from American restaurant waiters. "Everybody is very friendly, and we have time for each other," explained Becky, fifty-two, who speaks in the distinctive drawl of her native state. "This isn't for everyone, and a lot of people you see around here want everything to be just exactly as it is in the United States and Canada. They can't relax because it's too slow-paced for them. But the Mexicans are always very, very polite, and I feel safer here than I did in Maryland."

Retirement in Mexico has been traditionally associated with American senior citizens sixty-five years of age and older. But the Palinskis typify the new wave of American immigrants who are settling down in Mexico today. They are often baby boomers who realize they are approaching their golden years with not enough savings to afford a comfortable retirement in the United States. Some have gone through expensive divorces, while others can't afford the astronomical costs of health care in the United States. According to a recent report by the American Association of Retired Persons, more than 76 million Americans born between 1946 and 1963 will reach retirement age over the next twenty years, and fully one-fourth of them have no health insurance or significant savings to fall back on.[15] An expatriate in Mexico can qualify for full medical coverage under the country's government-run social security institute after only three years of full-time residence, and the cost of prescription drugs and dental care is usually a fraction of what is charged in the States.

Another category consists of baby boomers like Marianne Carlson who have seen their jobs eliminated by cash-strapped companies looking to trim payrolls. Carlson joined the ranks of the downsized in the spring of 1999 when the Pacific Gas and Electric energy company eliminated her clerical position at a nuclear power plant in central California. Carlson was only fifty-one years old at the time, and while she had some savings, Marianne knew she couldn't make it on her nest egg through the year 2010 when Social Security benefits would start to kick in. She had been traveling to Mexico on a fairly regular basis since the late 1960s, and she started searching on the internet for towns with a temperate climate and a fairly sizable population of American expatriates who might offer a customer base for the kind of small business that Carlson was planning to establish. Though she had traveled extensively throughout Mexico, she hadn't heard of Ajijic until she went online—and when Carlson arrived in the Lake Chapala district on a scouting expedition, it was love at first sight. "The minute I drove into town I said, 'This is it,' I felt I had come home," recalls Carlson. "If you're like me, once you get down to mainland Mexico you're hooked. I love Mexican people, and I didn't have any adjustment to go through."

Marianne Carlson has gone native in more ways than one. She moved into a three-bedroom, two-bathroom house in the heart of Ajijic and later opened a Mexican folk art gallery within walking distance of her home. Carlson runs an online business trading in handmade miniature dolls, baskets, pottery, and dishes, and she plans to become a Mexican citizen in the near future. "It's a very creative environment here, and my talents have just blossomed since coming to Mexico," she explains. "My rhythm has changed, time has a whole new meaning to you here. I don't wear a watch, and I like the fact that some days I don't know what day it is." The advent of baby boomers like Carlson is altering the demographic profile of the American community in the Lake Chapala region. "When I first decided to move down here, I was definitely the young kid," she says. "But things really changed, and there are more and more younger people moving down here." Her living expenses run at around $1,500 a month, less than a third of what she needed to live in California. Carlson says she has no plans of ever leaving her adopted country. "I could never go back to doing what I used to do," she says. "I will die here."

Other baby boomers see in Mexico an enticing refuge from the cultural wars raging across an increasingly divided United States. Constance Gavras has been thinking about retirement in Mexico ever since her seventy-five-year-old mother moved down to Ajijic in the late 1990s. When I met Gavras on the outdoor patio of a local hotel in the fall of 2004, she and her American fiancé had made a decision to buy a house or a lot in the area no later than the following year. A coin dealer by profession, Gavras reckons that she can continue to run her company from Mexico, and the Miami native acknowledges that in moving south she will be consciously fleeing an American society she no longer feels comfortable in.

But Constance Gavras will never be mistaken for an unreconstructed New Age hippie in Birkenstock sandals who cannot stomach the thought of remaining in a country governed by George Walker Bush. Quite the opposite: Gavras is a smartly dressed businesswoman in high heels, red lipstick, and two-toned Bebe sunglasses who describes herself as "a recovering feminist," and she says she can no longer abide the stifling political correctness of some Americans. By way of illustration, Gavras recounts an incident in a Minneapolis gym in which the manager overheard her using the word "fat" to describe someone. "He comes over and says, 'You have to come into my office,'" she says. "He tells me, 'You do not use that word around here.' I asked him why. 'First of all, it's demeaning,' he said. 'And it's not nice.' Then he tells me that if I said anything else like that, I would be suspended. I said, 'You know what? I'm on some strange planet.'" Gavras pauses between sips from a glass of iced tea. "There's a real us-versus-them mentality in the United States," she explains. "People are fearful and hateful even before they get to know each other. Everything becomes so Balkanized in the United States, and a lot of us are just very, very tired of the divisiveness."

Unlike Marianne Carlson, Gavras has no starry-eyed illusions about Mexico. When I asked her about the drawbacks of living south of the border, she immediately thought of three—a growing crime problem in the Lake Chapala area, the insufferable machismo of some Mexican men, and a language barrier that confronts any gringo who has only minimal fluency in the local tongue. "I don't speak proficient Spanish so I don't know what they think or feel," Gavras says bluntly. "Theft is a huge problem, Mexicans are always stealing from Mexicans, and every other person here has been cleaned out by the movers or the maid. Common sense tells you to lock your doors and turn on the security alarm system. But it's a very polite society for the most part, and when people are polite you think they are very nice and honest. It's like we leave our brains behind at the border."

But in spite of the disadvantages that come with the territory in her mind, Gavras remains firmly committed to starting anew in Mexico. "I definitely don't romanticize Mexico, there are a lot of wonderful things here and there are some negative things here," she notes. "But I feel very much at home here. I like the coins, the Spanish escudos, I love all this religious statuary and the crosses. I've established a good rapport with some Mexicans. The ones we get on best with are those who have traveled, they are real, and they are people who don't define their core being in political terms."

Too Many Americans?

As more and more Americans move to Mexico to live there full-time or snap up vacation homes along its sandy beaches, a question inevitably arises: are towns like San Miguel de Allende and Ajijic becoming too overrun with gringos? The thought has crossed my mind on more than one occasion. The city of Guanajuato has a distinct whiff of Catholic provincialism that partly explains why the family of the renowned muralist Diego Rivera fled to Mexico City at the end of the nineteenth century. But I have always preferred its overwhelmingly Mexican flavor and the relative scarcity of foreign tourists to the more Americanized ambience of San Miguel. And for me, a native Californian whose father grew up in a lakeside town called Jocotepec just down the road from Ajijic, it was a bit jarring to hear a gray-haired American woman reading aloud in English from the sometimes bawdy script of Eve Ensler's acclaimed play *The Vagina Monologues* at a hotel in Ajijic one summer evening a few years ago.

Some Mexicans share my opinions, but not all. Carolina de la Cajiga was a young mother of two when she and her husband, Francisco Ortiz, temporarily relocated from Mexico City to San Miguel de Allende in the summer of 1982. The peso devaluation of that year had devastated Francisco's construction business, and the young couple eventually immigrated to the Canadian city of Vancouver in 1984. Now in her late fifties,

Carolina finally returned to San Miguel in the fall of 2004, and she was instantly captivated by the town's dynamic cultural scene and cosmopolitan vibe. Perhaps owing to the many years she lived abroad, Carolina does not resent the throngs of Americans and other foreigners who have poured into San Miguel. If anything, she's actually made more friends among the expatriate population than with her own compatriots since she and Francisco bought a house in the city center.

That said, Carolina has sensed a certain disgruntlement among some of the town's native residents. "There is a tension with a few Mexicans we've had a chance to chat with, and some of them feel that foreigners are taking over," she told me. "It's a very subdued feeling that something is happening, that the whole center area is being bought by foreigners, and so people are being displaced. But they don't say that because it's impolite, and they don't use the word 'gringo' to describe Americans." Carolina found herself wondering aloud to an American friend in San Miguel whether the town was being irreversibly changed by the influx of expatriates. "Foreigners come here because of the atmospheric feel, but will there be a point when Mexicans will need to be imported to sit on benches in San Miguel?" she remembers asking the American. "Will this become an American city disguised as a Mexican town? Do I really want to live in a place where there are so many foreigners?"

In Carolina's case the answer to that last question remains an emphatic yes. But there is one downside of the gringo invasion that has affected her in a very direct way: the soaring price of real estate anywhere in Mexico where Americans congregate. Francisco and Carolina paid $160,000 for a house located on a 1,350-square-foot lot in San Miguel that she describes as the size of a handkerchief. "It's as if we were purchasing in the middle of Manhattan," marvels Carolina, who apparently hasn't shopped for real estate in New York City of late. "We were told that it was a cheap lot for San Miguel, but it's ridiculously expensive."

The trend is equally pronounced in the Lake Chapala area. In 2003 a retired Texas couple bought a two-story house with spectacular views of the lake and nearby hills in the fashionable neighborhood of Hacienda del

Oro for the bargain price of $175,000. When they decided to move back to the States two and a half years later, they sold the residence for almost double that. "People are paying asking prices for desirable houses," says Charlie Smith, a former U.S. Navy pilot who heads up the Lake Chapala Society. "We're getting a lot more baby boomers who intend to retire here one day, and they're buying land or a house because real estate prices are going up so fast."

Other recent arrivals in the area feel the same way about the cost of food and other basic necessities. In the spring of 2005 Rick and Kaye Brokaw moved into a palatial two-story house in the rural, gated community of Vista del Lago. The house sits next to a nine-hole golf course and offers, as the name of the residential complex suggests, spectacular views of Lake Chapala. A retired vocational education instructor, Kaye grew up on a farm in Michigan and was enchanted by the prospect of living in the countryside where cows and horses might cross her path on a daily basis. But she was not prepared for the prices charged at a local supermarket for a number of imported food products in the nearby town of Chapala. "A jar of pickles costs four dollars and a gallon of milk costs three," she says with a shudder. "That isn't cheap by any stretch of the imagination. Canned tomatoes cost more than they do in the United States, and quite often I just buy Mexican bread because it's closer to what I'm used to paying. It's more expensive to live down here than what I had thought."

At the same time, the Brokaws and other Americans are the first ones to admit that they are the ones largely responsible for the pricey cost of living. "Without intending to, we've inflated prices," says Rick Brokaw, an Arizona native who retired from Boeing on medical disability in 2001. "The craftsmen all expect more money from Mexicans because they can charge gringo prices to the Americans who build houses."

But not all the surprises lying in store for Americans moving to Mexico are necessarily unpleasant. To a man and a woman, all the expatriates I met in Ajijic and San Miguel said they had yet to experience any overt anti-Americanism from their Mexican neighbors. And in a country that is synonymous with male chauvinism for many outsiders, lesbian couples have encountered a remarkably high degree of acceptance from locals and foreigners alike. Nancy Creevan and her Mexican partner moved from San Jose, California, to Ajijic in 1999, and the few complaints she has overheard about the number of gays and lesbians living in the area have typically come from non-Mexicans visiting from out of town. "I'm more 'out' here than I ever was in California," she says. "The people who come here are usually quite adventurous and are more open to people. You're moving to a different country with a different culture and language and customs. You can't be a closed-minded bigot and stay here for very long." (Less than two years after Creevan shared these thoughts with me, the Mexico City council and the legislature of the northern state of Coahuila passed groundbreaking laws that legalized civil unions for same-sex couples.)[16]

There is a creeping sense among some American expatriates that their corner of paradise may soon be ruined by the swelling numbers of compatriots who will follow in their footsteps in the coming years. "A lot of us are now saying, 'Shhh, we don't want any more people, they can visit but not live here,' " says Becky Palinski with a laugh. Four new light signals were recently installed to ease traffic congestion along the stretch of highway on Lake Chapala's northern shore that slices through Ajijic. Crime is on the rise as carloads of unruly teenagers drive down from Guadalajara on the weekends to prey on unsuspecting *yanquis*. Some newcomers to the area are already steering clear of Ajijic on account of the more affordable housing and less Americanized atmospherics of nearby towns. "I actually like the town of Chapala, it has a certain Mexican feel about it," allows Constance Gavras, the coin dealer who has grown weary of living in the United States. "I hear people say, 'Ajijic is a little too much for me, it's just too American.'" The same can be said of Mexico's best-known beach resort, even though most of the Americans who go there are just passing through.

CHAPTER 8

The Gringo Riviera

"What's the difference between Cancún and Miami?" a Mexican tourism official asked me during my first visit to the world famous resort. I shook my head and said I had no idea. "In Cancún, everybody speaks English." The pithy truth of that joke stuck with me throughout the four days I spent in Cancún in March 2005. On the last night of my stay, I hailed a taxi in the city's hotel zone and told the driver in Spanish, "Please take me to the Hacienda El Mortero restaurant." "Sure," the cabbie replied in English without missing a beat. As we headed toward the restaurant he apologetically switched to Spanish and told me a little about his life story. Leonel García Sánchez once owned a clothing import business in his native Guadalajara that required him to make regular trips to Los Angeles, where nearly all of his clients spoke Spanish. When the clothing business went belly up, García moved to Cancún in 2002, and these days he spends more time speaking English as he plies the streets of the resort city than he ever did in southern California. "Here in Cancún I don't feel like I'm in Mexico," he explained. "I feel like I'm back in the United States because nobody speaks Spanish."[1]

Cancún was a place I had studiously avoided during my four-year assignment as *Newsweek*'s Mexico City bureau chief in the mid-1980s. One of the main reasons I chose journalism as a profession in the first place was to live outside the United States, and the last thing I wanted to do on my vacations inside Mexico was to sprawl on a beach packed with fellow

Americans swilling piña coladas by the pitcherful. In those days, the closest I ever came to Cancun was a foray to the majestic Mayan pyramid of Chichén Itzá, where I saw Americans with lobster-red sunburns coming in by the busloads for a quick tour of the famous archaeological ruins before heading back to their seaside hotel rooms.

"You Will Always Feel at Home"

My worst fears about the place were amply confirmed when I finally made it to Cancún twenty years later. Envisioned originally as an exclusive resort for wealthy, sophisticated American tourists, the hotel zone of Cancún occupies a narrow, twelve-mile-long sand spit just off the Yucatán Peninsula's northeastern tip, and it stands as a monument to made-in-the-U.S.A. consumerism and marketing. The prevalence of English became apparent as soon as I reached the baggage claim area of Cancún's congested international airport; even the advertising posters of local companies were worded in the global language ("No matter how far you travel," said one ad for the Mexican cellphone company Telcel, "you will always feel at home").

From the back seat of the tour bus whisking me to my hotel, I glimpsed a steady parade of the same restaurants, fast-food chains, and hotels found in American shopping malls from sea to shining sea. Hooters, T.G.I. Fridays, Hard Rock Café, Planet Hollywood, Bubba Gump Shrimp Co., McDonald's, Burger King, Subway, Hilton, Ritz-Carlton, Hyatt, Marriott—you name it, they were present in this market. Manicured lawns, green ferns and golf courses flashed by my window seat as the tour bus made its rounds depositing other American passengers at their respective hotels. The vehicle's radio was tuned to a pop music station that blared old hit songs from the likes of Gloria Gaynor, the Beach Boys, and the Fifth Dimension. As the Telcel poster foreshadowed, the raison d'être of Cancún is all about making the American vacationer feel as though he has never left the U.S. of A.

Tourism is big business in Mexico. It represents the country's third largest source of foreign exchange after oil exports and the remittances sent back by Mexicans living in the United States, and the industry keeps setting new records in annual revenues. In 2006 foreign tourists spent a record $12.18 billion in Mexico,[2] a 3.2 percent increase over the previous year (when a hurricane shut down the resort for several weeks), and that figure rose to $12.9 billion in 2007. Americans make up the vast majority of holidaymakers who visit Mexico: of the 21.35 million foreigners who traveled there in 2006, over 17 million came from the United States.

Mexico's tourism sector took a big short-term hit from the 9/11 attacks in New York and Washington as millions of Americans canceled plans to take a vacation anywhere outside the United States. But over the medium term, the industry actually got a shot in the arm from the American travel attitudes post-9/11.[3] Once Americans overcame the initial shock of 9/11 and were once again ready to venture overseas, they considered travel destinations closer to home and farther away from Osama bin Laden. Mexico suddenly seemed more appealing than ever, and among its various resorts Cancún was the biggest winner of all.

"Americans didn't stop coming to Cancun after 9/11," says Fernando Martí, a journalist-turned-publisher from Mexico City who came to Cancún in 1988 to open the first in a series of profitable local magazines. "They don't like the fact that there's terrorism in Spain and many aren't quite sure where Egypt or Iran are located, whereas here they feel right at home."

In financial terms, Cancún is the cash cow of the Mexican tourism industry. In 2004 the resort raked in a total of $2 billion in revenues from a record 3.4 million visitors. Most of them were Americans, and the hotel zone is perfectly suited to the kind of tourist whose idea of experiencing the real Mexico is to throw back another cold Corona. The Mexican restaurants located in the hotel zone serve up Tex-Mex fare like fajitas for the American who couldn't tell the difference between molasses and *mole poblano*, the thick, chocolate-tinged sauce from the central Mexican city of Puebla. In physical terms it is laid out as an enclave: the road leading from the airport brings visitors directly onto the island, enabling foreigners to completely bypass the city of Cancún on the Yucatán peninsula if they so wish. The only setting in the entire hotel zone where Mexicans and Americans rub shoulders on more or less equal terms is onboard the municipal buses that shuttle tourists up and down the island and ferry construction workers to and from their homes on the mainland.

Los Spring Breakers

I deliberately scheduled my visit to Cancún to coincide with the annual invasion of American college students during the spring vacation period. A few years ago Cancún was *the* destination for young Americans not yet old enough to buy a drink in their hometowns, and MTV would send camera crews to film *"los spring breakers"* in all their alcohol-fueled debauchery. Over time the spectacle of naked frat boys cavorting in hotel pools and topless coeds staggering down the main thoroughfare known as Kukulcán Boulevard inflicted a black eye on the resort's marketing image.

The resort received 150,000 spring breakers every year at the peak of Cancún's popularity among American college students. Their numbers have thinned out considerably since local bartenders and hoteliers struck a deal to stop serving grossly intoxicated patrons and to phase out contests that promoted heavy drinking. But the youthful revelers are still a conspicuous sight in the months of March and April. As night falls, Kukulcán Boulevard becomes clogged with American college students carrying plastic cups of beer in search of alcoholic stupor and a one-night stand.

The hedonistic appeal of the resort is bluntly described by a website called studentspringbreak.com. Forget about the "luxurious beaches, the lush jungles, ancient ruins and the beautiful hotels," the webpage tells its mostly young readers. "Benefits of going to Cancun are many, yes, but most students just care about the abundance of alcohol, alcohol and wait, you guessed it, more alcohol. Your yearly intake of alcoholic consumption could happen in one small week in Cancun, Mexico on Spring Break. Do I have to say more?"[4]

That was enough to sell Tatiana Brooks on Cancún. In the spring of 2005 the University of Nebraska student came down to Cancún with her boyfriend, over his parents' objections, to party, party, party, party. On the morning I met Brooks, she was a very satisfied if visibly hungover customer. "We knew we wanted to go to Mexico because we can't drink in the

United States," she explained four days into her spring getaway. "I was really nervous coming down here because if you don't speak the language, you can't do anything about it. But I love it here, the people are so nice, the atmosphere is great. It makes you feel you are at home even though you are in a foreign country."

Tatiana is a far cry from the kind of tourist that Cancún's founders had in mind. While most guidebooks recycle the popular myth that the resort site was picked out by a computer on the basis of data input in a Mexico City government office, Cancún was in fact the brainchild of two senior officials at the country's central bank who were asked to identify suitable locations along Mexico's shores for the construction of new tourist resorts catering to affluent American visitors. One of those officials was Antonio Enríquez Savignac, who would later serve as tourism minister under President Miguel de la Madrid, and he spent two years scouring the country for virgin beaches that might one day surpass Acapulco and Puerto Vallarta as magnets for international tourists. Enríquez Savignac settled on five spots: Ixtapa and Huatulco on Mexico's Pacific Coast, Loreto and Cabo San Lucas on the Baja California peninsula, and Cancún.

When construction commenced on a handful of luxury hotels in Cancún in 1972, the area's resident population consisted of several dozen fishermen living in the nearby village of Puerto Juárez. The local economy was still reeling from the collapse of the henequen industry, the main source of employment in the Yucatán Peninsula throughout the late nineteenth and early twentieth centuries, and in the early 1970s the then territory of Quintana Roo ranked dead last in per capita income nationwide.

For the government of President Luis Echeverría, Cancún held out the region's best hope for generating large numbers of new jobs fast. The federal government invested massive amounts of money to develop Cancún from scratch: it paved roads, installed sewage and potable water facilities, and built a new airport fit for a world-class tourism mecca. Within the first ten years 10,000 hotel rooms had opened, and in those days eight of every ten tourists in Cancún came from the United States, according to hotelier Abelardo Vara. Only 2 percent of the resort's clientele was Mexican. "We concentrated on promoting Cancún to the United States," says Vara, a native of the border state of Coahuila who owns the Omni Cancún Hotel and Villas complex. "That's what was working well. We didn't want Mexicans, we were very happy with American dollars."

Another 12,000 hotel rooms were added between 1983 and 1993, and the ensuing glut of accommodation combined with a natural disaster sent Cancún's fortunes into a tailspin. Hurricane Gilbert struck in 1988, killing over 300 people and tearing up many of the beaches along the hotel zone. The unprecedented scale of devastation forced many hotels and tour operators to slash their prices, and before long a different kind of American started to frequent Cancún—one who was less worldly and discriminating and considerably more budget-conscious. As Cancún became the destination of choice for a new generation of American students, many in the local tourism industry watched in horror as their resort morphed into a tropical Sodom and Gomorrah.

In 2002, travel agents, hotel managers, and bar owners decided enough was enough. They signed a "pact of civility" that required local businessmen to withhold service to obviously intoxicated customers. Upon arrival, tourists were handed leaflets at the airport explaining the new campaign to clean up Cancún and warning what would constitute unacceptable behavior. Word spread across U.S. college campuses that Cancún's anything-goes vibe had become a thing of the past, and American undergraduates began looking elsewhere for sunny, spring-break destinations.

Courting the Local Tourist

Some local businessmen also learned that Cancún had an image problem of a different sort among their fellow Mexicans. The national tourism market had long been neglected by Cancún's private sector, and many Mexicans came to think of the resort as a destination that was out of their reach. "It was perceived as an expensive resort where Mexicans could not go to relax," says Lizzie Cole Guerrero, the head of promotion at the tourism ministry of the Quintana Roo state government. When millions of Americans canceled foreign trips in the immediate aftermath of the 9/11 attacks, government officials and tourism entrepreneurs decided the time was ripe to target the heretofore overlooked Mexican holidaymaker. "September 11 was a watershed," admits Cole Guerrero. "We had become very dependent on the American tourist, and we needed to take some decisions to change that situation."

A series of tourism caravans crisscrossed the country to aggressively promote Cancún along with the nearby resorts of Playa del Carmen, Cozumel Island, and the Riviera Maya region. The response surpassed the most optimistic of expectations: within a year, Mexicans had become the resort's biggest clientele base after Americans, and today they make up nearly three in ten Cancún-bound tourists. "We had a sensational response," says the hotel owner Abelardo Vara. "It dawned on us that we had lost a great opportunity in the past because we had a gold mine right here in this country."

Different Mexicans react in different ways to Cancún. Fernando Martí, the magazine publisher who also serves as the resort's unofficial historian, says that his *chilango* friends from the capital don't care much for the place. "They don't feel at ease in Cancún, they find it to be too built up," he explains. "Just like they don't care for Miami, none of my friends goes to Miami." But for others, the American feel of the resort can be a plus. María Hernández moved from Puebla to Cancún in 2000 to take a job at a local ecological theme park as a restaurant cashier. Hernández left in 2003 but came back to Cancún with her family for a week-long vacation two years later and was enchanted by everything in the resort she once called home—including the mostly American guests at the Oasis Viva hotel where she stayed. "You learn from them, and we like to crack jokes that they can't understand," she said with a smile. "It's a good thing because Mexico can continue to grow."

Abel Gutiérrez and Magdalena Trujillo decided to spend their honeymoon in Cancún after consulting some friends in the city of Guadalajara who had recently stayed at the resort. Curiosity was a major factor for the young couple, who had previously taken vacations in Puerto Vallarta and Mazatlán on the country's Pacific Coast, and the newlyweds were pleasantly surprised by the Mexican-flavored interior decor and furniture of the hotels and restaurants they visited. "The places don't have the American look," said Trujillo. "They use local color schemes and traditional furniture. There may be places that do have that American style, but we didn't see them." The only sour note came when they toured some of the other properties belonging to the Spanish company that owns the hotel where they stayed, and the crowds of rowdy spring breakers made the couple feel out of place. "There they looked at a Mexican as something strange," recalled Abel. "It was a bit unpleasant," agreed Magdalena. "There was a lot of noise, and young people of all ages were drunk."

Some Mexicans complain of second-class treatment in the hotel zone. Gerardo García, the editor of the now defunct Cancún newspaper *La Voz del Caribe*, came up with an ingenious way of documenting the double standards that sometimes apply to Mexicans and foreigners in the resort. He told two of his swarthy reporters to drink in public along Kukulcán Boulevard in open violation of the recently signed pact of civility and later sent one of their American-looking colleagues to do the same. The "darkies," as García called them, were hassled by local cops while the fair-skinned reporter caroused in the streets with total impunity. A local elementary school teacher named Javier Martínez has witnessed the same pattern of discrimination in the restaurants and nightclubs of the hotel zone. "At the entrance to discos, they first admit foreigners and only later do they admit Mexicans," says Martínez. Damaris Mena echoed her husband. "They prefer the foreign tourist," says Mena, who, like Martínez, grew up on Holbox Island north of Cancun. "They don't offer the discount ticket packages to the local tourist, they try to get the attention of foreigners instead."

TROUBLE IN PARADISE

Tourism accounts for 85 percent of Cancún's local economy, and its newspapers publish statistics that track on a daily basis hotel occupancy rates and the number of flight arrivals. Tourism revenues have boosted the mainland city's population to 600,000, but Cancún's explosive growth has also brought with it the usual host of social ills associated with rapid urbanization. Squalid shantytowns have sprung up on the city's outskirts. Youth gangs terrorize the residents of poor neighborhoods that tourists never see. Taxi drivers run the same risk of being robbed at gunpoint as do their Mexico City counterparts. During my visit in March 2005, the front pages of the local newspapers were filled with stories about the brazen robbery in broad daylight of an expensive jewelry store inside the mainland city's top-drawer shopping mall.

The resurgence of major drug trafficking operations in the area has further tarnished Cancún's image. The state of Quintana Roo became a key transit corridor in the 1990s for Colombian cocaine headed for the United States. Drug kingpins thrived under the corrupt administration of governor Mario Villanueva, who vanished from view after his term in office ended and was finally taken into custody in 2001 on narcotics charges. Evidence of a revived drug smuggling trade surfaced in the fall of 2004 with the discovery of five bullet-riddled bodies near Cancún.[5] Three of the victims were members of Mexico's elite Federal Agency of Investigation, and twenty-seven state, federal, and local police officers were later arrested on suspicion of involvement in the murders and drug-trafficking activity.

Some of Cancún's tourism entrepreneurs accuse the news media of exaggerating the mainland city's crime and development problems. Eduardo Paniagua is a slender, twitchy man who moved from the Chiapas state capital of Tuxtla Gutiérrez to Cancún eight years ago. His thriving travel agency specializes in the Japanese tourism market, and he spent over two years living in Japan to master the language. He eyed me with a certain wariness when we sat down to talk about the resort, and I soon realized why: Paniagua vigorously objected to newspaper stories that portray Cancún in anything but the most glowing of terms. "Cancún is our brand, it's what we sell to the outside world and we have to protect that," said Paniagua, the president of the Quintana Roo state association of travel agents. "If the press continues to speak badly about Cancún, they'll wind up destroying our goose that lays the golden eggs. Within a few years, they'll have to go somewhere else to find work."

But other businessmen acknowledge that Cancún has grown too big too fast. Overdevelopment has replaced spring breakers as the bane of the resort's short-term future: current plans call for the construction of another 8,000 hotel rooms that could stretch Cancún's already overburdened infrastructure to the breaking point. The towering symbol of the resort's uncontrolled growth is the Rius Palace, a whitewashed, eight-story monstrosity that opened its doors in 2004 and resembles a cross between a gigantic lighthouse and a belle époque hotel. "A series of excesses has occurred here in this day and age," admits hotelier Abelardo Vara. "All these billboards have caused a kind of visual pollution, there's been a lot of corruption, and laundered drug money has entered the tourism industry. Success isn't easy to control."

Cancún is hardly unique in that respect. Similar problems have surfaced in Cabo San Lucas, the equally Americanized beach resort on the southeastern tip of Baja California. Like their counterpart in the Yucatán, Cabo San Lucas and its sister resort of San José del Cabo are focused squarely on the gringo's tourist dollar. The cover story of the March 2007 issue of Aeroméxico's in-flight magazine touted that end of the Baja peninsula as "the perfect vacation spot for Americans, especially those from California, where the state's position as the world's fifth largest economy translates into lots of disposable income for many of its residents." And as if to underscore the point, the fourteen-page magazine spread spotlighted a new luxury housing development under construction called Puerto Los Cabos that will feature a desert theme park, a marina with 462 boat slips, lots for 1,500 new homes, and two state-of-the-art golf courses designed by two of the sport's legends, Jack Nicklaus and Greg Norman.[6]

But the explosive growth of the "Cabos" has come at a price. The hotel construction boom along the beaches of Cabo San Lucas has largely robbed the town's Mexican residents of their sea views, and the opening of American-styled strip clubs has lent the resort a whiff of sleaze. Mark Casagranda has been sailing to Cabo San Lucas on a regular basis since 1980, and on a recent fishing trip the San Francisco real estate developer was approached by a well-dressed Mexican prostitute in her early twenties.

The incident struck him as an ominous sign that Cabo San Lucas may be headed in the wrong direction. "There were guys on side streets selling drugs, and the whole place had been transformed," recalls Casagranda. "Now you're hard pressed to find a Mexican restaurant. It's become a bad version of Las Vegas, and Mexicans don't take kindly to this. You can ill afford to have people going back to the United States and saying, 'Cabo, what a toilet. It's got hookers and drugs.'"[7]

Others share Casagranda's disenchantment. When Los Angeles mortgage broker Amir Nassirzadeh began shopping for a vacation home in 2006, he and his wife considered Cabo San Lucas for a time but dropped the idea because it seemed "a little too much like the United States." They settled instead for a $600,000 hillside condominium overlooking the mainland resort of Puerto Vallarta.[8]

SAYULITA: THE ANTI-CANCÚN

At the other end of the spectrum of resorts catering to *yanqui* tourists is Sayulita on the Pacific coast of Nayarit state. A forty-five-minute drive from Puerto Vallarta, Sayulita was once unknown to the outside world, a sleepy fishing village that brought back memories of what Puerto Vallarta was like before Liz Taylor and Richard Burton put it on the map in the 1964 film *The Night of the Iguana*. But Sayulita today has become a magnet for young American surfers and backpackers traveling on a shoestring. The lone reminder of Sayulita's quiet past is a two-story, whitewashed building in the town center that houses the offices of the local farmers' cooperative association.

Sayulita is packed with Internet cafes, art galleries, massage parlors, and real estate agencies that have signs written in English. Local restaurants offer a selection of Chinese, Italian, and Argentine cuisine, and a surprisingly large number of their employees are what some Mexicans call "gringo wetbacks"—Americans who settle down for a few months and have no legal work visas but still manage to find jobs. "They stay here as undocumented workers, they take care of people's homes or become tourist guides," says

Francisco Loza, an artist from the city of Guadalajara who first came to Sayulita in 1988 when he was in his early twenties. "But they're treated well simply because they're Americans."[9] An Oregon native who owns a restaurant with her lesbian partner in the quiet town of San Francisco to the north of Sayulita has noticed the changes. "In Sayulita you feel there are more foreigners than Mexicans," says Gloria Honan, a paramedic by training who moved to Mexico in 1991. "Once we were having coffee in Sayulita and overheard some Americans discussing a petition to make a disco turn down the noise. This is a very loud culture, it's part of the reason why people like the culture. I fell in love with it and have learned to embrace those differences, but some people come down here to change the culture."

There are no hotels in Sayulita, and none of the U.S. restaurant and sports bar chains that became fixtures in Cancún has yet opened a branch. But an ultra-expensive Four Seasons hotel has opened its doors a few miles down the coast at Punta Mita, and the influx of Americans has driven real estate prices through the roof. José de Alba Cruz remembers a very different Sayulita when he arrived in 1986 with his wife and nine children. In the old days, it was just another Mexican hick town suffering from a bad case of neglect by the state, he says. The streets were unpaved, livestock wandered through the town, and work was hard to come by. "Not even the houses were painted," recalls the paunchy pensioner. "It was dirty, there was no one who collected the garbage."

The arrival of Americans in large numbers forced government officials to spruce up the town's appearance and improve public services quickly. De Alba Cruz says that living conditions in Sayulita have taken a turn for the better. "It's been practically invaded by so many Americans," he says, "and that has generated a lot of progress. They spend a lot, there's work for people and there are more public services." The artist Francisco Loza uses different imagery to describe the transformation that Sayulita has undergone. "Once upon a time it was difficult to get a good cup of coffee," he told me over breakfast one morning as I weighed my options of ordering an espresso or a cappuccino. "Everybody used to drink Nescafe, but eventually people learned."

WILMA

In October 2005 a category four hurricane named Wilma packing winds with speeds of up to 170 miles per hour slammed into Cancún and dumped massive quantities of rainfall on the resort for two consecutive days. At least sixteen people died in the worst natural disaster to hit Cancún since Hurricane Gilbert ripped through the region in 1988. The storm washed away many of the hotel zone's trademark white-sand beaches and stranded nearly 40,000 foreign tourists who didn't manage to get out before Wilma came ashore. In a horrific year that broke all existing records for hurricane activity, Wilma proved to be Mother Nature's final blow to the U.S. Gulf Coast and the Caribbean. The havoc wrought by Wilma did not even begin to approach the levels of destruction caused by Gilbert: the final death toll was a tiny fraction of the 318 lives lost in the 1988 storm. But in the immediate aftermath of the hurricane, looters took to the streets of the city and the hotel zone, filling up shopping carts with food and household appliances that inspired unflattering comparisons with the lawlessness that engulfed New Orleans in the wake of Hurricane Katrina earlier that year. The front-page headline in a regional newspaper stressed government efforts to contain any damage the looting episodes could inflict on the resort's reputation: "Resolve to minimize harm to the tourism image of [Cancún]."[10]

I traveled to the Yucatán state capital of Mérida four days after Wilma made landfall to help a *Newsweek* colleague named Susan McVea make arrangements to leave the stricken area. McVea and her boyfriend Francesco Iacono arrived at my hotel in Mérida visibly exhausted and desperate to board a flight bound for New York City. It was not Susan's first visit to Cancún: she had taken a number of vacations at the resort in the past and had always enjoyed her stays. But it was hard to imagine any of the legions of angry foreigners camped out that week at the airport in Mérida coming back to Cancún in the foreseeable future. Many complained they had been given almost no information by Mexican officials throughout their four-day ordeal, spent inside makeshift shelters waiting to be evacuated. What would happen to the Mexican economy if the crown jewel of its second most important industry saw its reputation irreparably tarnished by the fallout from Wilma?

If my own experience was anything to go by, I would bet on Cancún's capacity to rebound and thrive once again. I was working for *Newsweek* in the Middle East when radical Islamist terrorists attacked an archaeological site in the Egyptian city of Luxor in November 1997 and killed over sixty foreign tourists. Upon my return to Cairo six months later, the city's usually teeming international airport was deserted. It took Egypt's tourism industry, which typically draws nearly four million foreign visitors annually, a full year to recover from the public relations debacle of Luxor. But it did—and if militant extremists couldn't dim the lure of the pyramids and a cruise down the Nile River, then surely a hurricane would not erase Cancún from the map of tourism destinations for the typical sun-starved gringo. They would surely return in their droves, I thought at the time after I said my goodbyes to Susan and Francesco at the airport that fall.

And so it came to pass. Although the resort had not fully recuperated from Wilma by the early months of 2006, Cancún still managed to attract 2.43 million tourists that year and racked up revenues of over $1.8 billion. Tens of thousands of American tourists were in Cancún in August 2007 when another monster hurricane named Dean was gathering force on its way toward the Yucatán Peninsula. Most of those Americans were evacuated in orderly fashion, and in the event Dean spared Cancún. Two years after the trauma of Wilma had passed, my colleague Susan McVea told me she fully intended to return to Cancún because she "absolutely loved it there." But I could not picture myself going back to the Mexican resort where everyone speaks English, unless my job called for it.

The abundance of Americans on the streets of Ajijic and San Miguel de Allende and in the bars of Cancún and Sayulita will maintain them as enclaves of expats and tourists in the Mexican landscape for a long time to come. But as other corners of the country can readily attest, you don't need hordes of gringos wandering around in flip-flops and oversized T-shirts to see how the United States impacts twenty-first-century Mexico.

CHAPTER 9

The Umbilical Cord
of Remittances

The rather impertinent question came at the tail end of Felipe Calderón's first joint press conference with George W. Bush as president of Mexico, in March 2007. "President Calderón, it's been reported you have relatives working in the United States," began Stephen Dinan, the White House correspondent of the conservative newspaper *Washington Times*. "Do they want to become citizens? Are they there legally?" Dinan's query elicited some nervous giggles inside the room, and Bush himself seemed slightly taken aback. But Calderón maintained his composure and tackled the question head-on. "Yes, I do have family in the United States, and . . . these are people who work and respect that country," replied the Mexican chief of state. "They pay their taxes to the [U.S.] government, these are people who work in the field . . . they probably handle that which you eat, the lettuce, et cetera. . . . I have not seen them in a long time and do not know their migratory status."

Subsequent press reports have cast doubt on the veracity of Calderón's account, given his family's comfortably urban, middle-class origins.[1] But whether or not the Mexican president actually has blood relatives toiling in the fields of some American farmer doesn't negate two larger points that Calderon was making in his answer. As he later noted in passing that day, up to half of the four million people from his home state of Michoacán are believed to be working and living in El Norte. And in an era when the remittances that Mexican immigrant workers send home each year represent the country's second-largest source of hard currency income after petroleum exports, it is no longer shameful for a family to have a kinsman who has immigrated to the United States. "These are our best people," said Calderón at the press conference. "These are bold people, they're young, they're talented, they have overcome tremendous adversity."[2]

It wasn't always that way. When my father moved from his native state of Jalisco to California in the 1930s to join an uncle living in Pasadena, many Mexicans regarded immigrants as renegades who had turned their back on the homeland in pursuit of the almighty dollar. But times have changed, and the estimated ten million Mexican legal and illegal residents in the United States are being courted by Mexican politicians and bankers like never before. When he took office in December 2000, Vicente Fox hailed them as "our beloved immigrants" who were nothing short of "heroic."[3] Small wonder: in 2004 those workers pumped an estimated $16.6 billion into the Mexican economy, a sum that represented a 24 percent jump over the previous year, and in the final year of Fox's presidency that figure surpassed the $23 billion mark. Under his stewardship, Fox pledged, Mexican consulates in the United States would become "the best allies of immigrants' rights," and his government later issued a comic book guide to the perils of entering the United States illegally that gave prospective migrants tips on how to stay safe.

Calderón made Mexican immigrants the number-one priority of his first presidential trip to the United States. His itinerary raised eyebrows on both sides of the border not only because four of the five United States cities he visited in February 2008 have large Mexican populations, but because Calderón chose to bypass Washington altogether. As he said on the eve of his departure, the trip was intended to show solidarity with his fellow Mexicans at a time when some Republican presidential candidates had declared war on undocumented workers and vowed to deport millions of them. "The fundamental message is that we are with them," said Calderón. "We are ready to help them with their problems."[4]

The factors that drew my father to southern California over seventy years ago exert an even stronger pull on Mexicans today. A comprehensive opinion poll commissioned by the *New York Times* in 1986 found that four in ten Mexicans would live in El Norte if given the opportunity.[5] That figure leapt to 81 percent in a May 2003 survey, with only 14 percent saying they would pass up the chance.[6] And as for those Mexicans still living in their native nation but with relatives in the United States, a 2004 poll sponsored by the Inter-American Development Bank and the Washington-based Pew Hispanic Center estimated that nearly one in five Mexicans regularly receives remittances from relatives employed in the United States,[7] making Mexico one of the largest beneficiaries of such financial transfers worldwide.[8]

THE BINATIONAL STATE OF ZACATECAS

Remittances have become an indispensable lifeline that has made modern Mexico's financial health even more dependent on El Norte. And nowhere is the economic importance and political clout of the Mexican immigrant more evident than in the central plateau state of Zacatecas. The name of the state comes from a word the Chichimeca Indians used to describe the place where the grass grows, but it is the U.S. greenback that reigns supreme in Zacatecas today. According to financial data compiled by Mexico's Central Bank, immigrants from Zacatecas transferred $352 million into the state's economy in 2003. And if the wads of cash that migrants physically carry back on periodic visits to their hometowns are factored in, that figure swells to an estimated $480 million, says Rodolfo García Zamora, an economics professor at the Autonomous University of Zacatecas. No state in Mexico has seen a higher percentage of its inhabitants move to the United States, and the remittances they send home make up 8.2 percent of the state's annual gross domestic product (GDP), another nationwide high. A more populous state like Calderón's native Michoacán has more immigrants living in the United States in absolute terms and therefore receives more money in remittances. But the $1.8 billion those workers sent home in 2003 amounted to only 4 percent of Michoacán state's annual GDP, according to García Zamora.[9]

The exodus of its native sons and daughters is a telling measure of how far the fortunes of Zacatecas have fallen over the centuries. The state was the original fountainhead of New Spain's wealth, beginning in September 1546 when the commander of a detachment of Spanish troops named Juan de Tolosa set up camp at the foot of a mountain known as La Bufa. During the previous twenty-five years, Spaniards had fanned out of Mexico City in search of mineral riches, but none of the mines excavated near the towns of Pachuca, Sultepec, or Taxco had yielded the windfall of silver that the original conquistador Hernán Cortés had dreamt of finding. The Indians whom Tolosa met led him to a cluster of rocks they thought might be of interest to the European adventurer. Those rocks contained the precious metal that the Spanish crown coveted, and in short order a mining settlement was established on the present-day site of Zacatecas city. It became the first ever silver-mining boom town of New Spain, and with the discovery of more deposits in the nearby towns of Sombrerete and Fresnillo the ensuing stampede of Spanish settlers and indigenous laborers made Zacatecas the colony's third-largest city after Mexico City and Puebla. By 1574, silver was being mined in seven settlements scattered across what is now Zacatecas state, and the region came to rival the Andean city of Potosí as Madrid's leading source of silver throughout much of the late seventeenth and early eighteenth centuries.

Three hundred years later, the state that first became famous for exporting silver now exports people. When the silver mines were mostly exhausted by the late nineteenth century, *zacatecanos* began leaving in droves. The initial flight of workers gravitated toward the mines and fledgling industries of Chihuahua and Nuevo León states, but some kept heading north and crossed the border to seek jobs in Texas, New Mexico, and Arizona. The booming American railroad industry was the principal magnet of employment that drew *zacatecanos* to the United States during the early years of the twentieth century, and the introduction of the *bracero* guest-worker program during World War II brought thousands more into the agricultural valleys of central and southern California.

Mexico's National Population Council estimates that 600,000 natives of Zacatecas now live in the United States, a figure that is equivalent to 40 percent of the state's resident population of 1.5 million. If that base population is supplemented by the number of children and grandchildren who have been born on the Other Side, the total number of Mexicans and Mexican Americans of *zacatecano* origin living in the United States exceeds the number of people who have stayed behind. In a state where the cultivation of beans, chili peppers, guava, and other farm produce still provides the leading source of income and employment, the economic well-being of Zacatecas is now overwhelmingly linked to the earnings of its native sons and daughters living in the United States and their willingness to keep sending money home. "The private sector has declined a lot, and the only area that has demonstrated any kind of economic dynamism is the immigrant sector," says García Zamora of the Autonomous University of Zacatecas. "No other sector has quite the same importance."

That unique confluence of circumstances has created what some *zacatecanos* call Mexico's first truly binational state. In 2003 the state legislature approved a bill that gave U.S.-based emigrants the right to run as candidates in municipal and statewide elections. Voters responded a year later by electing two emigrants to the thirty-seat state assembly and installing two more longtime residents of the United States as mayors in the towns of Jerez and Apulco. A fifth emigrant was elected to the town council of Fresnillo, the state's second-largest city.

In that same vote, Amalia García Medina became the first woman in the history of Zacatecas to be elected governor, and she credits her victory in part to the impact of immigration on the politics and demographics of a state where women make up 53 percent of its inhabitants. "Women in Zacatecas are very active politically, and there was an enormous identification with my candidacy," says the left-of-center governor. "But above all, Zacatecas' very extensive links with the United States have had a major impact on how we see the world. *Zacatecanos* don't find it strange that a woman is governing them. That doesn't create any conflicts; they see it as something natural."[10]

THE THREE-FOR-ONE PROGRAM

During the first 100 days of her administration, García Medina made five trips to American cities to meet with fellow natives of Zacatecas. Those peregrinations were intended as a kind of tribute to the vital contributions made by *norteños*, as the immigrants are known back home. But that did not arise spontaneously: the recognition is in reality the hard-won fruit of over thirty years of grassroots organization and community self-improvement projects spearheaded by people like state lawmaker Manuel de la Cruz.

A mechanical engineer by training, de la Cruz used false documents to enter the United States for the first time in 1972, and he soon settled in the Los Angeles suburb of Norwalk. De la Cruz landed work as a carpenter in the construction industry, and within a year of his arrival his wife delivered the first of their four U.S.-born children. On a visit to his suburban Los Angeles home, de la Cruz's mother asked her son for some money to build a chapel in the family's native village of El Tejujan—and that request eventually spawned an innovative program that has transformed dozens of towns and villages across the state of Zacatecas. To raise funds for the chapel, de la Cruz founded a social club called Ranchos Unidos (United Ranches) de Fresnillo. In 1986 the club joined a fledgling network of *zacatecano* clubs in southern California that later forged a productive working relationship with the Mexican consulate in Los Angeles. In 1992 de la Cruz was elected president of the federation and a year later the program *Dos por Uno* (Two for One) was established under a landmark agreement reached with the Mexican foreign ministry.

Under the accord, Mexico's federal and state governments pledged to donate one dollar each for every dollar the federation raised for public works and community projects. In 1999 the program was renamed *Tres por Uno* when municipal governments signed up, and over a twelve-year period the immigrant clubs have helped finance over 1,500 projects in Zacatecas, ranging from the pavement of streets and the construction of health clinics to the installation of sewage and drinking water facilities. Approximately 300 clubs of Zacatecas-born Mexicans have been established in thirteen U.S.

states, and Zacatecas governor García Medina says that $5 million was raised in 2003 alone for 308 community projects under the auspices of the Three for One program. The success of the initiative garnered an official endorsement from President Fox soon after he took office, and the program has since spread to twenty-two other states in Mexico.

The influence of the state's large migrant population can be seen throughout Zacatecas. The state capital city's international airport offers more direct flights to destinations in the United States (four) than in Mexico (three)—and one of those Mexican cities is Tijuana, a well-known launching pad for successive generations of U.S.-bound immigrants. In December the streets of towns like Jalpa, Juchipila, and Jerez fill up with Ford F-150 pickup trucks, Toyota Previa minivans, and Chevrolet Tahoe sports utility vehicles bearing the license plates of U.S. states from whence Mexican workers have come to spend the Christmas holidays with relatives and friends. Real estate agents and car dealers in Zacatecas routinely quote prices and fees in U.S. dollars. Governor García Medina says it is impossible to make a reliable estimate of the state's unemployment rate because so many members of the workforce go back and forth between Zacatecas and the Other Side. "We are more linked to Los Angeles than to Mexico City," notes Miguel Moctezuma Longoria, a researcher specializing in immigration issues at the Autonomous University of Zacatecas. "Zacatecas is the most binational state of all in Mexico."[11]

The Immigrant Vote

Until recently, the money sent by migrants to their hometowns never brought them any political dividends. Under their nation's election laws, Mexican workers living in the United States had to physically return to the country to vote, and successive PRI governments resisted proposals to grant migrants dual residency status and the right to cast absentee ballots from abroad. A population who had voted with their feet seemed like a poor bet to support a party that had governed Mexico for seventy-one years and stood to be held accountable for the corruption and mismanagement that drove millions of Mexicans to leave the country in the first place. The many years these migrants spent living in a foreign country with a true, functioning democracy was an additional deterrent for PRI politicians, argues Manuel de la Cruz, who won his seat in the state legislature in 2004 as a candidate of the left-wing Party of the Democratic Revolution (PRD). "Their greatest fear is the participation of immigrants in elections because we have learned a lot about democracy from living in the United States where there are two real political parties," says de la Cruz. "That democracy will destroy [the PRI's] castle of glass."[12]

The longstanding demands of politically active immigrants like de la Cruz for voting rights finally received a presidential imprimatur when Vicente Fox took office. When his government introduced a bill that would allow up to 4.2 million migrants to mail ballots from abroad in the 2006 presidential election, PRI congressmen had little choice but to join their colleagues from other parties in approving the legislation. The role of the migrant vote on that election turned out to be negligible, however. Under the cumbersome regulations set out by the legislation, only those Mexican emigrants with valid voter registration cards were eligible to cast ballots from outside the country. Those who lacked the document had to apply in person at a Mexican consulate in the United States or at offices of the Federal Electoral Institute (IFE), the body in charge of organizing and supervising elections, in towns and cities along the U.S. border. In 2006 the emigrant vote was restricted to the presidential contest, and a ruling by the IFE barred candidates from campaigning in the United States or any other foreign country. Political parties were similarly prohibited from spending money outside Mexico to promote their presidential nominees.

In the event, less than 1 percent of the total number of emigrants eligible to vote requested absentee ballot forms in time for the 2006 election that Calderón won by the narrowest of margins. New ground was broken nonetheless, and the importance of the immigrant vote in future elections will rise as migrants become more used to the idea of exercising their civic rights from homes in the United States. "Now they've become new political and social players who have been politically recognized and are acting in a bi-national way," says Moctezuma Longoria of the Autonomous University of Zacatecas. "The political class fears that these new players will take hold of their own destiny. They have the capability to negotiate, they're carrying out development programs in their communities and they are questioning the politicians."

THE TRANSFORMATION OF THE ZACATECAS COUNTRYSIDE

The town of Valparaíso in the northwestern corner of Zacatecas state depends almost entirely on the remittance pipeline from El Norte for its survival. Its tacky downtown is home to a half-dozen foreign exchange outlets and the branches of two major Mexican banks that process the estimated $100,000 pouring into Valparaíso on a daily basis. Like many other towns in Zacatecas, Valparaíso has seen its population shrink over the past fifteen years, and many of its present-day inhabitants have all or nearly all of their immediate family members living in the United States Delfino Blanco Pasillas is an attorney and father of three who runs a successful law practice in the town of 11,000, and he is the only member of his immediate family who still lives in Valparaíso. His parents moved to Chicago when he was fourteen years old, and all nine of his brothers and sisters live in the United States "There was a time when it was unusual to have a relative over there," recalls Blanco, a diminutive man with an impish grin and a seemingly insatiable appetite. "Now it's unusual *not* to have relatives over there."[13]

To illustrate his point, Blanco takes me on a tour of the rural hamlets outside Valparaíso on a crisp early winter morning. Cattle ranching was once king in this corner of the Zacatecas high desert, but that industry has been in decline since the government broke up the large farming estates known as haciendas in the aftermath of the Mexican Revolution. Our first stop is Las Pilas, a tangle of hovels separated by stone fences just off the highway linking Valparaíso to the neighboring state of Durango. Las Pilas is a good example of what Blanco calls the ghost towns of Zacatecas, abandoned villages whose younger residents long since left in search of greener pastures up north. Statewide, Blanco tells me, only three of Zacatecas's fifty-seven municipalities posted net population growth between 1990 and 1995. It's easy to understand why after talking with the few remaining inhabitants of Las Pilas. All six of Reyes Lozano Muñoz's children now live in Texas and California, and the sexagenarian corn farmer is one of the few year-round residents of Las Pilas. "There are four of us left who run the ranch," says the grizzled *campesino*. "You feel poorer, more empty, more alone."

The mixed blessings of immigration are visible at our next stop, a settlement of eighty residents called Cruces. The Three for One Program helped pay for the construction of the local cemetery and the refurbishing of a sixty-year-old Catholic chapel. But the three-room primary school was closed down a few years ago because there weren't enough children under the age of twelve to justify its continued operation. "There are very few people," says Tadeo Álvarez Reyes, a seventy-two-year-old father of four children who are living in St. Louis and Fort Worth, Texas. "This ranch used to be full, but now all the people have gone to the United States."

A short time later a young man who has returned to Cruces for the holidays saunters by. Rigoberto Navejas left at the age of eighteen and settled in Wisconsin where he works in construction. Now thirty-six, Navejas says he comes back to Cruces two or three times a year with his wife and two U.S.-born sons. Standing side by side, he and the white-haired Álvarez exemplify the two halves of Mexico's binational state. The aging *campesino* wears the clothes of his generation and social station—straw cowboy hat, faded jeans, and handmade *huarache* sandals. Navejas's garb is more reminiscent of an American tourist—dark blue New York Yankees cap, red Nike sweatshirt, brown hiking boots.

In his own way, Delfino Blanco also personifies the binational culture of Zacatecas. The country lawyer regularly quotes his fees in dollars and often ends a phone conversation with the English-language phrase, "Okay, I see you, bye." He is remarkably philosophical about the immigration phenomenon that has left him without any parent or sibling living nearby. "For a fourteen-year-old boy, the goal is to cross the border," he says on the drive back to Valparaíso. "It's an escape valve for impetuous youngsters. We're not giving them opportunities to find work, and if they stay here there will be more robbery and other crime." He doesn't view his compatriots who have left the country as any less Mexican or patriotic than himself. "They leave but they continue to be Mexican," says Blanco. "They may no longer live in the town, they've lost their membership in the club, but they will never lose their identity. And they will be fully accepted when they come back."

That has been the happy experience of Silvia Rodríguez Ruvalcaba. Born in Santa Monica, California, she was a girl of eleven when her immigrant father moved the family back to his native Zacatecas village of Contitlán ("he didn't want us to acquire American customs," she explains with a sheepish smile). Rodríguez married young and returned to southern California with her immigrant husband five years later. Then at the age of twenty-nine, the mother of two children was uprooted for the third and last time when Rodríguez and her family moved back to Contitlán. When Rodríguez first arrived in Zacatecas with her parents in the late 1960s, there was no electricity, sewage or drinking water in Contitlán. Her new schoolmates instantly dubbed her "la pocha." "I spoke Spanish with a slight accent," she explains. "I would crop my words, and I had to share my cookies with other kids so they would play with me."[14] When she swore allegiance to the Mexican flag at her new school, Rodríguez had conflicted feelings and worried that she was somehow betraying the land of her birth.

Times have changed in ways big and small in Contitlán, and the hometown of her parents bears scant resemblance to the rural backwater of Rodríguez's youth. The return of several families who prospered in the United States has transformed the community into a miniature version of a middle-class American suburb. A number of houses boast two-car garages, satellite dishes, and the Spanish red tile roofs commonly seen in southern California neighborhoods. Nearly all the streets are paved and equipped with speed bumps to slow down passing traffic. The biggest house in Contitlán, a sprawling two-story mansion painted the color of vanilla ice cream with green trim, belongs to one of Rodríguez's in-laws. Rodríguez has dual nationality and says she feels equally at home on either side of the border. And as she readily admits, Rodríguez and other onetime immigrants who have returned to Mexico for good find themselves enjoying the best of both worlds. "We liked the way of life over there and we wanted to bring it over here," she explains. "We want all the modern conveniences of the United States—the dishwasher, the icemaker—along with the customs and traditions of Mexico."

Up the road from Contitlán, I stumble upon another example of Zacatecas's binational character. Young men and teenagers in the town of Apozol have donned cleats and pinstriped uniforms bearing the names "Halcones" (Falcons) and "Diablos" (Devils) for a Sunday afternoon game of baseball. That would not have surprised me in a border state, where the proximity of the United States has put baseball nearly on a par with soccer as the spectator sport of choice and produced major league players like Baja California's Esteban Loaiza and Sonora's Fernando Valenzuela. But deep in the heart of the Mexican interior, the sight of grown men in batting helmets standing in an on-deck circle piques my curiosity. A small crowd of local residents stands behind the batting cage and along the first-base line, many of them drinking bottles of Corona beer while the public address system blares *ranchera* music between innings.

I approach one of the younger looking players after the game in search of an explanation. Raúl Islas Medina tells me that baseball was introduced into this part of Zacatecas by returning immigrants in the 1940s. The eighteen-year-old construction worker started playing *beisbol* at the age of ten, and his favorite player is the New York Yankees' star shortstop Derek Jeter. But lest I get the wrong impression as an outsider, Raul says that soccer is also big in Apozol, and he himself coaches a local club. "The same people who like to watch baseball also come out for the *futbol* games," says Raúl.[15]

Not everything about the immigration experience has been positive for Zacatecas. The handful of companies that opened *maquiladora* in-bond assembly plants in the state over the years had to close down operations because they could not meet inflated salary expectations based on the wages earned by immigrants in the United States. The incessant flow of people between the two countries has brought the AIDS epidemic into Zacatecas, where over 700 people have been diagnosed HIV-positive owing to sexual intercourse with returning migrants who picked up the disease in El Norte.[16]

The social fabric of some towns and cities has been disrupted by the forcible repatriation of teenaged gang members who were born in Zacatecas but grew up on the mean streets of inner-city neighborhoods in the United States. Tens of thousands of such youths have been deported to the Latin American countries of their birth after being found guilty of committing felonies, and many of the youngsters bring with them the bad habits of drug use and street gang activity they acquired on the Other Side. "There are youngsters who come back from the United States with different attitudes," notes university professor Rodolfo García Zamora. "They dress like the youth gangs of East Los Angeles, they speak more English than they do Spanish. Their values are different, they regularly get into fights with family elders and they don't fully adapt."

Zacatecas is an instructive microcosm of modern Mexico's rising dependence on remittances. The steady decline of the state's mining and agricultural sectors forced successive generations of *zacatecanos* to seek employment in other parts of Mexico and later in the United States. The swelling stream of money transfers from El Norte to Zacatecas brought many benefits to the state and saved the local economy from total collapse. But it also removed any incentive to attract investment from outside the state and promote homegrown industries. A sudden severing of the umbilical cord of remittances would spell disaster for Zacatecas and other states in central Mexico that have been expelling young members of their labor forces for decades. And unfortunately for Zacatecas and for Mexico as a whole, a xenophobic consensus has emerged on the right wing of American politics that doesn't augur well for the long-term future of that lifeline.

THE BROKEN BORDERS SYNDROME

The immigration issue is to U.S.-Mexican relations today what drug trafficking was in the 1980s, a never-ending source of tension and mutual recrimination between the neighboring countries. A shrill, anti-immigrant lobby has arisen in the United States led by CNN anchorman Lou Dobbs, who never misses an opportunity to bash Mexico and constantly hectored the Bush administration to do something about the country's supposedly "broken borders." The broadcaster's nightly rantings found a sympathetic ear on Capitol Hill, where the U.S. House of Representatives approved a bill in the closing weeks of 2005 that earmarked money to erect new fencing along over 700 miles of the country's southern border and make it a crime to knowingly provide assistance to an undocumented worker.

Had it been approved by the U.S. Senate, the measure would have turned millions of Mexicans into lawbreakers by their mere presence on American soil. President George W. Bush publicly backed the harsh legislation, and his livid Mexican counterpart responded with a scathing critique of the bill. "To us, this wall [sic] is a disgrace," declared Vicente Fox during a ceremony in his home state of Guanajuato to salute the contributions made by Mexican emigrants to improve economic conditions back home. "It is inconceivable that we are building walls in the twenty-first century between two countries that are neighbors, brothers and partners. It's a terrible signal that doesn't speak well of a country that prides itself on being democratic."[17] Standing up for his fellow Mexicans didn't just make good sense for Fox's approval ratings. It also reminded his constituents how crucial those migrants and their remittances had become for the Mexican economy.

The clauses that would have criminalized undocumented workers living in the United States and any assistance given to them were eventually dropped from the bill. But the fencing proposal was approved and funded by the U.S. Congress in 2006, much to the astonishment and outrage of Mexicans from across the political spectrum. Critics of the border fence initiative attacked it on two counts: the newly built barriers would ultimately fail to deter Mexicans from trying to enter the United States, and they would poison what had been until then a fairly harmonious bilateral relationship. The first assertion was later called into question by mounting evidence that the deployment of 6,000 National Guard troops along the U.S. side of the border in 2006 and the introduction of drone planes and remote surveillance technology were indeed reducing sharply the number of Mexicans willing to hazard life and limb to enter El Norte illegally.[18]

But there was no doubting the corrosive effects that construction of new fencing and other border security measures taken by Washington would inflict on U.S.-Mexico ties in coming years. Fox and Felipe Calderón may have been on the same page with George W. Bush on free trade, counter-narcotics initiatives, and many other issues. But when it came to immigration, both Mexican presidents took the United States to task. "We strongly protest the unilateral measures taken by the U.S. Congress and government that have only persecuted and exacerbated the mistreatment of Mexican undocumented workers," declared Calderón in his first state-of-the-union address in September 2007. "The insensitivity toward those who support the U.S. economy and society has only served as an impetus to reinforce the battle . . . for their rights. Where there is a Mexican, there is Mexico."[19]

THE REMITTANCE CULTURE

The importance for so many Mexican families of the monthly check or wire transfer from *norteño* relatives has given rise to what University of Southern California professor Roberto Suro calls a "remittance culture." "Remitting is like praying," says Suro, the U.S.-born son of Ecuadorian and Puerto Rican immigrants. "If you are a good migrant, you remit. People like to boast about how much they remit, and if you don't you're considered a lowlife, an idiot."

Alfonso Rodríguez is one such "good migrant." The middle-aged gardener left his native village of El Remolino in southern Zacatecas state in 1975 at the age of nineteen. He settled in Los Angeles, started a family, and founded his own club for fellow *zacatecanos* in 1996. Over the ensuing nine years, the club named after Rodríguez's hometown has raised over $50,000 for a variety of projects under the auspices of the Three for One program, from the rehabilitation of a primary school to the construction of a medical clinic and a local museum.

I met "Poncho" Rodríguez in December 2004 in the city hall of Juchipila, the municipality which has El Remolino within its jurisdiction.

He had arrived the previous day from Los Angeles with his wife Hortensia and their nine-year-old U.S.-born daughter Alejandra for the family's annual journey to Zacatecas. Some supporters of the Three for One scheme say it is picking up the slack left by inefficient government agencies that should be undertaking public works projects with taxpayer revenues, and Poncho's chest swelled with pride as he took me on a tour of the improvements his club has financed in El Remolino. "We have always concentrated on community projects," explained Rodríguez. "If the government comes in and builds a basketball court, it will be scratched up and ruined within two months after it's finished. That's why I'm in favor of the way we in the clubs do things now. It requires an effort on the part of all of us to do these projects, and for that reason it's unlikely that a community project will be ruined."[20]

When Rodríguez headed to Los Angeles to look for work in the 1970s, the typical married immigrant usually left his wife and children behind. Today however, increasing numbers of migrants go to the United States with entire families in tow, and that has accelerated the depopulation of many towns and villages across Zacatecas. When Rodríguez was growing up, El Remolino had upwards of 2,000 year-round residents. The town's permanent population has fallen to half that figure today. "Ways of thinking changed for obvious reasons," he explains. "Entire families left on account of the scarcity of jobs, and the population accordingly declined."

WARNING SIGNS

But that recent trend could undermine the remittance pipeline in the long run. The authors of a *Foreign Affairs en Español* article warn that the generous sums of money sent home by immigrants are likely to decline over time as larger numbers of these workers assimilate into American society. As more women and children cross the border in coming years to reunite with their husbands and fathers, the tug of the folks back home could lessen over time. Turkey's experience with remittances may be a cautionary tale for Mexico. Money sent by Turkish *gastarbeiters* living in Germany boomed throughout the 1980s and 1990s, but they have been plummeting since the peak of 1998, when those guest workers remitted $5.3 billion to their home country. Within three years that figure was cut almost in half, largely because of family reunification in Germany. "On the supply side, the pioneer immigrant has fewer incentives to return to Turkey since so many of his relatives now live in Germany," wrote Jerónimo Cortina, Rodolfo de la Garza, and Enrique Ochoa-Reza. "On the demand side, both the pioneer immigrants as well as those who came later no longer have anyone to send remittances to. The same will happen in Mexico if future immigration trends produce the reunification of Mexican families in the United States."[21]

The American academic Roderic Ai Camp believes that tendency is already surfacing among some Mexican immigrant communities in the United States "The longer they live in the United States," wrote Camp, "the less frequent the contact [with relatives in Mexico], and the less likely they are to provide financial assistance to family members who remain in Mexico."[22] Yet another voice of caution came from U.S. ambassador to Mexico Tony Garza, himself the Texas-born grandson of Mexican immigrants. In a July 2005 speech to the American Chamber of Commerce in Mexico City, Garza declared that "reliance on remittances from the United States is not a viable economic policy. This only increases dependence on the United States and delays Mexico's full participation in the global economy."[23] A 2006 study by an investment fund of the Washington-based Inter-American Development Bank (IDB) reached a similar conclusion. "No one should celebrate [the fact that] Mexico is the world's number one recipient of remittances," stated the fund in its report. "This signifies that the national economy isn't generating enough jobs."[24]

By the first half of 2007, clear evidence was emerging that the flow of remittances might show signs of abating in the not too distant future. In its annual survey, the IDB found that an estimated 64 percent of Mexicans working in the United States sent money back home during the first six months of that year, down from the 71 percent reported by the bank for the same period in 2006. In those states like Georgia and North Carolina where the presence of Mexican immigrants is a relatively recent development, the drop was considerably steeper, from 80 percent who said they had sent remittances in the first half of 2006 to 56 percent for the same time frame in 2007. The quantum leaps in the volumes of cash sent to Mexico in recent years are also likely to become a thing of the past, according to the IDB. Remittances between January and June of 2007 reached $11.5 billion, only slightly above the $11.42 billion that was sent to Mexico by immigrants during the same period of the previous year. Overall, bank officials projected a very modest 0.6 percent increase in total remittances for the calendar year 2007.[25]

The slowing trends in the volume of remittances and the rise of a fierce anti-immigrant lobby in the United States are warning signs that Mexican policymakers cannot ignore. The recession that took hold in the U.S. economy in the final months of George W. Bush's presidency will eliminate some of the low-paying jobs traditionally filled by undocumented workers, and future Mexican leaders will have to wean their nation's economy off its reliance on financial transfers from "good migrants" to supplement the foreign exchange earnings generated by oil and tourism. Failure to do so will eventually reduce states like Zacatecas and Michoacán to economic paupers utterly dependent on handouts from the national government for their survival. The bi-national identity of Zacatecas is a function of the Americanization that is changing modern Mexico. The most striking example of this process among the country's major cities is the manufacturing powerhouse of Monterrey.

CHAPTER 10

The Southernmost City
in Texas

MONTERREY, NUEVO LEÓN

It hits you almost as soon as you leave the glittering terminal of Monterrey's international airport. First come the hotel signs with names so familiar to the American business traveler: Hampton Inn, The Courtyard, Best Western, Fairfield Inn. As you drive around Monterrey, the same restaurant and store logos that line American interstate highways dot the cityscape— Bennigan's, Applebee's, Office Depot, Chili's, Tony Roma's. With a hefty dose of irony and a dollop of verisimilitude, the capital of Mexico's Nuevo León state is sometimes called the southernmost city in Texas. Where else in Mexico would you find a major avenue in the heart of a city's down-town named after George Washington?

In spirit as well as geography, Monterrey is closer to Houston than to Mexico City. Its rise as a manufacturing giant dates back to the opening of the first major railroad to the Texas border, and for more than 150 years Monterrey's prosperity has been intimately tied to the steady integration of northern Mexico into the U.S. economy. The city's inhabitants live and work to the rhythms of a Sunbelt metropolis, and its upper-middle-class families like to spend their vacations on South Padre Island along the Texas Gulf Coast. The ultimate role model for *regiomontanos*, as the natives of Monterrey are called, is the self-made captain of industry. Its richest suburb evokes the palatial homes and swank boutiques of Beverly Hills and La Jolla, and Monterrey's upper crust is thoroughly steeped in

183

American culture and attitudes. "There is a kind of American way of life that has been introduced through the vision, habits, and daily routines of this elite," says Abraham Nuncio, a historian and journalist from the town of Texcoco, outside Mexico City, who moved to Monterrey in the mid-1970s. "They know the history of the United States better than the history of Mexico, they express themselves better in English than in Spanish. . . . Monterrey is perhaps the most Americanized city in the entire country, including even those on the border."[1]

A two-hour drive from the Texas border, Monterrey's extensive ties to the United States were a direct result of the Mexican War. At the stroke of a pen, the Treaty of Guadalupe Hidalgo, which ended the war in 1848, brought the town of 20,000 people within striking distance of what would eventually become the world's richest economy. The outbreak of the American Civil War ushered in the city's first bona fide economic boom, as cotton planters in the southern United States re-routed their merchandise through northeastern Mexico to skirt the federal blockade of the Confederacy's seaports. The dawn of the railroad age in northern Mexico heralded an industrial boom that would make Monterrey the nation's steel-making capital and attract large flows of American capital. The city's elites were among the first Mexican families to send their children to American universities. The constant contact with American entrepreneurs, technicians, missionaries, and adventurers has left its mark on the metropolis of four million people—and if Mexico City lies at the heart of the country's Hispano-indigenous past and present, then Monterrey surely sits on the cutting edge of its Americanizing future.

HIGH-FIVES AND FLIP-FLOPS

The inroads of Americanization are most evident among Monterrey's young people. On a midsummer evening in 2004, dozens of soccer fans were drinking beer in a bar at the Sheraton Ambassador Hotel as they watched a game between the city's top clubs, Tigres and Monterrey, on huge TV screens. Each time their favorite team scored a goal, the youths exchanged high-fives in the time-honored tradition of American sports bars. Two days later I visited the flagship campus of the Monterrey Institute for Technological and Higher Studies (ITESM). Founded in 1943 with seed money from the city's top captains of industry to churn out future generations of engineers, managers, and accountants for the private sector, the "Tec" caters primarily to the sons and daughters of the city's well-to-do families. On the Saturday morning when I visited the university, the ground floor of its smoke-free main library was full of students dressed in loose-fitting T-shirts, flip-flops, and baseball caps seated in front of their laptop screens. None of them would have looked out of place in the lecture hall of a typical American university.

One of those students is Sofía Elizondo Jasso. Both of her parents can trace their family roots in the area back to the nineteenth century, and she envisions spending most of her adult life in her native country. But Sofía is a thoroughly bilingual Mexican who spent her seventh grade year at a boarding school outside Cleveland, Ohio, and didn't regularly read books in Spanish until she was in high school. "I used to dream in English," the twenty-year-old international relations student told me. Like many products of the posh Monterrey suburb of San Pedro Garza García, Sofia punctuates her spoken Spanish with English words. "*Soy bien* picky *cuando vamos* shopping [I am picky when I go shopping]," she notes with a smile. She has seen firsthand how imported ideals of feminine beauty have shaped the tastes of her peers. "There is a strong tendency for girls to become blonder as they get older," jokes the fair-skinned brunette.

Perhaps owing to her privileged upbringing, Sofia has no trace of the inferiority complex that so many Mexicans feel in the presence of their northern neighbors. "I relate to the United States in a very different way than an illegal alien trying to cross the border," she explains. "I think of going there for college or frat parties."[2] (That was no idle remark: not long after I spoke with Sofía, she transferred to the Ivy League's University of Pennsylvania in Philadelphia to pursue her undergraduate studies.)

Sofia's spirit of self-confidence is mirrored at the highest levels of government in her hometown. One of Monterrey's best-known native sons is

José Natividad González Parás, a French-educated lawyer who won the governorship of Nuevo León state as the PRI candidate in 2003, and he makes no bones about the state's future prosperity being inextricably linked to that of the United States. "As time goes on there are more synergies and positive encounters, along with the recognition of our respective virtues and differences," he says. "What Monterrey and northern Mexico in general have done is assimilate systems of economic organization that operate efficiently in the United States. Certain American paradigms of success are seen by us as accepted frames of reference."[3]

"Nati" González has an ambitious vision for Monterrey—to transform it into what he calls the City of Knowledge, a Mexican version of Boston that would one day become a focal point for new investment and scientific research. To that end, he and three other Mexican border state governors signed a 2004 agreement with their Texas counterpart Rick Perry to promote the five states' economic development on a joint basis. Negotiating a regional economic pact with an American state governor outside the channels of the Foreign Ministry in Mexico City would have been unthinkable for a Mexican politician not so long ago, and all the more so for a card-carrying PRI member like Gonzalez. But the governor shrugs off such protocol considerations and exudes the pragmatism that many northern Mexicans display toward the United States. "Mexico urgently needs to make its regions and production sectors more competitive," explains González. "If we don't, we'll squander our chance to achieve economic development."

The *Regiomontano* Mindset

Perhaps owing to my own father's roots in the central state of Jalisco, I grew up thinking of its capital city of Guadalajara as Mexico City's main metropolitan rival. But Monterrey has emerged as the most competitive urban center besides the national capital city in twenty-first-century Mexico. Part of it has to do with Monterrey's identity as home to some of the country's most dynamic companies. Part of it has to do with a more equitable distribution of income: Monterrey has long boasted the highest indices of consumption per capita among the nation's major cities.

The *regiomontano* mentality is more in tune with the challenges facing Mexico in a globalized world. One of the city's most prominent journalists is Ramón Alberto Garza, the son of a crop-duster pilot who started working at Monterrey's award-winning *El Norte* newspaper as a teenager and became editor-in-chief of his hometown paper at the age of twenty-six. At the behest of the owners of *El Norte*, the Junco family, Garza moved to Mexico City in 1993 to launch the new broadsheet called *Reforma*, and he left the company seven years later over a bitter financial dispute with the publisher Alejandro Junco de la Vega. But he continues to shuttle regularly between his hometown and the national capital, and over lunch one day at the Monterrey airport, Garza explained the different mindsets of the country's three principal cities. "In Guadalajara, it's very important to know what family you come from," he noted, speaking to me in Spanish. " 'Oh, so you are so-and-so!' In Mexico City, it's very important to know who are the contacts you know. 'Ah, so you're a friend of so-and-so. How marvelous!' In Monterrey, it's more important to find out what your project is, what it is you're proposing to do. The *regiomontano* is very conscious that [and here Ramón effortlessly slipped into English] time is money."[4]

In Garza's view, that typically American association of time with money has its roots in history and geography. "Monterrey is a state of mind of fighting against adversity," he said. "It is located in a rather inhospitable area of the north that is physically disconnected from the center of the country. Historically, the city has been closer to Texas and the United States than to Mexico, and that gave rise to an important generation of entrepreneurs in the late nineteenth and early twentieth centuries who struggled against that adversity." I asked him to describe prevailing attitudes toward the United States. "Most friendly," Garza answered without hesitation. "There is a lot of mutual understanding between Monterrey and the United States. The Mexico City resident aspires to spend his vacation in Paris, Rome, or Madrid. The *regiomontano* is happy to go to Houston, New York, or Los Angeles."

The city's pronounced affinity for the United States goes well beyond the preferences in holiday destinations of its jet set. Some top companies in Monterrey like the conglomerate IMSA and the tortilla maker Maseca view the United States as a market at least as important as Mexico. The constantly expanding ties between the United States and the city were frankly acknowledged by the head of Monterrey's most successful transnational company. "Mexico isn't Latin America, Mexico is North America, and that's the end of the discussion," CEMEX president Lorenzo Zambrano once told a *Reforma* newspaper reporter. "We have nothing to do with Latin America, period."[5]

That sweeping statement is contradicted by some of the foreign acquisitions made by CEMEX under Zambrano's stewardship. Between 1994 and 1999 the corporation bought or made major investments in cement companies in Venezuela, the Dominican Republic, Colombia, Chile, Costa Rica, and Panama. But those acquisitions were later dwarfed by the corporation's $2.8 billion purchase of Houston-based Southdown, Inc., in 2000, a transaction that represented the largest ever Mexican acquisition of a U.S. company. That investment made CEMEX the industry's third-largest producer worldwide and signified a powerful affirmation of the direction in which Zambrano thinks his company—and by extension, the country as a whole—should be heading. Consider the educational backgrounds of the company's top executives: Zambrano obtained his master's degree in business administration from Stanford; North American operations chief Francisco Garza got his MBA from Cornell; and executive vice president for development Armando García received his MBA at the University of Texas.

Dozens of American companies reciprocate Monterrey's affinity for the United States. The list of U.S. corporations operating in the state of Nuevo León reads like a who's who of American big business: Chrysler, General Electric, IBM, American Express, Bank of America, and Price Waterhouse Coopers, to name but a few. Coca-Cola's principal bottler in Latin America is based in the city and Simmons mattresses are manufactured in Monterrey. In 1999 *Fortune* magazine declared Monterrey to be the most business-friendly city in Latin America,[6] and when the U.S.

home improvement retail chain Lowe's announced plans to take the south-of-the-border plunge in 2007, it chose to locate its first stores in the northern Mexican city.[7]

If Monterrey's booming steel plants and breweries in the early twentieth century once invited comparisons with the Pittsburghs and Milwaukees of the U.S. rust belt, today it bears a stronger resemblance to a forward-looking epicenter of modern corporate America like Atlanta. "Monterrey is the laboratory for NAFTA," says pollster Desiderio Morales Pérez. "It would be ideal for the United States if all of Mexico were like Monterrey."[8]

FROM FRONTIER OUTPOST TO BATTLEGROUND

The fast-paced metropolis has come a long way since its days as a forgotten outpost of the Spanish empire. Founded in 1596 by Diego de Montemayor and a dozen families of mostly Jewish origin, Monterrey had neither the silver deposits, good roads, or nearby ports generally coveted by the viceroys who ruled New Spain. The city's commercial fortunes didn't really brighten until after the country won its independence and a port was opened in 1826 at the northeastern town of Matamoros near the mouth of the Rio Grande. But as late as the eve of the Mexican War, Monterrey was still considered a remote backwater whose townspeople rarely traveled to Mexico City or Guadalajara. "You could still count its streets with your fingers, four or six streets at most," wrote the historian Israel Cavazos Garza. "The streets running from north to south were called alleys because they were narrow." As its residents prepared to celebrate the 250th anniversary of its founding in the fateful year of 1846, Monterrey was, in the words of Cavazos Garza, "very small, a provincial . . . city, much as it had been during the colonial period. Monterrey was totally isolated from the rest of the country because of the natural barrier of the Sierra Madre [mountain range]."[9]

The city's first direct encounter with *norteamericanos* was not auspicious. In the winter of 1846, President James K. Polk ordered General

Zachary Taylor to take U.S. troops into a strip of disputed territory lying between the Rio Grande and the Nueces River in what is today south Texas. Hell-bent on acquiring the Mexican territories of California and New Mexico during his term in office, Polk reckoned that the incursion of Taylor's forces into land that was clearly Mexican according to all existing international treaties would be treated as a grave provocation. Mexico's de facto president, General Mariano Paredes, did not disappoint Polk: he duly ordered Mexican troops to cross the lower Rio Grande and confront the invading American forces, and in late April 1846 Mexican units ambushed a U.S. reconnaissance patrol near Matamoros. Over the ensuing three weeks the two opposing armies fought two full-fledged battles, the Americans captured Matamoros, and at Polk's instigation the U.S. Congress declared war on Mexico. By July 1846, Taylor was ready to set out from Matamoros in the direction of Monterrey, the largest town in the northeastern part of the country.

On September 19, the eve of the fiesta celebrating Monterrey's patron saint, the Virgin Mary of the Immaculate Conception, Taylor's 6,640 soldiers set up camp at a shady grove three miles outside the town. The ensuing siege and three-day battle featured some of the fiercest hostilities seen during the entire U.S.-Mexican War, and on the first day of fighting alone, Taylor's poorly planned and coordinated assault on the city cost his forces 394 casualties. The battle of Monterrey ended with the surrender of the high-walled fortress known as The Citadel by General Pedro de Ampudia on September 25.

The Mexican army and many of Monterrey's residents resisted the Americans with great valor. Some of the women who remained in the city to fight alongside their husbands, fathers, and brothers particularly distinguished themselves. María de Jesús Dosamantes journeyed to Monterrey from the city of San Luis Potosí with her soldier-husband to confront the invaders, and she reported for duty dressed as a man and even crossed the line of fire. One U.S. soldier recounted the courage of a local woman in his personal diary. "I saw a Mexican female carrying water and food to the wounded men of both armies," wrote the soldier. "I saw her lift the head of one poor fellow, give him water, and then take her handkerchief from her own head and bind up the wounds. . . . I heard the crack of one or two guns and she, poor good creature, fell. . . . She was dead! I turned my eyes to heaven and thought, 'Oh God, and this is war!' " The unidentified woman was later immortalized as the Maid of Monterrey in contemporary American accounts of the battle, and American songwriters and playwrights commemorated the battle for the city in stirring lyrics and prose.[10]

For a city that would be later held up as a telling example of how the United States has imprinted itself upon modern Mexico, Monterrey covered itself in glory in Mexican annals of the war. While the denizens of bigger cities like Puebla and Jalapa did almost nothing to halt General Winfield Scott's triumphant march from Veracruz to Mexico City in the spring and summer of 1847, many *regiomontanos* braved enemy fire alongside uniformed Mexican troops in the early autumn of 1846. The battle of Monterrey marked the first engagement that saw U.S. casualties run into the hundreds. The town itself paid a steep price in physical damage as American soldiers advancing toward the city center smashed down the doors of dwellings and punched holes in walls to insert shells in bloody hand-to-hand fighting. But Monterrey would fare far better during the next major armed conflict involving American men in uniform.

MONTERREY AND THE AMERICAN CIVIL WAR

The secession of eleven pro-slavery southern states from the American Union in 1860 and 1861 led President Abraham Lincoln to impose a naval blockade on the Confederacy's coastline, from Port Isabel, Texas, to Norfolk, Virginia. In the process, President Lincoln unwittingly converted Monterrey into a vital link to the outside world for the fledgling Confederate States of America. A pro-slavery American expatriate founded the city's first English-language newspaper, the *Monterrey Era*, during the Civil War, and the city became a key way station for cotton exports coming out of Texas en route to the Gulf Coast port of Tampico. Led by the Spaniards Valentín Rivero and Mariano Hernández and an Irishman named Patrick Mullins, some of the city's top merchants made fortunes from selling gun powder, copper, tin, coffee, clothing, sugar, and other commodities to the rebel states.[11] Mullins, who later changed his name to Patricio Milmo, had already built up a thriving textile trade prior to the American Civil War and produced large quantities of military uniforms for the rebel forces.

But not all the foreigners who made a killing off the Civil War were European immigrants. Charles Stillman first struck it rich during the U.S.-Mexican War when he won a contract to bring provisions up the Rio Grande to supply General Taylor's army of occupation. When that war ended, Stillman bought up vast properties on the northern side of the river and set up a trade and manufacturing network on the Mexican side that was anchored in Monterrey. The federal naval blockade of the Confederacy's seaports furnished Stillman with another fabulous opportunity to make millions, and between 1862 and the end of the U.S. Civil War he and two American partners bought up cotton from growers in western Louisiana, Arkansas, and Texas and hauled it to Stillman's warehouses in Monterrey and Matamoros on large, two-wheeled carts known as *carretas*.[12]

Over a three-year period ending in 1864, Stillman and his partners averaged $60,000 a month in commissions and storage and marketing services, and without being identified by name their endeavors were chronicled by the U.S. consul in Monterrey. "[The city] receives large quantities of cotton and sends sufficient provisions to supply the entire rebel army," wrote the consul in a September 1862 dispatch to Lincoln's secretary of state, William Seward. "There are [Confederate] agents all over the place buying up corn and wheat from here [to the Mexican city of] San Luis Potosí. Great caravans leave daily for the Rio Grande, the majority bound for [the Mexican border town of] Piedras Negras laden with bedspreads, shoes, hides, fabrics, sulfur, medicines, etc. for the rebels. The agents have brought over $500,000 for their purchases."[13] From that point onward, Monterrey and much of northeastern Mexico became a virtual appendage of the expanding U.S. economy.

The Rise of the Sultan of the North

The dawn of the industrial revolution in Mexico transformed Monterrey into a vital pillar of the national economy. It began in 1882 with the opening of a major railroad line from Mexico City to the Texas border town of Laredo that ran right through Monterrey. That helped trigger a surge in citrus fruit production in southeastern Nuevo León state that saw oranges overtake traditional crops like corn and sugar cane.

In 1890 the U.S. Congress approved a steep tariff on foreign imports that inadvertently spurred the industrialization of Monterrey. Prior to the imposition of the tariff, the Philadelphia Smelting and Refining Company had imported large quantities of Mexican ores for processing at a smelter in Pueblo, Colorado. The new import duty posed a direct threat to the company's mineral pipeline from Mexico and led its owners, the wealthy Guggenheim family, to contemplate a major investment south of the border. "Why give up on Mexico?" asked the family's patriarch, Meyer Guggenheim. "If we can't bring Mexican ores to Pueblo, let us take a smelter to Mexico."[14] Monterrey's proximity to the U.S. border and its strategic location astride Mexico's expanding railroad network convinced the Guggenheims to select the city as the site for the Gran Fundición Nacional smelter that opened in 1891. It was a wise choice: from their Monterrey facility, the Guggenheims steadily expanded throughout north-central and northeastern Mexico until, by 1907, they acquired a virtual monopoly over smelting in that part of the country.[15]

By the turn of the century, American-style capitalism was firmly planted in the arid desert highlands of Nuevo León state. American technicians were recruited to install and maintain the machinery of the Cervecería Cuauhtémoc, which became one of the country's leading beer companies within a few years of its founding in 1890.[16] The brewery's insatiable demand for bottles spawned the creation of the Vidriera Monterrey, which soon emerged as one of Mexico's biggest glass factories. Headed by the brewery's main partners Manuel Cantú Treviño, Isaac Garza, and Francisco Sada, Monterrey's leading capitalists organized joint-stock companies to finance and regulate the city's unprecedented economic growth. The city's meteoric ascent was crowned in 1903 by the founding of the Companía Fundidora de Fierro y Acero de México, a steel mill that eventually became the largest in Latin America, with a workforce of 2,000 and boasting the capacity to process a thousand tons of iron ore daily. Business leaders and the local press dubbed Monterrey the Sultan of the North and hailed it as a city of "progress," a code word in the Porfirio Díaz era for entrepreneurship, urban development, and modernization.

By the early years of the twentieth-century Monterrey became for Mexico what Pittsburgh was to the United States—a hub of heavy industry that was playing a pivotal role in its country's rapidly modernizing economy. The city's industrial boom brought with it some early examples of American influence, though the phenomenon actually predated the economic transformation of Monterrey. Religious missionaries first made their presence felt in 1852 with the arrival in Monterrey of Melinda Rankin, who opened a mission for the American Biblical Society. Twelve years later, two Baptists followed in Rankin's footsteps and founded the Primera Iglesia (First Church) in Monterrey, which was described at the time as "the first Spanish-speaking evangelical church in Latin America."[17] By 1898, a correspondent for the Mexico City newspaper *El Imparcial* was noting that the señoritas of the city's upper classes "speak English with admirable correctness."[18]

At the turn of the century, the city hosted one of the largest American expatriate communities in the country. That was reflected in the founding of two English-language newspapers, the *Monterrey Daily News* and *El Monterrey News*, and in the sons of Monterrey's elite families who "formed the vanguard of 'high culture' for the first two decades of the twentieth century, albeit an imported culture." It was these privileged young men who introduced English words like "cocktail," "lunch," and "surprise" into the common parlance of the day.[19] Before long, some of the city's wealthiest industrialists started sending their designated heirs north of the border for a university education, led by Eugenio Garza Sada, who was among the first natives of Monterrey to graduate from the Massachusetts Institute of Technology in 1917.

"*Y EN EL* MEANTIME, MERRY CHRISTMAS TO ALL!"

The Americanization of Monterrey proceeds apace a century later. It can be glimpsed in its residents' practical adaptation to the local climate. Perhaps owing to its unchallenged status as the country's historic and political capital, Mexico City has a rather formal urban ethos. Suits and neckties abound in its restaurants on weekday afternoons, and walking shorts are rarely seen on the legs of anyone except foreign tourists. But when the mercury rises in the dry summer months in Monterrey, a fair number of *regiomontanos* exchange their trousers for shorts, a concession to the elements that few *chilangos* would make no matter how high the temperature might rise.

But Americanization extends far beyond local habits of dress. In 2005 Nuevo León became the first state in Mexico to introduce U.S.-styled oral courtroom trials that require prosecutors and defense attorneys to present their arguments in open court instead of in writing. Rocked by successive peso crises in the 1970s, 1980s, and 1990s, much of the city's private sector views Mexico City and its vast bureaucracy with the same mix of distaste and suspicion that a Dallas oilman harbors toward Washington and its paper-pushing network of federal regulatory agencies.

Tatiana Clouthier Carrillo is struck by the differences between Monterrey and other parts of the country. The daughter of Manuel Clouthier, the late leader and onetime presidential candidate of the center-right National Action Party (PAN), Tatiana moved from the Pacific Coast state of Sinaloa to Nuevo León in 1983 to begin her university studies at the Monterrey campus of the "Tec." After graduating with a degree in English, Tatiana remained in the city, became active in local politics, got married, and later started a family. A mother of two who was elected to the national Chamber of Deputies in 2003 from the PAN slate of candidates, Clouthier detects many signs of U.S. influence in Monterrey, from the routine quoting of rents in dollars instead of Mexican pesos to the insistence of many *regiomontanas* on buying their clothes in the Texas cities of McAllen and San Antonio. "There are three things that stand out," she says. "Drug use, the young girls who from the time they're teenagers or are in college become sexually promiscuous, and the arrival of many religious denominations—evangelicals, Mormons, and Protestants. People from other places [in Mexico] come here and say, 'My goodness, it's really Americanized here.'"[20]

The different vibes that distinguish Monterrey from the Mexican capital are hard to miss. Mexico City has a strongly nationalist flavor, and its equivalent of the Eiffel Tower or the Statue of Liberty is a patriotic landmark, the soaring Angel monument commissioned by Porfirio Díaz to celebrate the centennial of Mexican independence in 1910. The closest thing to the gold-plated Angel on the streets of Monterrey pays homage to the city's private sector, a featureless concrete column with the pedestrian name the Guiding Light of Commerce that trains laser beams heavenward at night.

Upper-middle-class *chilangos* have almost defiantly retained Mexico City's leisurely approach toward the workday, and the extended, late afternoon lunch break remains a hallowed tradition among the national capital's business and political elites. But their counterparts in Monterrey have largely surrendered to the frantic pace of the globalization age, eating lunch earlier and with greater haste. At 7 A.M., a time when the freeways and boulevards of major American cities are already packed with commuters heading into work, the streets of Mexico City's Hipódromo district where I lived for three years are almost deserted. Not so in Monterrey: when I asked for an interview with the president of the Supreme Court of Nuevo León state on a recent visit to the city, his secretary penciled me in for an 8 A.M. meeting. The judge was already at his desk when I arrived at the state government courthouse on the appointed morning.

Some *chilangos* look down on Monterrey as a provincial, money-grubbing place where wealth is celebrated, loyalty is rewarded, and dissent is discouraged. "It's a company town, and the identity of its residents is defined by the workplace," says the Mexico City–born journalist Rossana Fuentes-Berain. "Intellectuals are not very well regarded, you look up to people who are self-made, who are entrepreneurs. Money is of lesser importance in Mexico City than it is in Monterrey."[21]

Not every Monterrey resident is thrilled with the relentless Americanization of his city or country. A local radio talk show host named Oscar Múzquiz once urged his male listeners to be on the lookout for symptoms of what he termed creeping "gringofication" among their wives. On his morning program, called *Educating Your Woman*, the irreverent Múzquiz warned about the telltale signs of such strange behavior— a spouse who sleeps until nine in the morning, serves frozen dinners, watches TV all day, and rarely shaves her legs.[22] In a more serious vein, the feminist author and academic Rosaura Barahona published a prescient column for the newspaper *El Norte* in December 1993, just nine days before NAFTA was scheduled to formally take effect. "A dear friend who is also a respected sociologist was telling us on Saturday that Mexico will become like the United States, whether we like it or not," wrote Barahona. " 'It may take 100 or 150 years, but it's inevitable.' Though we may not live to see it, it saddens us. . . . Of course the influence of the dominant country is so strong that we have ceased to use the Spanish word '*influjo*' and instead write *influencia*, and we sing 'Happy Birthday' instead of 'Las mañanitas' and 'Glory, Glory, Alleluia' instead of 'Los pastores de Belén [The Shepherds of Bethlehem].' " The perspicacious Barahona ended her column with a sentence in the Spanglish spoken by so many of her neighbors: "Y *en el* meantime, Merry Christmas to all."[23]

A FUTURE CITY OF KNOWLEDGE OR A KILLING FIELD?

For all the advantages that proximity to the United States has brought Mexico—direct access to the largest market of consumers mankind has ever known, a safety valve for alleviating the country's chronic inability to generate enough jobs for its young people, a bountiful wellspring of

investment capital and gringo tourist dollars for the Mexican economy—
there are also some serious downsides. None is more pernicious than the
scourge of drug trafficking, which first took off in the late 1960s and
became a major flashpoint of friction between the Reagan and de la
Madrid administrations in the mid-1980s. But despite the physical near-
ness of the U.S. border, Monterrey for a long time had been spared the collateral damage inflicted by the murderous turf wars of rival drug cartels
that have convulsed border cities like Tijuana, Ciudad Juárez, and Nuevo
Laredo. Sadly, however, the Sultan of the North's insulation from Mexico's
narco wars is now a thing of the past.

The March 2003 arrest of Mexican kingpin Osiel Cárdenas Guillén
earned the government of then President Vicente Fox words of high praise
from U.S. law enforcement officials. The leader of the so-called Gulf
Cartel had a $2 million bounty on his head at the time, and the capture of
Cárdenas seemed to signal a greater readiness by Mexican authorities to
round up the country's top drug lords once and for all. But the apprehension of Osiel Cárdenas did not put a damper on narcotics trafficking in
Mexico. Quite the contrary: his detention ushered in a new and even
bloodier phase in the country's drug-fueled violence as a rival syndicate
based in the western state of Sinaloa challenged the weakened Gulf
Cartel's control over Nuevo Laredo, a key entrepôt on the border for U.S.-
bound narcotics shipments. The ensuing bloodshed turned that town into
a killing field—and it was only a matter of time before the carnage in
Nuevo Laredo would spill into the streets of Monterrey a mere 150 miles
to the southwest.

Monterrey's outward calm was shattered in the spring of 2005 when two
reputed gangsters were shot dead in a Dave & Buster's restaurant as they
were eating with their families. In August of that year, Nuevo León state
police raided another local eatery and nabbed twenty-three suspected drug
cartel hit men including a kingpin from Nuevo Laredo named El Tuby. The
arrests amounted to a public relations coup for Marcelo Garza y Garza, the
young commander of the state police's investigations unit who stated at
the time that "everyone must contribute their grain of sand." Payback

arrived when Garza y Garza was fatally gunned down in September 2006 as he walked alone on a sidewalk in the wealthy Monterrey suburb of San Pedro Garza García. During the course of that year, six municipal police chiefs were assassinated in Nuevo León along with two federal prosecutors assigned specifically to investigate narcotics cases.[24]

The dawn of a new year brought no respite. Monterrey registered 162 homicides in the first six months of 2007, nearly as many as were recorded in all of 2006. One of those murders seemed particularly brazen: in June, a Nuevo León state legislator was gunned down in broad daylight in front of the Monterrey city hall. Suspicions surrounding the identity of Mario Rios Gutiérrez's killers only heightened in the wake of disclosures that the slain lawmaker had been arrested by state police in the mid-1980s for allegedly possessing twelve kilos of marijuana (the charges were subsequently dropped).[25]

During one particularly murderous rampage in late March 2007, eight persons were killed in four separate attacks linked to drug traffickers. One of the corpses bore a note apparently addressed to the Nuevo León state attorney general Rogelio Cerda that read: "Look fool, even with all of your bodyguards you will die, Rogelio Cerda, together with your family, all the officials who are with you, and the Sinaloa cartel. P.S. This will continue until you get it."[26] Two of the victims were cops, bringing to sixteen the number of lawmen killed in Monterrey and environs during the first quarter of the year. The death toll also fueled speculation that some of the victims had been killed by drug lords because they had been accepting money from rival kingpins. "Without a doubt," said the state's deputy attorney general, Aldo Fasci, "this is due to a concrete strategy by organized crime that consists of generating terror in the population."[27] If so, the campaign was achieving its intended goal: at least fifty policemen in Monterrey and the surrounding suburbs walked off the job during the first three months of 2007.

Within a matter of months, Monterrey's blood-spattered image was looking a lot more like Al Capone's Chicago in the 1920s than Governor Nati González's vision of a twenty-first-century Boston. The same city

that was saluted as the safest in Latin America by an international consulting group in 2005 was a year later losing its luster for some foreigners, and
a senior executive for one of Monterrey's top-drawer companies told me
he was deeply worried about the long-term damage the violence might
inflict on the city's regional and international image. González and other
officials discovered that hundreds of state and municipal cops were on the
payrolls of warring drug lords. "We can no longer [call Monterrey] the
safest city . . . in the country," conceded the president of the city's chamber of commerce at the November 2006 funeral of a suburban police chief
killed just twenty-three days after assuming his duties.[28]

U.S. diplomats stationed in Mexico also took notice. A February 2007
consular information sheet addressed to American citizens who were
planning a trip to Mexico noted that Monterrey and four other cities were
plagued by "high levels" of crime. In Monterrey, Ciudad Juárez, Nuevo
Laredo, and Tijuana, "shootings have taken place at busy intersections and
at popular restaurants during daylight hours."[29] An edition of the same
consular information sheet issued only six months earlier made no men-
tion of Monterrey anywhere in its pages. The State Department reiterated
the warnings in April 2007 with a travel advisory that mentioned "execu-
tion-style murders of Mexican officials" in five states including Nuevo
León, "especially in and around Monterrey."

In hindsight, the governor may have unintentionally brought the
plague of violence upon himself and his beleaguered state. When the epidemic of gangland killings in Nuevo Laredo was spiking in the spring of
2005, "Nati" González discreetly advised some of the feuding kingpins in
that border town that they could get their families out of harm's way by
moving them to Monterrey. According to the South American ambassador stationed in Mexico City to whom the governor gave this account,
González was stunned when the narcos brought their murderous ways as
well as their loved ones to Monterrey.[30] Whatever presidential ambitions
the governor may have once entertained simply evaporated in the blast
furnace of the city's drug wars and the negative news coverage they
received.

The narcotics-related violence that has become a staple of life in modern Mexico is sometimes portrayed as a largely internecine affair that mostly claims the lives of bad guys and crooked cops. But the collateral damage of drug trafficking in Mexico is not limited to innocent bystanders getting caught up in the crossfire of gangland wars. The country's booming narcotics industry has also brought with it several harmful side effects like rising corruption in the armed forces, and perhaps the most insidious spin-off is the soaring rate of recreational drug use inside Mexico today, one of three quintessentially American social diseases that have entrenched themselves south of the border.

Part IV

CHAPTER 11

Made-in-the-U.S.A. Diseases

The descent of Pedro Rocher into the sordid world of crack cocaine addiction is a sad but familiar tale for millions of American families. The son of a Mexico City secretary began drinking alcohol at the age of fourteen and smoked marijuana for the first time a year later. It wasn't long before Rocher started snorting powder cocaine, in part because he wanted to set himself apart from the poorer boys in his neighborhood who could only afford to smoke marijuana and sniff glue. "In the movies you'd see guys snorting cocaine, and I wanted to try it and find out how it feels to be high," says Rocher. "In my neighborhood my brother and I had the best clothes, and doing coke gave you a certain social status, like saying I'm better than you are." One of the movies that made a big impression on the young Mexican was Quentin Tarantino's 1994 *Pulp Fiction*, and Rocher vividly remembers the hypnotic scene in which a long-haired John Travolta injects himself with heroin before a rendezvous with a gangster's wife, played by Uma Thurman.

But Rocher's real downfall started in 1998 when his older brother brought home a friend who was carrying some crack cocaine. He knew his brother was already smoking crack and Rocher, then eighteen years of age, was acutely aware of the drug's ferociously addictive qualities. "I didn't like the idea because the thought of trying it scared me," he recalls. But his initial resistance soon flagged, and before long Rocher had become a full-blown crackhead. He spent a large chunk of his earnings as a restaurant waiter on his new narcotic of choice, and when his tips failed to keep up with the spiraling cost of his addiction, Rocher sold off many of his worldly possessions one by one—jackets, watches, rings, chains, two pairs of expensive Adidas sneakers. All told, Rocher reckons he unloaded $3,000 worth of goods to sate his new drug habit.

Once an avid athlete who enjoyed playing basketball, volleyball, and American football, Rocher lost thirty-three pounds and dropped out of Mexico City's Ibero-American University, where he was studying to become a chef. When I met him at a rehabilitation center run by the government-funded Centers for Juvenile Rehabilitation (CIJ), Rocher hadn't touched crack in nearly two weeks and was getting back to his normal weight of 185 pounds. He was wearing the de rigueur uniform of the hip-hop generation: long, baggy dark blue shorts; an oversized light brown T-shirt bearing the only overtly Mexican detail in his clothing that morning, a logo of the Mexico City–based Pumas soccer club; gray Nike sneakers; and short white gym socks. But his fidgety manner and gaunt face attested to his recent bout with drug addiction. "I have to recognize my mistake and acknowledge it before my mother, my grandmother, and myself," says Rocher. "They saw that I was in bad shape and very stoned. They read me the riot act and wanted to throw me out of the house."[1]

Traditionally regarded as a country where drugs are produced or transshipped for the U.S. market, Mexico now has a major internal drug abuse problem on its hands. In October 2004 the Health Ministry's National Anti-Addiction Council (CONADIC) reported that an estimated 1.3 million Mexicans were addicted to some type of illicit drug. That same year Health Minister Julio Frenk said that 3.5 million people between the ages of 12 and 65 had tried illegal narcotics,[2] and the CONADIC survey found that 15 percent of Mexico City residents in that age category had sampled banned substances at least once.[3] "Mexico never prepared itself for the possibility that drugs would be consumed at home," says María Elena Morera de Galindo, president of the nongovernmental organization México Unido Contra la Delincuencia (Mexico United Against Crime).

"It was always thought that it would remain a country for transiting drugs."[4]

Most worrisome of all, the use of hard drugs has spiked over the last fifteen years. Only one in eight of the patients seeking treatment for drug use at the state-funded Centers for Juvenile Rehabilitation in 1990 said they had tried cocaine or crack. Ten years later that figure had jumped to nearly three in four. In 1994, less than 3 percent of those patients reported having used crystal methamphetamine at least once; by 2003 that number had quadrupled to 11.5 percent. "Today we face a problem that is totally different from what he had in the 1990s," says David Bruno Díaz Negrete, a psychologist who is deputy director of research at the CIJ's main offices in Mexico City. "In the 1970s and 1980s there were high levels of marijuana and glue-sniffing, and the problem was pretty stable. The 1990s saw a rise in the use of cocaine, and now many people start their drug use with crystal meth, crack cocaine and heroin."[5]

Drug use has expanded well beyond the ranks of young adult men like Pedro Rocher. Mexican authorities are alarmed by evidence that children as young as ten years old have begun experimenting with narcotics, and the consumption of synthetic drugs like methamphetamine is rising sharply among young women living in major cities and along the U.S. border.

Narcotics use has become a standard feature of campus life at high schools in the country's major cities. A poll of 54,694 students conducted by the national Public Education Ministry in five cities found that 41 percent had physically seen drugs and nearly one in three knew a friend at their school who used narcotics. While most Mexicans stoutly reject any talk of legalizing any controlled substances, a survey of 3,000 people commissioned by México Unido Contra la Delincuencia in 2007 found at least some acceptance of the notion among better educated and more affluent Mexicans. When asked if some drugs should be legalized, 22 percent of the poll participants with a university degree answered yes, and a similar percentage of Mexicans in the top three income brackets also supported the idea in principle.[6]

Recreational drug use has taken on disturbing proportions in the national capital. In March 2005, authorities revealed the existence of 2,111 "narco-retail" distribution points in the Mexico City metropolitan area, more than triple the number identified five years previously.[7] As the U.S. government has tightened up security along its southern border in the aftermath of the 9/11 attacks, the amount of cocaine available inside Mexico has exploded, causing prices for a "grapa"—local slang for a dose roughly equal to seven-tenths of a gram—to tumble from a high of around $30 to as little as $3. "Cocaine is flooding Mexico City," read the headline of a May 2005 article in the newspaper *Reforma* based on an interview with Mexico City security chief Joel Ortega. "All this is a result of the process of closing down the country's border [with the United States]," said Ortega. "A portion of the drugs that were bound for the United States are staying in Mexico."[8]

Outside the capital, the incidence of drug use shows a very direct correlation with the availability of narcotics. Consumption of crystal methamphetamine is particularly high in border towns like Tijuana and Mexicali where the synthetic drug is produced in backyard laboratories for export to the United States. With a total population estimated at 1.4 million people, Tijuana alone is host to over 100,000 methamphetamine addicts, according to San Diego State University sociologist Victor Clark-Alfaro. But only 6,000 of those addicts are receiving treatment at the border city's 109 rehabilitation centers.

Patterns of migration to the United States also appear to have an effect. "While waiting to enter the United States in Tijuana or Mexicali, [migrants] become addicted and take that addiction back south as they settle elsewhere in Mexico," noted a February 2007 report issued by the New Mexico–based International Research Center (IRC). Researchers have noted a marked increase in the use of heroin and crystal methamphetamine in states like Michoacán and Puebla, where high rates of immigration to the United States have existed for several decades. "A second theory sees migrants becoming addicted in the United States," said the IRC report. "When they are deported, they take that addiction back to

Mexico and Central American countries. As these same individuals make a second or third attempt to enter the United States, they carry with them an addiction that fuels meth demand along migratory paths."[9]

The insatiable demand for controlled substances in the United States has therefore impacted Mexico in two ways. It has spawned the rise of murderous drug cartels who threaten to turn the country into a North American version of Colombia, and it has simultaneously fueled a boom in narcotics consumption among young Mexicans. "The consumption of hard drugs is increasing at truly alarming rates . . . of as much as 20 percent annually," the country's attorney general Eduardo Medina Mora told a group of Mexican congressmen in January 2007. "Changing international [market] conditions have not only caused an increase in violence as they fight for markets, but have also focused organized criminal groups more toward the domestic market."[10]

Yet most Americans are totally oblivious to this byproduct of their society's voracious drug habit. In reality, drug use in Mexico is one of three quintessentially American social diseases afflicting Mexico in the young century. But you wouldn't know that from watching Lou Dobbs, the anti-immigrant, right-wing CNN broadcaster who never misses an opportunity, however tenuous or baseless in fact, to bash America's southern neighbor. Whether it be the outsourcing of American jobs to *maquiladora* assembly plants or the supposedly soaring costs that the children of Mexican immigrant workers are imposing on U.S. public school systems, Dobbs, who is married to a Hispanic woman, seems obsessed with depicting Mexico in the worst possible light. His one-man propaganda campaign hit a new low in June 2005 when he invited a San Diego medical attorney named Madeleine Cosman to talk about the diseases that Mexican immigrants are allegedly bringing into the United States. The list was long and scary—tuberculosis, dengue fever, polio, and hepatitis—and with prompting from Dobbs, Cosman blamed Mexican workers for importing "diseases that we've never seen or rarely seen in America, because they've always been diseases of poverty and the Third World."[11]

THE ADVENT OF AIDS

Public health problems are indeed crossing the U.S.-Mexican border. But for the most part, they are heading in the opposite direction from what Dobbs believes. Besides rising drug use at home, Mexico is coping with an alarming rate of obesity and now ranks second behind the United States among major industrialized countries worldwide. An even more clear-cut example of a deadly epidemic that Mexico has imported from directly across the border is the acquired immune deficiency syndrome, better known as AIDS. The disease claimed the lives of 4,944 Mexicans in 2006, and it has killed over 70,000 people to date. Estimates of the number of patients who have tested positive for human immunodeficiency virus (HIV) as of 2005 start at 182,000 and go as high as 220,000.[12] (The basic distinction between an AIDS patient and someone who has merely tested HIV-positive boils down to the presence of the illness's classic symptoms in the former and the outward absence of those symptoms in the latter.)

By the summer of 1983, fully two years after the Atlanta-based Centers for Disease Control reported the deaths of five young homosexuals in Los Angeles from an illness that would later be identified as AIDS, Mexican physicians had encountered only one patient with similar symptoms—a Haitian male living in Mexico City who later died from the disease. Only in the fall of that year did doctors diagnose a Mexican patient with AIDS: a thirty-two-year-old homosexual flight attendant who traveled regularly between Mexico City and New York for Mexicana Airlines and had by his own admission led a sexually promiscuous lifestyle. Although doctors at the Salvador Zubirán National Institute of Medical and Nutritional Sciences in Mexico City never managed to identify which of the flight attendant's many lovers had infected him, it was clear he had contracted AIDS during one of his frequent stays in New York. His was not an isolated case: according to Dr. Guillermo Ruiz-Palacios, the U.S.-trained head of the Institute's department of infectology who treated all of the early AIDS cases in Mexico, at least three other male flight attendants at Mexicana who worked on the New York and San Francisco routes also tested

HIV-positive in that period.[13] "The imported nature of the fledgling epidemic in Mexico became apparent," wrote Donato Alarcón Segovia, a colleague of Ruiz-Palacios at the Institute, in 2004.[14]

Between 3,500 and 4,000 new AIDS cases are diagnosed each year in Mexico, according to the National Center for HIV/AIDS Prevention and Control. The number of AIDS-related deaths placed the country sixth in the Western Hemisphere as of 2003. The epicenter of the phenomenon is Mexico City, where 213 people out of every 100,000 residents at the end of 2004 had contracted the disease, followed by the states of Baja California (140), Yucatán (123), and Morelos (122).[15]

The incidence of AIDS in Mexico has stabilized in recent years, and Ruiz-Palacios gave the government of President Vicente Fox high marks for adopting farsighted policies that provided anti-AIDS drugs like AZT free of charge to patients and for publicly encouraging citizens to get tested for the disease. "This program has been available to the general population for several years, and each state has its own treatment centers," notes Ruiz-Palacios. "If there hadn't been the same degree of commitment on the part of the government, we would easily be worse off than Brazil [where three times as many people died from AIDS in 2003]."

Experts have identified three distinct periods in the evolution of the AIDS epidemic in Mexico. The initial group of patients who numbered nearly 100 came from the country's jet set, affluent Mexican gays and bisexuals who made frequent visits to the United States and to New York City and San Francisco in particular. The second wave of AIDS cases consisted of Mexicans who received transfusions of contaminated blood from unscrupulous companies that collected some of their supplies from HIV-positive donors. That phase was effectively ended by passage of a law in 1985 that banned the commercial sale of blood. The third wave of cases occurred in the late 1980s and emerged from the ranks of Mexican immigrants to the United States who had contracted the disease through sexual relations with infected homosexuals and prostitutes. Many of these immigrants were closet bisexuals who had families they left behind at home, and the list of ten states with the highest incidence of AIDS today includes

Jalisco, Veracruz, and Guerrero, which have been sending large numbers of migrants to the United States in search of work for many years.

The country's gay and bisexual male population had been the driving force behind the AIDS problem in Mexico. But it no longer accounts for the overwhelming percentage of cases: whereas men who have sex with other men made up about 80 percent of the country's registered patients in the 1980s, that figure has fallen to between 60 and 65 percent in more recent years. Immigrants today represent an increasingly significant portion of the total population at risk from AIDS: roughly one in five Mexicans who have tested positive for HIV have spent some time in the United States, where they are believed to have picked up the virus. While the roughly 200,000 Mexicans who are HIV-positive amount to less than 0.2 percent of the country's 105 million inhabitants, studies indicate that the rate among Mexican migrant workers in the United States can be more than three times that found in the general population.

The effects of Americanization on this particular slice of the Mexican population have been documented by researchers, and in unusually graphic ways at times. The dangerous combination of social isolation in the United States, greater sexual liberty, and a ready supply of prostitutes often produces striking changes in the sexual practices and attitudes of Mexican migrants. The Argentine AIDS researcher Mario Bronfman interviewed immigrants from the Michoacán town of Gómez Farías in the 1990s who journeyed regularly to the California farming town of Watsonville for work. "The vast majority . . . stated that their sexuality had been changed by the migration experience," observed Bronfman in an article he cowrote with Nelson Minello. "In the first place, in comparison to people who stay in Mexico a higher percentage [of immigrants] have multiple sexual partners, and they have greater recourse to prostitution. . . . When it comes to practices they picked up, they repeatedly mentioned new positions in vaginal intercourse, oral sex (which they admitted to in much higher proportions than in Mexico) and, on occasion, anal sex with women."

One immigrant used particularly salty language to describe the new sexual horizons he had explored north of the border. "American women are different, and I got to know some who like to do it in different ways," he told Bronfman. "In Mexico I only knew how to do it in the missionary position, and I don't think any woman ever gave me oral sex. But over there, I give oral sex and I like to have it done to me. I learned better ways to have sex: in the sixty-nine position, her on top, standing, and anal sex on a few occasions. I have changed, they know other things over there and when I'm back home I feel free to do them with my wife."[16]

The wives of some migrants become infected by their HIV-positive husbands when they return from the United States. Their numbers are relatively small: as of 2004, only one woman had been diagnosed with AIDS for every four men who had picked up the disease. But the onset of AIDS usually catches the woman completely by surprise, and in some instances their husbands never even acknowledge their responsibility for having infected them in the first place. A *campesina* woman named Minerva began to notice an abrupt decline in her health during the winter of 1998. Her common-law husband Edgar Román had been working as a dishwasher in New Jersey and had returned to their home in the city of Córdoba, Veracruz, in the closing weeks of 1997 to spend the Christmas holidays with Minerva. Within weeks of Román's return to the United States, Minerva's hair started falling out, her skin turned a sickly shade of yellow, and her arms became covered with red blisters normally associated with herpes. Her appetite disappeared and she lost forty-four pounds. A fungal infection called candidiasis appeared along the membrane of her pharynx, the tube that connects the mouth and nasal passage with the esophagus.

Appalled by the realization that she may have acquired the deadly disease, Minerva sought treatment for her symptoms at a government-run hospital in Córdoba under a false name. "I felt ashamed," explains Minerva. "I said to myself, 'Ayyy, what are my neighbors going to say? They're going to judge me.'"[17]

Minerva was puzzled by the news that she had tested positive for HIV. She had not slept with another man nor had she received any transfusions of blood that might have been contaminated during the time when Edgar had been away in New Jersey. A devout Roman Catholic, Minerva had never tried illegal drugs, and by process of elimination she concluded that the disease could only have come from her husband. When he came back to Córdoba in December 1998 for the end-of-year holiday season, Edgar adamantly denied blame for her condition and instead grilled Minerva about how she might have become sick. That was the last time she ever saw Román: when he left Córdoba to go back to the United States in the new year, Edgar promised to send Minerva money to help pay for her treatment but then vanished for good.

Ailing and penniless, Minerva moved to the state of Puebla, where her sixty-three-year-old mother was living. In 2001 she registered as a patient at a hospital in the city of Puebla operated by the Social Security and Services Institute for Government Employees (ISSSTE), and doctors prescribed antiretroviral medication to treat her symptoms. For the past four years, Minerva has been taking a cocktail of drugs twice a day consisting of zinovudine, nelfinavir, and lamivudine. Her allotment of drugs carries a monthly price tag of $1,000 but is provided free of charge by the ISSSTE, and the medication has worked wonders for Minerva. Her straight, black hair has grown back and she has regained her normal dark brown skin color. Her CD4 white blood cell count is normal, and she has gained back half the weight she lost. Minerva's long-term prognosis is encouraging. Her doctor says she can lead a long, normal life as long as she maintains her twice-a-day dose of antiretroviral drugs. "I am no longer afraid of dying," says Minerva, who ekes out a meager existence working as a farm-hand on cornfields near her mother's home in the village of La María. But she is still troubled by knowledge that she is HIV-positive: she has told no one about her medical condition apart from her mother, brother, and doctor. Now in her late thirties, she has resigned herself to life as a single woman. "I have no partner," says Minerva, "nor do I want to have one."

MEXICO'S WEIGHT PROBLEM

The third unhealthy trend in Mexico that evokes striking parallels with modern American society can be seen in the bulging waistlines of its people. Mexico recently acquired the dubious distinction of having a rate of obesity second only to the United States among the thirty industrialized countries belonging to the Organisation of Economic Co-operation and Development.[18] A June 2003 study by the Mexican Health Ministry found that 36 percent of all women between the ages of eighteen and forty-nine were overweight and another 28 percent were classified as obese, a medical term applied to individuals who exceed their ideal body mass index by five points on a sliding scale based on height and weight.[19] By way of comparison, a similar survey conducted fifteen years earlier found that 24 percent of Mexican women were overweight and only 9 percent were obese.[20] The trend had also surfaced to a slightly lesser extent among adult men, of whom 41 percent were overweight and 19 percent fell into the obese category. And the problem is getting worse. A nationwide health and nutrition survey released by the National Public Health Institute for 2006 found that 71.9 percent of women and two of every three men older than twenty years of age were obese or overweight. That survey reported that three in ten adult Mexicans were obese, up from the 24 percent who fell into that category in 2000.[21]

All this might be a laughing matter were it not for the serious health risks associated with obesity. The number of Mexicans who die from diabetes, which is closely related to overeating and obesity, has been rising by around 5,000 every year since 2001. At first blush, that should come as something of a surprise. Diabetes is a disease that has been traditionally associated with rich nations, and Mexico remains a developing country, nearly half of whose 105 million inhabitants live below the official poverty line. But diabetes claimed the lives of over 59,000 Mexicans in 2003, and the World Health Organization ranks it as the leading cause of death among women and the second most common killer of men.[22] And with over 7 million diabetics in a population of 105 million, Mexico now has the highest per capita incidence of the disease among major countries worldwide, according to Joel Rodríguez Saldaña, president of the Mexican Diabetes Federation.[23]

It is tempting to blame Mexico's visibly fatter citizens on the proliferation of American fast-food outlets in the NAFTA era. Nearly every major

U.S. junk-food chain is represented in the country's major cities, from Carl's Jr. and Domino's to Kentucky Fried Chicken and Papa John's. Both Burger King and McDonald's have introduced the pernicious practice of giving customers the option of purchasing their burgers and French fries in larger, "super-size" quantities, and the concession stands of many movie theaters have followed suit by offering giant plastic cups of sugar-laced soft drinks and huge tubs of popcorn smothered in melted butter. An official of the Mexican National Restaurant Chamber has blamed the popularity of Big Macs and pizzas for a 50 percent decline in the sales of Mexican sandwiches known as *tortas*, a healthier choice, in the ten years since the NAFTA treaty took effect. At a time when tortilla sales are up in the United States, per capita consumption of the Mexican staple is down by 25 percent between 1998 and 2004, according to the National Corn Processors Chamber.[24]

The penetration of fast-food culture was brought home to Dr. Rodríguez Saldaña of the Mexican Diabetes Federation when he traveled to the southern state of Chiapas in 2004 to address a conference of physicians in the state capital of Tuxtla Gutiérrez. As a taxi ferried Rodríguez from the airport to the city center, he noticed the now familiar logos of major U.S. fast-food chains lining the principal boulevard of the city. " 'It gives me great pleasure to be in this city and enjoy the regional cuisine,' " Rodriguez remembers greeting his colleagues with tongue firmly in cheek. "That's all there was, fast food restaurants. That's what people find and that's what people eat."

There's no denying the penetration of Colonel Sanders and the Golden Arches in twenty-first-century Mexico. Miguel Darío Hernández Reseldes is a walking, breathing example of the health hazards that come with eating junk food. At a mere twenty-two years of age, the social services worker already sports a sagging double chin and a generous spare tire of fat around his waist. But that doesn't deter him from making regular visits to a Burger King outlet in downtown Mexico City. "I come here about twice a week after work and I order a Whopper, a soda, and French fries," Hernández says in a quiet, halting voice. "I don't get home until six in the afternoon, and so I want to eat something before I get home."

But it's not just a weakness for cheeseburgers and onion rings covered in fried batter that lures Mexicans to these tacky outposts of the American way of life. It's also the increasingly hectic pace of life in the country's big cities, which is in itself another symptom of Americanization. Many white-collar workers no longer have the luxury of dashing home in the middle of a weekday afternoon for the traditional three-course luncheon that might last up to three hours. "I choose Burger King because it's quick," explains José Manuel López, a civilian administrative employee of the Mexican army. "We don't have much time to eat in Mexico these days."[25]

In all fairness, a combination of factors is spurring the Mexican obesity trend and the associated rise in diabetes cases. Genetic factors predispose some Mexicans to develop diabetes at a lower level of obesity than is the case with other populations. Traditional Mexican cuisine has acquired a higher fat content in modern times. The abundance of American-style, twenty-four-hour convenience stores has made calorie-rich snack foods like potato chips and cookies more readily available than ever before. High crime rates, air pollution, and the growing numbers of people who own cars discourage the residents of Mexico's biggest cities from commuting to work on foot and promote a more sedentary lifestyle. "We live in an environment that is conducive to obesity," warns Dr. Juan Rivera Dommarco, head of the Center for Nutritional and Health Research at the National Public Health Institute in Cuernavaca. "It is a direct by-product of modernization, and now you have to be careful to avoid becoming obese."[26]

Obesity afflicts Mexicans from all walks of life. When Dr. Rivera first saw the data from a government-sponsored nationwide nutrition survey in 2001 that indicated a sharp rise in the percentages of Mexicans who were overweight or obese, he assumed the biggest increases would be concentrated in Mexico City and the northern states along the U.S. border. But the southern region of the country actually registered a higher increase than did the national capital. The phenomenon also encompassed the countryside, where 44 percent of rural residents were found to be overweight or obese. It was present in all income brackets: among

Mexicans belonging to the poorest one-fifth of the population, the percentage of people exceeding their ideal body mass index was nearly as high (52) as that in the richest one-fifth (54). The prevalence of weight problems was even higher among Mexicans in the three middle-income categories, 62 percent of whom were said to be overweight or obese.

The trend is also gaining ground among Mexico's children. One of every three adolescents was obese or overweight as of 2006, up from 25.5 percent registered in 1999. About one of every four Mexican kids between the ages of five and eleven was either obese or overweight in 2006, an increase over the 18.6 percent found to have developed weight problems seven years previously. The percentage of overweight and obese children under the age of five rose from 4.2 percent in 1988 to 5.4 percent by the end of the 1990s.[27] "We're talking about very serious problems affecting all of these groups," concludes Rivera. "Obesity and the diseases it leads to, like high blood pressure, diabetes, and premature death, are such serious problems that it's important to convince everybody of the need to change all this."

The American Contagions That Won't Go Away

The public health challenges that these social diseases pose to modern Mexico should be put in perspective. Mexicans still lag way behind their northern neighbors in the quantities of illegal drugs they consume, the prevalence of AIDS in the general population, and the size of their protruding bellies. Noteworthy progress has been achieved in the fight against the AIDS epidemic, which has stabilized in recent years thanks in good part to enlightened government policies. Fewer than 97,000 AIDS cases were reported in Mexico between 1981 and the fall of 2005,[28] and among Western Hemisphere countries Mexico ranks near the bottom in per capita incidence of the disease. The percentage of HIV-positive young people between the ages of fifteen and twenty-four has actually declined since 2001 except among intravenous drug users in the northern part of the country.[29] Owing to the anti-AIDS medication that government agencies provide free of charge, those Mexicans afflicted with the disease are no longer condemned to a premature death.

But curbing the country's other two made-in-the-U.S.A. social diseases will be much harder. The obesity problem is here to stay: Mexico has long held the dubious distinction of having the highest per capita consumption of Coca-Cola worldwide, and the waistlines of its citizens are bound to expand further as more Mexicans move to the country's cities and junk-food chains and convenience stores open more outlets. The World Health Organization predicts that 36.5 percent of all men and 47.6 percent of women in the country will be obese by the year 2015.[30]

Drug trafficking will also flourish for the foreseeable future as one of the nation's top growth industries—and that means more of the narcotics originally earmarked for the United States will wind up being smoked, snorted, or injected by Mexicans. That grim outlook won't improve until Washington either legalizes narcotics like cocaine and marijuana or undertakes a concerted effort to reduce illegal drug use among its own citizens. Yet when it comes to narcotics issues, most Republican and Democratic politicians are content to issue ringing calls for more aggressive enforcement of existing anti-drug laws in the United States and seem incapable of any fresh thinking on how to address the root causes of their society's voracious drug habit. The spillover effects on Mexico will likely last throughout the rest of this century. "The dimensions of the problem in the United States are having an impact," says psychologist David Bruno Díaz Negrete of Mexico's Centers for Juvenile Rehabilitation. "The supply and demand for drugs in Mexico are structurally related to the supply and demand for drugs in the United States. These are lifestyles that we are inheriting in some way from the United States." The Americanization of modern Mexican society transcends mere lifestyle choices. A very different import from El Norte is changing the ways that Mexicans worship, and that poses almost as great a threat to the country's Roman Catholic hierarchy as drug addicts, AIDS patients, and tubby teenagers do to the quality of public health.

CHAPTER 12

The Evangelical Challenge

In an era when the once omnipotent PRI finds itself outnumbered by two parties in the national congress and its candidate finished a distant third in the country's most recent presidential balloting, the central state of Hidalgo lives on as a steadfast bastion of Mexico's erstwhile ruling party. The state's voters elected the PRI's gubernatorial candidate in 1999, only a year before Vicente Fox ousted the party from power, and the PRI maintained a solid majority in the Hidalgo legislature throughout Fox's six years as president. The PRI reaffirmed its domination of the state's politics in February 2005 when its nominee for governor, Miguel Ángel Osorio Chong, trounced his rivals from Fox's National Action Party and the left-wing Party of the Democratic Revolution (PRD).[1] But the PRI's grip on power in Hidalgo finally showed signs of slipping a few months later in statewide municipal elections. The PRI won only thirty-seven of the eighty-four city halls at stake, while the PRD emerged as the big winner, posting a net gain of thirteen municipalities won by its candidates.[2]

Some political analysts in Mexico City attributed the PRD's strong showing to the coattails of its presidential candidate Andrés Manuel López Obrador, who had been campaigning nonstop since resigning as Mexico City mayor in the summer of 2005. López Obrador was still the front-runner in the polls when municipal elections were held in Hidalgo that November, but there were other forces at work behind the voting in some of the towns where the PRI came up short. One of those places was Ixmiquilpan, a dusty, unprepossessing town of 35,000 that dominates the fertile Mezquital Valley. There, voters shifted their allegiance in massive numbers to the PRD ticket. Best known for the *ayate* cloths woven by Otomi women from the fiber of maguey plants, Ixmiquilpan has been a flashpoint of friction between Roman Catholics and Mexico's growing population of evangelical Christians in recent years. One in six residents of the town and its surrounding villages practices a Protestant faith, and tensions flared in 2001 when some local Catholic militants threatened to destroy the homes of dozens of families who had joined evangelical churches. In August 2005, a prominent member of the town's evangelical community who had passed away was denied burial in the cemetery of a village outside Ixmiquilpan called San Nicolás, ostensibly because he had refused to donate money toward its upkeep. A month later Catholic residents of San Nicolás used a bulldozer to block the road leading to a private residence where evangelical Christians gathered for religious services.[3] The PRI-controlled neighborhood council vetoed the evangelicals' existing plans to erect a new temple in San Nicolás, even though they had obtained the necessary building permits from the appropriate government office in the state capital of Pachuca.

In the weeks leading up to the November 13 municipal elections, the evangelical community in Ixmiquilpan appealed to both state and federal authorities to intervene on their behalf with the intransigent officials of the San Nicolás neighborhood council. But their requests for a meeting to plead their case fell on deaf ears, and frustrated members of the community ended up taking matters into their own hands on the eve of the statewide municipal balloting. Hundreds of evangelical Christians erected a blockade along the main highway linking Ixmiquilpan to Pachuca and brought traffic to a standstill for five hours. A contingent of officials from the state capital arrived at the scene to beg the demonstrators to go back home, but the evangelicals refused to budge. "Our people unanimously vowed not to move until we had assurances that this situation would be resolved and we would have a meeting with the governor," explained Alejandro Nepomuceno, a pastor from the Independent Pentecostal Christian Church in Ixmiquilpan.[4] Desperate to lift the impromptu road-block, the state government officials who had rushed in from Pachuca promised the evangelicals an audience with Governor Osorio Chong to discuss their grievances after the municipal elections.

When the results of the November 13 balloting were announced two days later, the PRD's mayoral candidate in Ixmiquilpan had scored a convincing victory over his PRI rival. The party also triumphed in other municipalities in the Mezquital Valley like Tasquillo and Cardonal, where evangelical churches have made significant inroads among local residents, and Nepomuceno drew the obvious conclusion. "There was a vote to punish the PRI that could have been avoided," the pastor told a reporter from the Mexico City newspaper *Reforma*. "If the [state] government had received us sooner, the sequence of events would have been different. Now when I'm with other pastors and Christian folk, I see a difference in their appearance when they tell me, 'my vote was worth something, our actions had an impact.' "[5]

An Evangelical Christian Voting Bloc?

The outcome of the voting in Ixmiquilpan poses an intriguing question about the future of electoral politics in twenty-first-century Mexico. Evangelical churches have made great strides among Latin America's predominantly Christian populations for the past forty years, and today approximately one in five Mexicans no longer belongs to the Roman Catholic Church. Religious affairs expert Elio Masferrer of Mexico's National School of Anthropology and History estimates that between eight and ten million identify with Pentecostalism, a branch of evangelical Christianity with historical roots in the United States that emphasizes baptism in the Holy Spirit and achieves its classical expression when a convert speaks in usually unintelligible tongues.[6] What would happen to Mexican politics if this expanding sector of the national population harnessed its members to one political party, as has happened north of the border with evangelical Christians and the Republican Party?

Most Americans who have some knowledge of Mexico tend to think of it as a profoundly Catholic country, and with good reason. It is home to the world's second largest population of Roman Catholics after Brazil, and the Virgin of Guadalupe continues to rival the tricolor Mexican flag as a patriotic symbol. In the early years of independence the Catholic Church was the country's largest landowner and played an aggressive role in national politics through its alliance with Mexico's conservative factions. But its clout began to ebb during the mid-nineteenth century War of the Reform, which pitted the church's conservative supporters against their liberal enemies led by the country's constitutional president Benito Juárez. Its political fortunes later took a sharp nosedive after the church hierarchy endorsed France's imposition of a Habsburg archduke as emperor of Mexico in 1864. The 1917 constitution that emerged from the chaos and bloodshed of the Mexican Revolution contained several explicitly anti-clerical clauses and provisions and reaffirmed the liberal principle of separating church and state.

In more recent times, the exponential growth of the country's evangelical Christian community has taken place against the backdrop of an institutional crisis inside Mexican Catholicism. Like their American brethren, the country's Catholic hierarchy has been put on the defensive by accusations that it sheltered priests known to have sexually abused seminarians and altar boys. The resulting loss of prestige and credibility has been felt most keenly in the national capital, where the country's primate cardinal Norberto Rivera Carrera could do nothing to stop the Mexico City council from approving two landmark bills that legalized abortion and okayed civil unions for same-sex couples in 2006 and 2007. The contrasting fortunes of Mexican Catholicism and evangelical Christianity are dramatically reflected by the numbers of clergy who tend to their respective flocks. A census released by Mexico's Interior Ministry in April 2007 counted 33,326 evangelical preachers, a figure that represents over 57 percent of all the Christian ministers surveyed by the government nationwide and is nearly twice the number of Catholic priests (19,003) in the country. The gap between evangelical pastors and Catholic clergymen won't narrow anytime soon. While slightly over 300 priests are ordained each year in the thirty diocesan seminaries scattered across Mexico, ten times that number of evangelical pastors are appointed each year.[7]

THE LEGACY OF CHIAPAS

As the numbers of Mexican evangelicals continue to multiply on a literally daily basis, the movement is flexing political muscles that would have seemed unthinkable not so long ago. The most illustrative demonstration of the evangelical Christians' growing influence has occurred in the impoverished southeastern state of Chiapas. Though it is best known to the outside world as the cradle of the 1994 Zapatista rebellion, Chiapas has been far more destabilized by a campaign of religious persecution that has divided indigenous communities, left hundreds dead, and displaced tens of thousands of people. The religious troubles in Chiapas date back to the late 1960s, when PRI-affiliated political bosses known as *caciques* who viewed evangelical groups as a rival power base embarked on a systematic campaign to expel them from indigenous villages in the highlands of the state. In the town of San Juan Chamula and environs, as many as 35,000 indigenous evangelicals were driven from their homes and thousands more were chased out of nearby villages like Zinacantán and Tenejapa. Large numbers of the refugees fled the countryside and wound up in squalid shantytowns on the outskirts of the colonial city of San Cristobal de las Casas.[8]

The sectarian wars that ripped apart the social fabric in much of Chiapas subsided only in the early 1990s when the progressive Catholic bishop of San Cristobal reached out to the refugee communities with educational programs and economic self-help projects. About 15,000 indigenous evangelicals have returned to the highlands surrounding San Juan Chamula since then. Evangelicals are believed to make up about 30 percent of the state's population, giving Chiapas one of the highest concentrations of such Christians nationwide, and, in a tacit acknowledgment of their swelling ranks, the PRI handpicked one of their own, a Nazarene named Pablo Salazar Mendiguchía, for a seat in the national senate in the 1997 midterm election (the party also tapped a Baptist from Mexico City named María de los Ángeles Moreno Uriegas for another seat in the upper chamber of congress that same year). Salazar left the PRI two years later to head a coalition of opposition parties that would serve as a springboard for the governorship of Chiapas in 2000. The evangelical candidate won that vote handily and became the state's first non-PRI governor in several decades.[9] (The embers of religious intolerance have not been completely extinguished, however: in the same year that Salazar was elected governor, ninety-eight evangelicals were forcibly expelled from a village near San Juan Chamula when Catholic militants razed their houses, and some of their children were threatened with violence if they tried to attend the local primary school.)[10]

The cases of Chiapas and Hidalgo have raised at least the possibility that the evangelical Christian movement in Mexico could one day emulate the example of its American counterpart. High-profile leaders of the Christian Right like Ralph Reed and the late Jerry Falwell have been flexing their muscles inside the Republican Party for over two decades, and many political analysts attribute George Bush's narrow victory over his Democrat rival, John Kerry, in the 2004 presidential election to the estimated four million ballots that evangelical Christian voters cast in his favor. Mainstream Mexican politicians are starting to take notice of the evangelical Christian movement in their own country. In March 2005 former PRD presidential candidate Cuauhtémoc Cárdenas, then Interior Minister Santiago Creel of the PAN, and former Coahuila state governor Enrique Martínez of the PRI accepted invitations to speak at a conference hosted by the National Confraternity of Evangelical Christian Churches (Confraternice), a Mexico City–based umbrella organization of 220 evangelical associations.[11]

The president of Confraternice, Arturo Farela Gutiérrez, founded a nonpartisan political association called Truth, Integrity, and Democracy

in 2005 as a vehicle to mobilize evangelical laypersons interested in participating more actively in Mexican politics. The head of the Interdenominational Christian Church, Farela bases his argument for a higher political
profile on a passage from the Book of Proverbs in the Old Testament. In
it, King Solomon is quoted as saying: "When the righteous govern, the
people are happy." "I am telling a lot of laymen to exercise their rights
because participating in politics isn't a sin," explains Farela. "It is God's
will that they take part in order to sanctify politics."[12]

Throughout most of its seventy-one-year rule of Mexico, the PRI
enjoyed the rock-solid support of the country's evangelical Christian
minority. From its inception in the late 1920s, the PRI adopted a con-
frontational stance toward the country's Catholic hierarchy. In 1935
President Lázaro Cárdenas ratified the anticlerical ideology of party
founder Plutarco Elías Calles when Mexico's secretary of public education, a Presbyterian named Moisés Sáenz, invited a young missionary
from California named W. Cameron Townsend to work with indigenous
communities in southern Mexico and translate the Bible into their native
languages.[13] But the PRI's traditionally good relations with the evangelical
movement began to sour in the late 1980s as President Carlos Salinas de
Gortari undertook a concerted campaign to bolster ties with the Catholic
Church. As a goodwill gesture, Salinas de Gortari pushed through a historic constitutional reform that eliminated several old and largely ignored
laws such as a ban on the wearing of ecclesiastical clothing outside a place
of worship.

The political loyalties of the country's evangelical Christians have
become more diffused in recent years, with no single party enjoying their
support as the PRI once did. But the head of Confraternice sees the evangelicals' anti-PRI vote in the 2005 Hidalgo state municipal elections as
proof that no party can afford to ignore them. "That should be a warning
to [the then presidential candidates] Andrés Manuel López Obrador,
Felipe Calderón, and Roberto Madrazo that the evangelical vote matters,"
said Farela as the 2006 election campaign got underway. "If [the politi-
cians] continue to treat us with disdain, they shall be punished."

THE AMERICAN ROOTS OF MEXICAN EVANGELICALISM

American missionaries have played a crucial role in the history of Protestant and evangelical churches inside Mexico. The first Protestant denomination to organize a church in Mexico was a group of Baptists led by James Hickey, an Irishman by birth who had founded a Bible school in the border town of Matamoros in 1860.[14] Hickey's antislavery convictions forced him to flee Texas after the leaders of that state joined the Confederacy the following year. Hickey and his wife settled in Monterrey and established a church two years later with the baptism of three Mexican converts.[15]

Other non-Catholic denominations and churches followed in their wake, and their endeavors received the active support of President Benito Juárez after he was restored to power in 1867 following the military defeat of the French-backed Emperor Maximilian's forces. The principal author of the historic Reform Laws of the 1850s that sought to break the enormous economic and political power of the country's conservative bishops, Juárez welcomed the arrival of the U.S. Episcopalian Church's first missionary, Henry Riley, in 1868 and even donated a Catholic parish church to help the American Protestant get started. "I could wish that Protestantism would become Mexican by conquering the Indians," Juárez famously declared. "They need a religion which will compel them to read and not spend their savings on candles for the saints."[16]

Other denominations set up shop in Mexico in quick succession. A Quaker missionary named Samuel A. Purdie arrived in Matamoros in 1871, three missionary couples from the Northern Presbyterian Church in the U.S.A. moved to Mexico City in 1872, and the Northern Methodists sent down two bishops in the winter of 1873 to finalize the purchase of two large Catholic churches in Mexico.[17] Two Congregationalist couples landed in Guadalajara in 1872, but one of the missionaries, John L. Stephens, never left Mexico alive. Accompanied by a Mexican neophyte named Jesús Islas, he toured the villages of Jalisco state in search of converts, but violence erupted in the countryside a year after Stephens's arrival and he and Islas were stoned to death.[18]

Juárez's benign stance toward non-Catholic Christians was copied by Porfirio Díaz, who attended the inauguration of a Protestant church in 1885 and granted private audiences to representatives of various Protestant denominations. A senior Mormon leader named John Henry Smith received the full VIP treatment during a visit to Mexico in 1901 and later hailed Díaz as his church's "greatest benefactor . . . no more heroic man stands on God's green earth . . . than the man who stands at the head of the government of Mexico." At the height of the Protestant boom during Díaz's long reign, nearly 500 congregations claimed a membership in excess of 100,000, and the diverse faithful included schoolteachers, small landowners, and textile and railway workers.[19]

But mainstream Protestant churches today account for no more than 10 percent of Mexico's estimated 15 million non-Catholic Christians. They have been completely overtaken in recent decades by the Pentecostal movement, whose roots are also very American. The movement sprang up in 1901 when a Methodist minister from Iowa named Charles Parham Fox conducted a detailed study of the ministry of the Holy Spirit at his Bible college in Topeka, Kansas, and made the link between baptism in the Holy Spirit and the speaking of unknown tongues.

One of Fox's disciples who received the "gift" of speaking in tongues was a black hotel waiter named William Seymour, who later opened a mission in downtown Los Angeles and led a spiritual revival that is widely regarded as the flowering of modern Pentecostalism. Seymour's mission soon attracted a fervent following among the city's black and Hispanic communities that was chronicled in a disparaging newspaper account of the era. "Disgraceful intermingling of the races, they cry and make howling noises all day and into the night," reported the *Los Angeles Times* in 1906 on its front page under the headline "Weird Babel of Tongues." "They run, jump, shake all over, shout to the top of their voice, spin around in circles, fall out on the sawdust-blanketed floor jerking, kicking and rolling all over it. . . . These people appear to be mad, mentally deranged or under a spell. . . . They have a one-eyed, illiterate Negro as their preacher who stays on his knees much of the time with his head hidden between the wooden milk crates."[20]

One of the participants in Seymour's revival mission was a woman from the Mexican border state of Chihuahua named Romana Carbajal de Valenzuela who had arrived in Los Angeles in 1912. Romana soon converted to Pentecostalism along with her husband, and when the couple returned to her hometown of Villa Aldama two years later she founded Mexico's first known Church of the Apostolic Faith.[21]

The social and political anarchy that engulfed the country during the ten-year Mexican Revolution spurred the northbound exodus of a million people, and like Romana Carbajal some of these immigrants were exposed to the Pentecostal movement during their stays in the United States. Between 1914 and 1932, at least twenty-six Apostolic churches were founded in a dozen states in northern Mexico by migrants who had returned from the United States. Antonio Nava Castañeda was eighteen years old when the revolution erupted in 1910, and his father's refusal to let him take up arms against the Díaz regime led the Durango native to journey north. Nava found work in the cotton fields of California's Imperial Valley, and a fellow farm worker named Marcial de la Cruz introduced the young Mexican to Pentecostalism in 1916. Nava opened a ministry in Yuma, Arizona, two years later and spread the Pentecostal gospel among residents in the border towns of Mexicali and Calexico, California.[22]

Another Pentecostal pioneer was David Genaro Ruesga, a native of Morelia who served with the forces of Pancho Villa during the revolution and then moved to the United States when the fighting ended. Ruesga claimed to have heard the gospel during a serious illness, and after regaining his health he was immediately baptized. Ruesga moved to Mexico City in 1920 and set up a small church three years later that is regarded as the first Pentecostal congregation based in the Mexican capital.[23] The movement continued to gather momentum throughout the postrevolutionary period. "The 1920's and 1930's saw the birth and rapid growth of many Pentecostal groups in Mexico," wrote Lindy Scott in his 1991 book, *Salt of the Earth*. "Frequently it was Mexican *braceros* [temporary workers] who, embracing Pentecostalism in the United States, returned to their country spreading their newfound faith."[24]

"IT IS A VISION OF OUR OWN MAKING"

The made-in-the-U.S.A. genesis of the movement is a touchy subject for some Mexican evangelicals. That's understandable, given the way in which the foreign origins of Mexico's Pentecostal churches and mainstream Protestant denominations have been used as a weapon to question their members' patriotism and loyalties. Lindy Scott quotes a revealing diatribe from a delegate to the constituent assembly that drafted Mexico's landmark 1917 constitution. "It would be unjust and immoral to undermine the characteristics of our nationality by permitting the substitution of a national cult by that of a powerful and dominating neighbor," declared Félix Palavicini, a former cabinet minister who had recently founded the newspaper *El Universal.* "The Protestant minister organizes sporting clubs that popularize English terminology, he has organized the Young Men's Christian Association where music is played, where bad verse is recited, where the 'one-step' is danced. . . . I assure you that it is not the Mexican people who support the Protestant cult in the Republic. I assure you that the Protestant cult is financed with Yankee money."[25]

That mindset lives on among some twenty-first-century Mexican Catholics. When I visited Ixmiquilpan a couple of weeks after the November 2005 vote that wrested control of its city hall from the PRI, I looked up members of the neighborhood council in the outlying village of San Nicolás who had vetoed the local evangelical community's government-approved plans to build a new temple. A lawyer named Noé Gerardo Nicolás Guerrero minced no words about the provenance of his non-Catholic neighbors' particular brand of Christianity, which he described as a contagion similar to the AIDS epidemic. "That famous Protestantism definitely comes from the United States," he snorted. "It's the consequence of our compatriots having gone over there to work, and they bring back those values and dogmas. It is our people's nature to imitate others, and when we ask them why they have changed and abandoned Catholicism they tell us that in the United States, everyone who preaches that dogma is rich. They are drawn to that dogma because they too want to be rich."

Mexican evangelicals reject such characterizations as a bum rap. Some of Mexico's earliest evangelical churches cut their formal ties to sister organizations in the United States because they resented the efforts of their American colleagues in the 1920s to assert more direct control over the Mexican movement. And while most of the mainstream Protestant denominations in Mexico were founded by American missionaries in the nineteenth century, Pentecostalism has experienced a boom never enjoyed by those denominations because it was brought into the country mostly by fellow Mexicans who had been converted on the Other Side. "We don't see it as an imported church," says Butch Frey, a native of West Virginia who has been living in Mexico City since 1989 and runs a program sponsored by the Assemblies of God churches based in Springfield, Missouri, that sends dozens of American missionaries into Mexico each year. "Much of the growth of the Assemblies of God in Mexico has been owing to Mexican pioneers."[26]

Any questioning of the Mexican evangelical movement's links to its American equivalent can elicit a testy response. When I brought up the subject with Confraternice president Arturo Farela, he retorted, "We have no dealings with Bush. We are not dependent on the gringos in either economic or ecclesiastical terms. It is a vision of our own making." The remark took me aback because neither he nor I had mentioned George W. Bush up to that point. Yet the same Pentecostal pastor who recoils at the slightest hint of any institutional nexus with the United States also has strong words of praise for the historical circumstances surrounding the birth of Mexico's powerful neighbor. "The United States was founded on the Bible, and we believe that it was the United States' good fortune to have been conquered by people who brought the word of God instead of a single religion," said Farela. "What came to Latin America wasn't the word of God but rather [Catholicism, which is] a religion imposed from above."

Farela believes that millions of Mexicans have embraced evangelical Christianity in part because of the Roman Catholic Church's own failings. "The Mexicans failed to find in the Catholic religion the answers to their needs," said Farela, who converted to Pentecostalism at the age of twenty-three. "Catholics talk about pie in the sky and how good things will be in heaven. The evangelicals say no, heaven is here because the kingdom of God is right here on earth. While they are offering blessings for the future, the message of evangelical ministers is to look for blessings in the here and now."

In comparison with the traditional, hour-long Roman Catholic mass, a very different style of Christianity is on offer at an evangelical house of worship. Some of these groups don't even call themselves churches: Christian Friendship is registered with the government as a civil association, a detail that its pastors highlight during the religious services that are held on Sundays. At the suggestion of Farela's office, I visited the Emmanuel Evangelistic Center in a gritty, working-class neighborhood of Mexico City called Tránsito one Sunday morning. I was received by Guillermo Fuentes, a seventy-nine-year-old Pentecostal pastor who told me he was called to the ministry when he was barely in his teens. His temple belongs to the Missouri-based Assemblies of God, which saw their membership in Mexico triple over a fifteen-year period ending in 2004, when it stood at over 600,000.[27] The two-hour religious service on Sundays isn't called a mass but rather a general assembly, and it takes place in the austere interior of an auditorium that seats 2,500 people under a corrugated metal roof.

The service kicked off with thirty minutes of singing led by a young woman in her late teens who was accompanied by a three-man band and a backup singer. The lyrics of the catchy, pop music–flavored songs were projected onto a screen behind the raised stage that served as a kind of altar, and members of the congregation lifted their arms in a show of religious ecstasy as they chanted, "Alleluia, Alleluia, Our Powerful God Is King."

Judging from their modest dress and physical appearance, most of the assembled believers seemed to come from blue-collar and lower-middle-class backgrounds. When the opening round of singing concluded, Fuentes took the microphone and introduced a young man in the crowd who had just been released from prison. "We have come here primarily to do what?" the pastor asked the congregation. "To worship God!" the faithful answered in chorus. On cue the band struck up a song called

Vine Adorar a Dios (I Came to Worship God), and then a youthful-looking pastor took center stage to deliver a twenty-five-minute-long sermon.

When the sermon finished, the pastor asked for a show of hands from people who wanted to have a more intimate encounter with God. The volunteers were summoned to the foot of the stage where they were issued copies of the New Testament and then escorted out of the main hall for private sessions of instruction and counseling. The portion of the service bearing the strongest resemblance to the proceedings of a Catholic mass came near the end, when members of the congregation lined up in front of the altar to take part in a ritual called The Supper of the Lord, which strongly evoked the sacrament of Holy Communion. But apart from that one last detail, the evangelicals' "general assembly" exuded an air of informality rarely found inside the walls of a Mexican cathedral.

DRAWING POWER DOESN'T ALWAYS EQUAL POLITICAL POWER

The evangelical Christian movement has demonstrated its drawing power in dramatic fashion with interdenominational services that regularly fill up Mexico City's huge Azteca Stadium. But will the evangelical boom alter the course of the country's politics in coming decades? Confraternice president Arturo Farela thinks it will, and he foresees the day when a fellow evangelical will be elected to the nation's highest office. "They are encouraging their people to vote," says missionary Butch Frey of the U.S. Assemblies of God, referring to his Mexican colleagues. "I have never seen our pastors publicly urging their congregations to seek office, but they are extremely grateful when their church members are involved in politics."

Yet it remains a stretch to imagine Mexican evangelical Christians ever acquiring a semblance of the political clout wielded by influential pastors in the States. For starters, the Mexican constitution prohibits religious ministers from openly endorsing specific political candidates. Unlike their U.S. counterparts who have become powerbrokers inside the Republican Party, Mexican evangelical leaders have yet to find a home in any of the major political parties since the movement began to drift away from the

PRI in the 1990s. As long as the country's evangelical Christians fail to unite around a single politician or party, their impact on politics will be limited on a national level and confined largely to those towns and states where their concentrated numbers make them a force to be reckoned with. But that by itself represents a significant milestone in the rise of evangelical Christianity south of the border.

An Invaded Country

Few Mexican cities can boast a central plaza matching the beauty and elegance of Puebla's main square. The *zócalo* is dominated by the city's seventeenth-century cathedral and its 225-feet-high towers, the tallest of any church in the republic. On the opposite side of the plaza sits the Municipal Palace, an imposing, belle époque edifice that stands as a monument to the architectural fashions of the *Porfiriato* era. The square features a central fountain and has retained the trees and flower beds that were once a trademark of its namesake in Mexico City before it was reduced to a featureless slab of concrete. At night, the floodlit facades of the buildings overlooking the *zócalo* further enhance the physical beauty of the setting.

But the ground-level arcades of these buildings also harbor some of the best-known brands of the globe-spanning U.S. fast-food industry. Burger King, McDonald's, Carl's Jr., and Domino's Pizza all do a thriving trade among the crowds who stroll through the city's downtown, and just off the plaza a Kentucky Fried Chicken branch offers competitively priced alternatives to the burger-weary passerby. These totems of the American way of life look painfully out of place in a handsome city center that has been designated a world heritage site by UNESCO, but Puebla's teenagers don't seem to mind. When school lets out on weekday afternoons, they take over the sidewalk tables outside these fast food outlets, and you can pick out the sons and daughters of the city's middle class from the base-ball caps and Converse All Star sneakers they sport.

At no point in my extensive travels through Mexico have I seen a starker contrast between the country's Catholic, heavily Spanish-flavored past and its increasingly Americanized present and future than in the heart of Puebla. The writer Carlos Monsiváis memorably described the upper-middle-class residents of Mexico City's exclusive neighborhoods as the first generation of Americans to be born in Mexico, and these young *poblanos* look and act like their spiritual offspring. Later that evening, I sat down with a twenty-four-year-old liberal arts student at the Autonomous University of Puebla named Mary Carmen Méndez. Unlike most of her peers, Méndez has a frame of reference that transcends the North American continent: she lived in Spain until the age of thirteen and still affects the trademark lisp of Mexico's so-called *madre patría* (mother nation). And on account of that background, her own left-wing politics, and possibly her English-language first name, Méndez seemed more con-scious of the Americanizing influences washing over the country than most Mexicans of her generation. "I've acquired the American sense of humor, and I laugh more when I'm watching an American sitcom than when I watch a Mexican comedy," said Méndez. "Nearly all the movies we see come from over there. There's a tendency [now in Mexico] to work longer hours, and the employee who spends more hours in the office is considered to have a greater commitment to the company. I feel slightly invaded, but it would seem there's no way of stopping this."[1]

"Almost a Part of the United States"

Invaded. That single word best captures what is happening to Mexico in the twenty-first century. In varying degrees American fashion, food, phrases, status symbols, social diseases, department stores, tourists, pensioners, religious denominations, and belief in the gospel of free trade have all established firm footholds inside today's Mexico. The Americanization is especially pronounced in the cities and among the country's middle and upper middle classes. Modern Mexico resembles a de facto economic colony of the United States, where a leftist governor proudly proclaims her state to be 'binational,' the biggest employer in the private sector is Wal-Mart, the biggest bank is owned by Citigroup, and the heir to the country's largest broadcasting empire dispatches his wife to San Diego to bear their first child. It is a country where a large and almost unseemly percentage of the population says they would leave for El Norte if given the chance, where Big Macs and Whoppers are challenging the home-grown *torta* as the sandwich of choice, where Halloween trinkets are given preference on store shelves over the miniature skulls used to celebrate Mexico's traditional Day of the Dead.

The impression all this must leave on a Latin American who did not grow up in the shadow of the Great Colossus of the North was neatly summed up by Jorge Yoma, a veteran lawmaker from Argentina's ruling Peronist party who arrived in Mexico in 2006 as that country's ambassador. On the final day of Argentine President Néstor Kirchner's state visit to Mexico in the summer of 2007, Yoma told a gathering of Mexican and Argentine businessmen that "Mexico is almost a part of the United States." The refreshingly candid characterization of the bilateral relationship sent twitters of nervous laughter rippling across the conference room—but no one challenged the remark in a subsequent question-and-answer session.[2]

This trend in Mexican society has been gathering momentum for more than two decades. In his 1985 book *Distant Neighbors: A Portrait of the Mexicans*, the journalist Alan Riding accused the country's dominant television network Televisa of propagating "Americanized values" and warned of the dangers inherent in the Americanization of the country's upper social strata. "Most people—the peasants, the urban poor, those living in smaller provincial cities—struggling to deal with their problems in Mexican terms, living the present in harmony with their own past, never question their identity as Mexicans," Riding wrote. "The middle and affluent classes, in contrast, are caught up in a rootless future, avidly adopting non-Mexican customs and values and in many cases even believing they have the option to become Americans."[3] If the PRI catered to the Americanized values of these latter-day *malinchistas* (a pejorative term applied to Mexicans who prefer foreigners to their own people), he cautioned, the ruling party of the epoch would jeopardize the system of political control it had carefully built up over the course of over fifty years. "By trying to make the country more superficially democratic, more Western, more 'presentable' abroad, the system's roots in the population have weakened," noted the British journalist. "The more the system responds to the Americanized minority, the more blatant will be the contradictions within the country."[4]

The widely respected Mexican journalist Alma Guillermoprieto posed a couple of soul-searching questions in a story she wrote for *The New Yorker* magazine a little over a year before NAFTA took effect at the beginning of 1994. "What people want to know about the coming onslaught of modernity is: How Mexican is it to be modern? Or, rather, since everything modern comes from a large, powerful country to the north, how Mexican is it to be like the United States?"[5]

These issues trouble even some Mexican intellectuals who will take issue with the fundamental premise of this book. In a column he wrote for the Mexico City newspaper *Reforma* in December 2003 that compared the historical experience of Puerto Rico as a quasi-colony of the United States with that of Mexico, a pessimistic Lorenzo Meyer addressed the possibility that his country could wind up as a satellite of its neighbor in all but name. "What remains of the efforts going back two centuries to achieve independence and consolidate nationalism?" asked the left-wing historian. "At the end of the day, is Mexico heading in the direction of becoming a [Puerto Rico–style] commonwealth? Under current circumstances, is independence incompatible with economic growth? Will the preservation of our 'cultural identity' become the only thing we can salvage from this disaster?"[6]

NEIGHBOR BASHING

That cultural identity remains as distinctive as ever. It is a defining trait of Mexico that never fails to impress the first-time visitor: the French poet and critic André Breton once called it "the surrealist country par excellence," and that description is reinforced on a daily basis by its resplendently dressed mariachi bands, its masked professional wrestlers, its spectacularly colorful murals, and its mawkish *telenovela* soap operas.

There are also clear limits to this Americanization process. In the countryside for example, the impact of the phenomenon is largely restricted to the dependence of millions of families on remittances, the continuing loss of jobs in the agricultural sector, the introduction of AIDS, and, of course, the ubiquitous Coca-Cola sign. Much of the country's intelligentsia remains self-consciously anti-gringo, and the mainstream news media never passes up an opportunity to chide the U.S. ambassador for some real or imagined slight. The yuppie classes of Mexico City, Monterrey, and Guadalajara may pay tribute to the likes of Bill Gates and Steve Jobs, but their more politicized, left-wing peers still look to the Fidel Castros and Che Guevaras of a bygone era for inspiration.

There are incipient signs of a backlash against the Americanization of modern Mexico. Anti-Americanism has enjoyed a resurgence across all of Latin America in the new century, thanks in great part to the cowboy diplomacy and peculiar governing style of George W. Bush. In recent years, the Mexican Left has been encouraged by the populist tilt of voters in a number of important South American countries, and the Mexican politician who seemed ideally poised to ride that wave in the 2006 presidential election was Andrés Manuel López Obrador of the Party of the Democratic Revolution (PRD). One veteran analyst of Mexican politics expected both the PRD nominee and his PRI counterpart to play the anti-gringo card with gusto on the campaign trail. "They will all engage in U.S.-bashing," predicted ex–foreign minister Jorge G. Castañeda in the spring of 2005. "The political elite is more anti-American than ever for a simple reason. The PRI was not anti-American when it was in power because it couldn't be. Now that it's in the opposition, it's irresponsibly anti-American."[7]

Yankee-baiting was certainly acceptable outside the boundaries of conventional political parties. The Zapatista leader *Subcomandante* Marcos issued a ringing indictment of the nation's neoliberal status quo and the Americans it allegedly benefits when he launched his own political campaign in the summer of 2005 as an alternative to the electoral contest pitting López Obrador against the PRI and the PAN. "What is happening in Mexico is that it has become a place where people are born and die, only to work for the enrichment of foreigners, principally rich gringos," the *subcomandante* declared in a communiqué.[8] The language harked back to the signature slogan of political opposition leaders in the late nineteenth century that described the Mexico of Porfirio Díaz as the "mother of foreigners and stepmother to the Mexicans." Support for *Subcomandante* Marcos's thesis has come from one of the leading Mexico scholars of the modern era, historian John Mason Hart of the University of Houston, who has written about what he calls "a neo-Porfirian synthesis of elite Mexicans and more powerful Americans" in key sectors of the national economy.[9]

The man who eventually replaced López Obrador as the elected mayor of Mexico City also hopped onto the anti-U.S. bandwagon at one point. At the closing ceremony of a Cuban cultural festival held in the Mexican capital's leafy neighborhood of Coyoacán in July 2005, the PRD's mayoral candidate Marcelo Ebrard expressed words of high praise for the Cuban Revolution and its ideological kindred spirit in Venezuela. "For all of us, the struggle of the Cuban people is exemplary," stated Ebrard, who went on to win the 2006 mayoral race by a comfortable margin. "The dignity that you have demonstrated in front of the American boot has a historic significance for us." Speaking in the presence of the Venezuelan ambassador to Mexico and the chargé d'affaires of the Cuban embassy, Ebrard welcomed the recent launch of Venezuelan President Hugo Chávez's Telesur cable news network. "The news that we are going to have Telesur, a Latin American channel for all Latin Americans, gives us great pleasure," declared the then candidate, "because the information that comes to us in Mexico is that which the United States wants us to hear, not what you are doing."[10]

A Pragmatic View from the Left

But López Obrador did not succumb to the gringo-bashing temptation in the end. On the hustings he did promise to review the NAFTA accords if elected president, and he often ridiculed the country's outgoing chief of state Vicente Fox as "a puppet of the foreigners." But the premier standard bearer of the Mexican Left never spelled out who exactly those foreigners were, and the eventual winner of the presidential balloting, the conservative former energy minister Felipe Calderón, has pledged to uphold the U.S.-backed free-market policies that Fox promoted during his six-year term in office. Marcelo Ebrard abandoned the anti-American rhetoric for the rest of his campaign and did not revisit the topic after he was sworn in as Mexico City mayor.

Long after the sound and fury of Mexico's periodic election campaigns have died down, the Americanization of the country will relentlessly grind on. The primacy of the United States in Mexican foreign policy will be upheld throughout the Calderón era. In the early months of his presidency, the veteran PAN politician paid more attention to Latin America than had Fox, who gave the region short shrift throughout his tenure. But a senior official at the U.S. embassy in Mexico City told me in the summer of 2007 that the intensity and level of contacts between officials of the neighboring countries had actually increased since Calderon succeeded Fox the previous year.[11]

That won't change even if López Obrador stages a political comeback of historic dimensions and wins the presidential election in 2012. In a 2004 book, López Obrador took no pot shots at Uncle Sam and limited himself to platitudes about the need to defend the rights of Mexican workers in the United States and pursue a relationship based on the principles of "mutual respect and cooperation." His carefully chosen words reflected a pragmatic recognition of the ever-deepening ties between the two countries and the overriding importance that a healthy U.S. economy represents for Mexico's future prosperity. "[Our] geographic proximity to the largest market and its position as a cultural frontier gives

Mexico a strategic position of great relevance," wrote López Obrador. "It has to do with what is nothing less than the world's most intense bilateral relationship."[12]

A FULL PARTNER OR A MERE APPENDAGE?

For some seasoned analysts of international affairs, the current state of U.S.-Mexican ties should gradually evolve toward a model based on that of the European Union (EU). To support their case, these observers cite the enormous benefits that EU membership has delivered to relatively poorer member countries like Portugal and Ireland via massive economic assistance that has upgraded living standards and public infrastructure. The notion of a North American Union that would promote greater political, economic, and social integration among the three NAFTA countries has garnered widespread support across the political spectrum in Mexico, from López Obrador on the left to his nemesis Vicente Fox on the right. One of the concept's strongest advocates inside the United States is Robert Pastor, a former Carter administration official who is vice president of international affairs at Washington's American University. If the United States and Canada followed the examples of France and Germany and invested large sums of money in the Mexican economy and society, argues Pastor, the long-term benefits for Mexico's NAFTA partners would vastly outweigh the initial costs. "The U.S. contribution would be much less than European aid to its poorest member states and only one-half of the amount of the Bush Administration's aid to Iraq," Pastor wrote in *Foreign Affairs* magazine. "The return on an investment in Mexico, moreover, would benefit the U.S. economy more than any aid program in history."[13]

But greater integration with Mexico is not a concept that goes down well in the American political climate of today. Quite the contrary: spearheaded by right-wing broadcasters like CNN's Lou Dobbs and Fox News anchorman Bill O'Reilly, neighbor-bashing is very much in vogue within certain sectors of American politics. The Austrian-born actor

Arnold Schwarzenegger exploited simmering resentment of Mexican immigrants to get himself elected governor of California, and voters in the adjacent state of Arizona approved a controversial ballot initiative in 2004 to restrict government services for undocumented workers. Rising numbers of city councils in the United States have passed ordinances in recent years prohibiting employers and landlords from hiring or renting housing to such foreign immigrants. Several leading Republican presidential hopefuls advocated mass deportation of (mostly Mexican) illegal aliens during the early months of the 2008 presidential race.

The comprehensive immigration agreement that Vicente Fox sought nearly a decade ago to legalize the status of millions of Mexican workers seemed more elusive than ever as the era of George W. Bush finally came to a close in the winter of 2009. At a time when both houses of the U.S. Congress have approved the construction of new fencing along more than 700 miles of the two countries' shared border to deter Mexican migrant workers, there is frankly little enthusiasm for EU-inspired proposals to bring the two countries any closer than they already are. "Following the European model would eventually give Canada and the United States a better trading partner to the south, and a more prosperous Mexico would result in less illegal immigration," argued Rafael Fernández de Castro and Rossana Fuentes-Berain in the *New York Times* editorial pages in March 2005. "Undoubtedly, this level of cooperation would be a hard sell to Americans, who would assume they would have the most to lose."[14] Indeed, at one of the last NAFTA summits he attended as president, George W. Bush dismissed recent rumors that Canada, Mexico, and the United States would create a North American union by 2010 as "political scare tactics" on the part of his foes back home.[15]

The knee-jerk rejection of such a union seems selfish and short-sighted. There may come a point later in this century when the rise of China and India could force policymakers in Washington to reconsider the North American community idea. But for the time being, most American politicians and their constituents are not interested in a marriage of equals between the United States and Mexico. (To his credit, Democratic presidential candidate Barack Obama called for a bilateral relationship based on equality during the 2008 campaign, but his was a decidedly minority view.) They prefer to treat Mexico as the international equivalent of an appendage that is always ready to service certain indispensable needs of American society when it is required and can be disowned whenever it suits U.S. interests. That handy appendage attached to America's doorstep will continue to absorb and imitate the values, vices, lifestyle, and language of El Norte for the foreseeable future without any realistic hope that Washington might one day accept Mexico as a full partner.

As a California-born son of Mexican immigrants, I find the attitudes of so many Americans toward Mexico to be not just myopic but downright maddening. The Americanization of the country has infected Mexico with a number of unwelcome social diseases, a crass consumerism, and a dangerous dependence on the remittances of her migrants. But the balance sheet overall has been positive. The example of the United States has served to promote the rights of Mexican women, gays, and lesbians in recent years. Judicial reform based on the American legal system is advancing, the news media is freer than ever before, and Mexico's functioning democracy is a far cry from the PRI-run "perfect dictatorship" of the mid-twentieth century. More engagement with the United States would steadily narrow the gap separating the two countries on issues of immigration, workplace conditions, and the environment. Yet no matter how much more Americanized Mexico becomes in our lifetimes, she will still be viewed by much of the U.S. political establishment as a problematic neighbor that should be kept at a healthy remove. Poor Mexico, Porfirio Díaz might say if he could see the state of the nation nearly a century after his death. So close to the United States, so far from a relationship based on true equality and respect.

Acknowledgments

I like to think of the acknowledgments section of a book as a vehicle to express the author's gratitude to those who made vital contributions to the researching and writing of the work and also tell readers a little bit about its genesis. In that spirit, I wish to thank the New York literary agent Carol Mann for selling Rutgers University Press on the idea of publishing this book, which originally appeared in Mexico under the title *Tan lejos de Dios: El México moderno a la sombra de Estados Unidos.* I'd like to salute Adi Hovav, my editor at Rutgers University Press, who made helpful suggestions that immeasurably improved the manuscript and transformed what in large part had been a collection of articles into a more coherent product. A doff of the cap goes to Professor Roderic Ai Camp of Claremont McKenna College for his careful review of the original text and his many trenchant observations and criticisms that made this book more suitable for an American audience. And a round of applause goes out to Rick Delaney, whose meticulous copyediting made the text a smoother and more concise read.

My thanks also go out to the Barcelona literary agent Willie Schavelzon, who approached me with the offer of his services in 2004 and encouraged me to come up with a viable idea for a book. Equally vital was the role played by Ariel Rosales of Random House Mondadori who, over a round of tequilas at a restaurant near the publishing company's Mexico City offices, suggested I consider writing a book that compared and contrasted the Mexico of today with the country I lived in and got to know as a young foreign correspondent in the mid-1980s.

Many of the people who gave me their invaluable advice and perspectives are cited in these pages, and I offer them my heartfelt appreciation. I am indebted to Jaime Gutiérrez Casas, Eloy Masferrer Kan, Félix and Barbara Arredondo, Olga Wornat, Lindy Scott, and Nick Carter for their assistance in the reporting phase. Lastly, I wish to thank my parents, Olga and Joe Contreras, for instilling in me a pride and appreciation of our family's Mexican roots, sentiments which I am happy to report are being absorbed by their grandchildren several decades after they immigrated to the United States of America.

Notes

INTRODUCTION — THE UNITED STATES OF MEXICO

1. Paul Garner, *Porfirio Diaz* (London: Pearson Education Limited, 2001), 137.

2. Enrique Krauze, *Mexico: Biography of Power* (New York: HarperCollins, 1997), 4–5.

3. Garner, *Porfirio Diaz*, 139.

4. Ibid., 182.

5. Ibid., 177.

6. Guillermo Kahlo, *Mexiko* 1904 (Mexico City: Universidad Iberoamericana, 2002), 81–82.

7. Garner, *Porfirio Diaz*, 144–145.

8. Krauze, *Mexico*, 10–11.

9. Ibid., 773.

10. The Monsiváis interview can be accessed online at the Journal of American History's site, http://www.indiana.edu/~jah/mexico/cmonsivais.html.

11. *Bloomberg News*, November 10, 2005.

12. *El Universal* (Mexico), February 2, 2007, 1.

13. *Webster's Ninth New Collegiate Dictionary* (Springfield, MA: Merriam-Webster Inc., 1990), 78.

14. Remarks of U.S. Secretary of Commerce Carlos M. Gutierrez, Mexico City, February 1, 2007.

15. Carol and Thomas Christensen, *The U.S.-Mexican War* (San Francisco: Bay Books, 1998), x–xi.

16. Friedrich Katz, *The Life and Times of Pancho Villa* (Stanford, CA: Stanford University Press, 1998), 705.

17. Octavio Paz, *The Labyrinth of Solitude, the Other Mexico, and Other Essays* (New York: Grove Press, 1985), 357, 372.

18. Interview with the author, August 18, 2004, Mexico City.

19. Robert A. Pastor and Jorge G. Castañeda, *Limits to Friendship: The United States and Mexico* (New York: Vintage Books, 1988), 341.

20. *Reforma*, El Angel supplement, May 23, 2004, 5.

21. *Excélsior*, June 3, 1999.

22. *Journal of American History* website. http://www.indiana.edu/~jah/mexico/cmonsivais.html.

23. Jorge G. Castañeda, *Ex Mex: From Migrants to Immigrants* (New York: The New Press, 2007), 7–8.

24. Interview with the author, August 27, 2004, Mexico City.

CHAPTER 1 — A CHICANO COMES TO THE BIG ENCHILADA

1. Octavio Paz, *The Labyrinth of Solitude, the Other Mexico, and Other Essays* (New York: Grove Press, 1985), 14.

2. Julian Nava, *My Mexican-American Journey* (Houston: Arte Público Press, 2002), 145.

3. The Associated Press, January 26, 2005.

4. United Press International, February 23, 1984.

5. *New York Times*, February 28, 1984, A4.

6. *Newsweek*, April 2, 1984, 21.

7. Jack Anderson, "Mexico Makes Its Presidents Millionaires," *Washington Post*, May 15, 1984, C15.

8. *Time*, March 4, 1985, 8.

9. Hearings before the Subcommittee on Western Hemisphere Affairs of the Committee On Foreign Relations, United States Senate, *Situation in Mexico*, May 13, June 17 and 26, 1986 (Washington, DC: U.S. Government Printing Office, 1986), 28.

10. *Newsweek International*, March 17, 1986, 6.

11. Hearings, *Situation*, 27–28.

12. Robert A. Pastor and Jorge G. Castañeda, *Limits to Friendship: The United States and Mexico* (New York: Vintage Books, 1988), 186.

13. Miguel de la Madrid Hurtado, *Cambio de rumbo: Testimonio de una Presidencia, 1982–88* (Mexico City: Fondo de Cultura Económica, 2004), 422 and 425.

14. Pastor and Castañeda, *Limits*, 340.

15. Rossana Fuentes-Berain, "Where Roma Soap Meets Dove," *New York Times*, January 13, 2004, A25.

16. *Newsweek International*, October 19, 1987.

17. Hearings, *Situation*, 41–43.

18. De la Madrid, *Cambio de rumbo*, 514.

19. Ibid.

20. Ibid., 427 and 581.

21. Ibid., 614.

22. Pastor and Castañeda, *Limits*, 271–272.

23. Ibid., 167.

CHAPTER 2 — NOT SUCH DISTANT NEIGHBORS

1. Interview with author, August 27, 2004, Mexico City.

2. *Newsweek International*, June 26, 2000, 18.

3. *Newsweek International*, July 3, 2000, 2.

4. *Proceso*, May 13, 1991, 7.

5. The Associated Press, July 23, 2004.

6. *New York Times*, December 8, 1998, A8.

7. Edward M. Conley, "The Americanization of Mexico," *The American Monthly Review of Reviews* (1909), 725.

8. Anne Rubenstein, "Mass Media and Popular Culture in the Postrevolutionary Era," in *The Oxford History of Mexico*, ed. Michael C. Meyer and William H. Beezley (New York: Oxford University Press, 2000), 667.

9. Ibid., 648.

10. Stephen D. Morris, *Gringolandia: Mexican Identity and Perceptions of the United States* (Lanham, MD: Rowman & Littlefield, 2005), 190.

11. Ibid., 190–191.

12. Paulo Antonio Paranagua, ed., *Mexican Cinema* (London: British Film Institute, 1995), 9.

13. Alan Riding, *Distant Neighbors: A Portrait of the Mexicans* (New York: Alfred A. Knopf, 1985), 19.

14. Andrés Oppenheimer, *Miami Herald*, January 8, 2004.

15. *El Universal*, February 1, 2007, B1.

16. *Newsweek International*, September 27, 2004, 31.

17. Jorge Castañeda, "Los ejes de la política exterior de México," *Nexos*, December 2001, 72.

18. Vicente Fox and Rob Allyn, *Revolution of Hope: The Life, Faith and Dreams of a Mexican President* (New York: Viking, 2007), xii.

19. David Frum, *The Right Man: An Inside Account of the Bush White House* (New York: Random House, 2003), 86.

20. *Miami Herald*, May 28, 2004, 15A.

21. *Reforma*, April 26, 2005.

22. Interview with the author, May 14, 2005, Mexico City.

23. Interview with the author, October 14, 2005, Mexico City.

24. Interview with the author, May 14, 2005, Mexico City.

25. Jeffrey Davidow, *The U.S. and Mexico: The Bear and the Porcupine* (Princeton, NJ: Markus Wiener Publishers, 2004), 173.

26. Statement by Ambassador Antonio O. Garza, Jr., June 13, 2007.

27. *Proceso*, January 11, 2004, 14.

28. Interview with the author, September 2, 2004, Mexico City.

29. Interview with the author, August 27, 2004, Mexico City.

30. Interview with the author, August 27, 2004, Mexico City.

31. Samuel Huntington, "Clash of Civilizations," *Foreign Affairs* (summer 1993).

32. Denise Dresser, "Policy of Opposites Undoes U.N. Diplomat," *Los Angeles Times*, November 26, 2003, B13.

33. Interview with the author, May 14, 2005, Mexico City.

34. The Associated Press, May 29, 2007.

35. *Journal of American History* web site. http://www.indiana.edu/~jah/mexico/cmonsivais.html.

36. Interview with the author, August 17, 2004, Mexico City.

37. *Crónica* (Mexico), March 4, 1999.

38. Interview with the author, August 27, 2004, Mexico City.

39. Andrés Oppenheimer, *Miami Herald*, January 25, 2004, 20A.

CHAPTER 3 — LOOKING NORTHWARD

1. Charles A. Hale, *Mexican Liberalism in the Age of Mora* (New York: Random House—Knopf, 1968), 214.

2. Ibid.

3. Lorenzo de Zavala, *Journey to the United States of North America* (Houston: Arte Público Press, 2005), 193.

4. Ibid., 39.

5. Ibid., 194.

6. Ibid., 2–3.

7. Enrique Krauze, *Mexico: Biography of Power* (New York: HarperCollins, 1997), 143.

8. Enrique Krauze, "Mirándolos a ellos: Actitudes mexicanas frente a Estados Unidos," *Letras Libres*, June 2007, 39.

9. John Mason Hart, *Empire and Revolution: The Americans in Mexico since the Civil War* (Berkeley: University of California Press, 2002), 14–16.

10. Krauze, "Mirándolos a ellos," 40.

11. Friedrich Katz, *The Life and Times of Pancho Villa* (Stanford, CA: Stanford University Press, 1998), 46.

12. Paul Garner, *Porfirio Díaz* (London: Pearson Education Limited, 2001), 138.

13. Charles A. Hale, *The Transformation of Liberalism in Late Nineteenth-Century Mexico* (Princeton, NJ: Princeton University Press, 1989), 242–243.

NOTES TO PAGES 68–79

14. Jules Davids, *American Political and Economic Penetration of Mexico, 1877–1920* (New York: Arno Press, 1976), 166–167.

15. Hale, *Transformation*, 241.

16. Krauze, *Mexico*, 6.

17. Ibid., 252.

18. Katz, *Life and Times*, 43.

19. Carlos Fuentes, *Nuevo tiempo mexicano* (Mexico City: Aguilar, 1994), 47.

20. Daniel Cosío Villegas, *The United States versus Porfirio Diaz* (Lincoln: University of Nebraska Press, 1963), 237–238.

21. Katz, *Life and Times*, 616.

22. Krauze, "Mirándolos a ellos," 42.

23. Krauze, *Mexico*, 417–418.

24. Ibid., 419.

25. Stephen D. Morris, *Gringolandia: Mexican Identity and Perceptions of the United States* (Lanham, MD: Rowman & Littlefield, 2005), 19–20.

26. Rafael Segovia, "El nacionalismo mexicano: los programas políticos revolucionarios 1929–1964," in *Lecturas de Política Mexicana* (Mexico City: El Colegio de México, 1977), 37–53.

27. Howard Cline, *The United States and Mexico* (New York: Atheneum, 1973), 316.

28. *Time*, March 17, 1947.

29. Cline, *United States*, 388.

30. Leopoldo Solís, "La política económica y el nacionalismo mexicano," in *Lecturas de Política Mexicana* (Mexico City: El Colegio de México, 1977), 55–75.

31. Krauze, "Mirándolos a ellos," 43.

32. Morris, *Gringolandia*, 21.

33. Katz, *Life and Times*, 395.

34. Ibid., 312.

35. Ibid., 394–395.

36. Ibid., 549.

37. Morris, *Gringolandia*, 173.

38. Ibid., 202–203.

39. Charles Ramirez Berg, *Cinema of Solitude: A Critical Study of Mexican Film, 1967–1983* (Austin: University of Texas Press, 1992), 25.

40. Andrés Oppenheimer, *Bordering on Chaos: Guerrillas, Stockbrokers, Politicians, and Mexico's Road to Prosperity* (Boston: Little, Brown, 1996), 99.

41. Ibid., 99–100.

42. Ibid., 100.

43. Morris, *Gringolandia*, 43.

44. Interview with the author, August 3, 2004, Washington, DC.

45. Morris, *Gringolandia*, 14.

46. Rodolfo O. de la Garza, "Foreign Policy Comes Home: The Domestic Consequences of the Program for Mexican Communities Living in Foreign Countries," in *Bridging the Border: Transforming Mexico–U.S. Relations*, ed. Rodolfo O. de la Garza and Jesus Velasco (New York: Rowman and Littlefield, 1998), 71.

47. María García Castro, "Identidad nacional y nacionalismo en México," *Sociología* 8 (21) (1993), 38.

48. Morris, *Gringolandia*, 41.

49. Chicago Council on Foreign Relations, Centro de Investigación y Docencia Económicas and Consejo Mexicano de Asuntos Internacionales, *Global Views 2004: Mexican Public Opinion and Foreign Policy* (Ann Arbor, MI: Inter-University Consortium for Political and Social Research, 2005), 9–10.

50. Roderic Ai Camp, "Learning Democracy in Mexico and the United States," *Mexican Studies/Estudios Mexicanos* 19 (1) (Winter 2003), 13.

51. Carlos Monsiváis, *Mexican Postcards* (London: Verso, 1997), xiv.

52. Carlos Monsiváis, "Muerte y resurrección del nacionalismo mexicano," *Nexos* 109 (1987), 21.

53. Monsiváis, *Mexican Postcards*, 20.

54. Carlos Monsiváis, "De la cultura mexicana en vísperas del Tratado de Libre Comercio," in *La educación y la cultura ante el Tratado de Libre Comercio*, ed. Gilberto Guevara Niebla and Nestor García Canclini (Mexico City: Nueva Imagen, 1992), 200.

55. Ibid., 192.

56. *San Diego Union-Tribune*, January 27, 2002, A19.

57. Carlos Monsiváis, *Los rituales del caos* (Mexico City: Procuraduría Federal del Consumidor y Ediciones Era, 1995), 33–34.

CHAPTER 4 — NAFTA: THE DOUBLE-EDGED SWORD OF FREE TRADE

1. Malcolm Lowry, *Under the Volcano* (New York: J. B. Lippincott, 1965), 3–4.

2. Fred Rosen and Irene Ortiz, "Mega-stores Destroy Historic Site," *NACLA Report on the Americas* 37, No. 4 (January 2004), 11–12.

3. Ibid.

4. Interview with the author, May 18, 2005, Cuernavaca.

5. *Chicago Tribune*, September 9, 2002, A1.

6. *New York Times*, December 6, 2003, A1.

7. Paul Garner, *Porfirio Diaz* (London: Pearson Education Limited, 2001), 145.

8. Robert Pastor, "North America's Second Decade," *Foreign Affairs* 83 (1) (January/February 2004), 127.

9. Jorge Castañeda, "Los ejes de la política exterior de México," *Nexos* (December 2001), 67.

10. Lorenzo Meyer, "La visión general," in *Una historia contemporánea de México: Transformaciones y permanencias*, ed. Ilán Bizberg and Lorenzo Meyer (Mexico City: Océano, 2003), 27.

11. *New York Times*, December 27, 2003, A1.

12. An analysis of NAFTA's effects on the Mexican manufacturing sector can be accessed online at the web page of the Council on Hemispheric Affairs. http://www.coha.org/2007/08/08/the-tail-end-of-free-trade-a-preliminary-evaluation-of-the-impact-of-nafta-on-the-manufacturing-sector.

13. Pastor, "North America's Second Decade," 130.

14. Interview with the author, August 17, 2004, Mexico City.

15. *New York Times*, November 19, 2003, A8.

16. John J. Audley, Demetrios G. Papademetriou, Sandra Polaski, and Scott Vaughan, *NAFTA's Promise and Reality: Lessons From Mexico for the Hemisphere* (Washington, DC: Carnegie Endowment for International Peace, 2004), 6 and 12.

17. Reuters, January 31, 2007.

18. Various interviews with the author, November 26, 2005, Nopalucan de la Granja, Mexico.

19. "Special Report: Mexico and Globalisation," *The Financial Times*, December 13, 2005, 3.

20. The Associated Press, March 13, 2007.

21. The Associated Press, April 12, 2005.

22. Interview with the author, May 16, 2005, Mexico City.

CHAPTER 5 — THE NEW BREED OF MEXICAN BUSINESSMEN

1. Claudia Fernández and Andrew Paxman, *El Tigre: Emilio Azcárraga y su imperio Televisa* (Mexico City: Grijalbo, 2000), 39.

2. Interview with the author, February 20, 2003, Mexico City.

3. The Associated Press, May 11, 2005.

4. "U.S.-Mexico Economic Relations: Trends, Issues and Implications," *Congressional Research Service* (updated July 11, 2005), 6. For 2004 figures, see http://www.state.gov/r/pa/prs/ps/2006/63553.htm.

5. Interview with Casa Cuervo chief executive officer Juan Domingo Beckmann, February 19, 2003, Mexico City.

6. Reuters, July 6, 2006.

7. Interview with the author, February 24, 2003, Mexico City.

8. Phone interview with the author, March 7, 2005.

9. Roderic Ai Camp, *Mexico's Mandarins: Crafting A Power Elite for the Twenty-first Century* (Berkeley: University of California Press, 2002), 247–248.

10. *Reforma*, February 1, 2005.

11. *Chicago Tribune*, February 1, 2005, A2.

12. Interview with the author, May 2, 2007, Mexico City.

13. *New York Times*, September 15, 2006, C3.

14. *New York Times*, April 29, 2005, C5.

15. Phone interview with the author, May 10, 2007.

16. Sarah Babb, *Managing Mexico: Economists From Nationalism to Neoliberalism* (Princeton, NJ: Princeton University Press, 2001), 133.

17. Ibid., 200.

18. Enrique Krauze, *Mexico: Biography of Power* (New York: HarperCollins, 1997), 247.

19. Camp, *Mexico's Mandarins*, 248.

20. Phone interview with the author, December 7, 2005.

CHAPTER 6 — THE MODERN MEXICAN NEWS MEDIA

1. Interview with the author, December 15, 2005, Mexico City.

2. Julia Preston and Samuel Dillon, *Opening Mexico: The Making of a Democracy* (New York: Farrar, Straus and Giroux, 2004), 433.

3. Interview with the author, August 18, 2004, Mexico City.

4. Interview with the author, December 12, 2004, Monterrey.

5. Interview with the author, August 25, 2005, Monterrey.

6. Raymundo Riva Palacio, *La prensa de los jardines: Fortalezas y debilidades de los medios en México* (Mexico City: Plaza Janés, 2004), 61.

7. Ibid.

8. Sallie Hughes, *Newsrooms in Conflict: Journalism and the Democratization of Mexico* (Pittsburgh: University of Pittsburgh Press, 2006), 139.

9. William A. Orme, Jr., ed., *A Culture of Collusion: An Inside Look at the Mexican Press* (Miami: North-South Center Press, 1997), 5.

10. Hughes, *Newsrooms in Conflict*, 167–168.

11. Ibid., 169.

12. Ibid., 178–179.

13. Interview with the author, October 19, 2005, Mexico City.

14. Jeffrey Davidow, *The U.S. and Mexico: The Bear and the Porcupine* (Princeton, NJ: Markus Wiener Publishers, 2004), 28.

15. Ibid., 28–29.

16. *El Universal*, November 30, 2005.

17. Interview with the author, November 25, 2005, Mexico City.

18. Interview with the author, November 21, 2005, Mexico City.

CHAPTER 7 — THE MEXICAN DREAM

1. All interviews in San Miguel Allende quoted in this chapter were conducted on October 23 and 24, 2005.

2. David Weber, *The Mexican Frontier, 1821–1846: The American Southwest under Mexico* (Albuquerque: University of New Mexico Press, 1982), 166.

3. William Schell, Jr., *Integral Outsiders: The American Colony in Mexico City, 1876–1911* (Wilmington, Del.: Scholarly Resources, 2001), xvi–xviii.

4. John Mason Hart, *Empire and Revolution: The Americans in Mexico since the Civil War* (Berkeley: University of California Press, 2002), 235–36.

5. Paul Garner, *Porfirio Diaz* (London: Pearson Education Limited, 2001), 200.

6. Hart, *Empire and Revolution*, 238–243.

7. Ibid., 398.

8. *Dallas Morning News*, March 14, 2005, 1A.

9. The Associated Press, August 21, 2004.

10. Interview with the author, March 29, 2007, Mexico City.

11. *San Diego Business Journal*, March 28, 2005.

12. Interview with the author, March 15, 2005, Cancún.

13. The Associated Press, March 7, 2008.

14. All interviews in Ajijic and the surrounding Lake Chapala district of Jalisco state quoted in this chapter were conducted between October 26 and 28, 2005.

15. *Dallas Morning News*, March 14, 2005, 1A.

16. *Newsweek International*, September 17, 2007.

CHAPTER 8 — THE GRINGO RIVIERA

1. All interviews in Cancún that are quoted in this chapter were conducted between March 14 and 18, 2005.

2. The tourism industry revenue statistics for 2006 can be found at the website of the publicity service firm PR Leap http://www.prleapcom/pr/68418.

3. *The Economist*, October 9, 2004, 56.

4. The description of Cancún's tippling scene can be found at the Student Spring Break website. http://www.studentspringbreak.com/dests/cancun.shtml.

5. The Associated Press, December 1, 2004.

6. *Escala* (magazine), March 2007, 54–69.

7. Phone interview with the author, January 12, 2005.

8. Phone interview with the author, February 9, 2007.

9. All interviews in Sayulita and San Francisco, Nayarit state that are quoted in this chapter were conducted on December 13 and 14, 2004.

10. *El Mundo* (Mérida), October 25, 2005, 1.

CHAPTER 9 — THE UMBILICAL CORD OF REMITTANCES

1. *Los Angeles Times*, March 23, 2007.

2. White House web site. http://www.whitehouse.gov/news/releases/2007/03/20070314–2.html.

3. *Houston Chronicle*, December 11, 2000.

4. *New York Times*, February 9, 2008.

5. *New York Times*, November 16 and 17, 1986.

6. Alduncin y Asociados, "Emigración de México a Estados Unidos y monto de las remesas," n.d., 17 (Copy in author's possession). Other surveys found a lower percentage of Mexicans who were willing to try their luck on the Other Side, such as a May 2005 poll by the Washington-based Pew Hispanic Center showing that 46 percent would live in the United States "if they had the means and the opportunity." Jorge G. Castañeda, *Ex Mex: From Migrants to Immigrants* (New York: The New Press, 2007), 48.

7. *Los Angeles Times*, June 16, 2004, C2.

8. *Houston Chronicle*, February 3, 2007.

9. Interview with the author, December 15, 2004, Zacatecas.

10. Interview with the author, December 17, 2004, Zacatecas.

11. Interview with the author, December 15, 2004, Zacatecas.

12. Interview with the author, December 16, 2004, Zacatecas.

13. Interview with the author, December 17, 2004, Valparaíso.

14. Interview with the author, December 20, 2004, Juchipila.

15. Interview with the author, December 19, 2004, Apozol.

16. See chapter 11.

17. *New York Times*, January 14, 2006, A3.

18. The Associated Press, August 11, 2007.

19. *Arizona Republic*, September 3, 2007, A2.

20. Interview with the author, December 20, 2007, El Remolino.

21. *Foreign Affairs en Español* (July-September 2005).

22. Roderic Ai Camp, "Learning Democracy in the United States," *Mexican Studies/Estudios Mexicanos* 19 (1) (Winter 2003), 5.

23. http://www.usembassy-mexico.gov/Ambassador/eA050303chamber.html.

24. *Houston Chronicle*, February 3, 2007.

25. The Associated Press, August 8, 2007. The warnings of Ambassador Garza and the Inter-American Development Bank were confirmed months later when Mexico's central bank reported a net 5.9 percent drop in remittances in January 2008 from the same time period in 2007. Reuters, March 5, 2008.

CHAPTER 10 — THE SOUTHERNMOST CITY IN TEXAS

1. Interview with the author, August 25, 2005, Monterrey.

2. Interview with the author, August 23, 2004, Monterrey.

3. Interview with the author, August 26, 2004, Mexico City.

4. Interview with the author, December 12, 2004, Monterrey.

5. Gerardo Reyes, ed., *Los dueños de América Latina* (Mexico City: Ediciones B, 2003), 169.

6. *Fortune*, December 20, 1999.

7. *Miami Herald* (Mexican edition), January 25, 2007, 7.

8. Interview with the author, August 22, 2004, Monterrey.

9. Carol and Thomas Christensen, *The U.S.-Mexican War* (San Francisco: Bay Books, 1998), 130.

10. Ibid., 135.

11. Mario Cerutti, *Propietarios, empresarios y empresa en el norte de México* (Mexico City: Siglo Veintiuno Editores, 2000), 34–35.

12. John Mason Hart, *Empire and Revolution: The Americans in Mexico since the Civil War* (Berkeley: University of California Press, 2002), 22–25.

13. Cerutti, *Propietarios*, 43.

14. Juan Mora-Torres, *The Making of the Mexican Border: The State, Capitalism and Society in Nuevo León, 1848–1910* (Austin: University of Texas Press, 2001), 90–91.

15. Hart, *Empire and Revolution*, 141.

16. Mora-Torres, *The Making of the Mexican Border*, 249.

17. Hart, *Empire and Revolution*, 43–44.

18. Mora-Torres, *The Making of the Mexican Border*, 202.

19. Ibid.

20. Interview with the author, July 22, 2005, Mexico City.

21. Interview with the author, August 18, 2004, Mexico City.

22. *Christian Science Monitor*, February 18, 2003.

23. *El Norte*, December 23, 1993.

24. *Houston Chronicle*, December 17, 2006, A1.

25. *Reforma*, June 13, 2007, A6.

26. The Associated Press, March 23, 2007.

27. *San Antonio Express-News*, March 31, 2007, A26.

28. *San Antonio Express-News*, November 23, 2006.

29. U.S. Department of State web site. http://travel.state.gov/travel/cis_pa_tw/cis/cis_970.html.

30. Interview with the author, July 27, 2007, Mexico City.

CHAPTER 11 — MADE-IN-THE-U.S.A. DISEASES

1. Interview with the author, June 14, 2005, Mexico City.

2. *Reforma*, October 22, 2004.

3. *Reforma*, October 26, 2004.

4. Interview with the author, September 3, 2007, Mexico City.

5. Interview with the author, June 13, 2005, Mexico City.

6. Copies of surveys in author's possession.

7. *El Universal*, March 4, 2005.

8. *Reforma*, May 15, 2005.

9. The International Relations Center report on soaring methamphetamine use inside Mexico can be found at the center's website. http://americas.irc-online.org/am/3976.

10. The Associated Press, January 23, 2007.

11. "Lou Dobbs Tonight," *CNN*, June 8, 2005.

12. *El Universal*, November 30, 2005, A23.

13. Interview with the author, October 20, 2005, Mexico City.

14. Donato Alarcón Segovia and Samuel Ponce de León Rosales, eds., *El SIDA en México: 20 años de la epidemia* (Mexico City: El Colegio Nacional, 2003), 14.

15. *Reforma*, July 24, 2005.

16. Mario Bronfman and Nelson Minello, "Hábitos sexuales de los migrantes temporales mexicanos a los Estados Unidos de América. Prácticas de riesgo para la infección por vih," in *Sida en México. Migración, adolescencia y género*, ed. Mario Bronfman, Ana Amuchástegui, Rosa María Martina, Nelson Minello and Gabriela Rodríguez (Mexico City: Editorial EDIPESA, 1995), 61.

17. Interview with the author, November 25, 2005, Puebla.

18. *Dallas Morning News*, December 12, 2003.

19. *Houston Chronicle*, August 3, 2003, A28.

20. *Dallas Morning News*, December 12, 2003.

21. *El Universal*, September 27, 2006.

22. The statistics on the fatality incidence of diabetes among adult men and women can be found at the World Health Organization website. www.who.int/countryfocus/resources/ccsbrief_mexico_mex_06_en.pdf.

23. Phone interview with the author, July 28, 2005.

24. The Associated Press, July 23, 2004.

25. Interviews conducted by research assistant Nick Carter, July 25 and 26, 2005, Mexico City.

26. Phone interview with the author, August 1, 2005.

27. *El Universal*, September 27, 2006.

28. *El Universal*, November 22, 2005.

29. The declining HIV incidence among young Mexicans can be found at the World Health Organization website. www.who.int/countryfocus/resources/ccsbrief_mexico_mex_06_en.pdf.

30. The future projections for the percentage of obese and overweight Mexicans in 2015 can be found at the World Health Organization website. http://www.who.int/ncd_surveillance/infobase/web/InfoBasePolicyMaker/reports/Reporter.aspx?id=1.

CHAPTER 12 — THE EVANGELICAL CHALLENGE

1. *The Financial Times*, February 22, 2005.

2. *Latin American Newsletters*, Mexico & NAFTA Report, December 2005, 5.

3. *Los Angeles Times*, December 15, 2005, A1.

4. All interviews in Ixmiquilpan that are quoted in this chapter were conducted on December 1, 2005.

5. *Reforma*, November 28, 2005.

6. Phone interview with the author, November 23, 2005.

7. *Reforma*, April 6, 2007, A1.

8. Paul Jeffrey, "Evangelicals and Catholics in Chiapas: Conflict and Reconciliation," *The Christian Century* 114, No. 6 (February 19, 1997), 195.

9. Elio Masferrer Kan, *¿Es del César o es de Dios? Un campo antropológico del campo religioso* (Mexico City: Plaza y Valdés Editores, 2004), 200–201.

10. *New York Times*, August 13, 2000, A3.

11. Cox News Service, March 24, 2005.

12. Interview with the author, November 28, 2005, Mexico City.

13. Luis (Lindy) Scott, *La sal de la tierra: Una historia socio-política de los evangélicos en la ciudad de México (1964–1991)* (Mexico City: Editorial Kyrios, 1991), 45.

14. John Mason Hart, *Empire and Revolution: The Americans in Mexico Since the Civil War* (Berkeley: University of California Press, 2002), 43.

15. Scott, *La sal de la tierra*, 99.

16. Ibid., 35.

17. Ibid., 37.

18. *Dallas Morning News*, December 20, 2003, 1G.

19. Paul Garner, *Porfirio Diaz* (London: Pearson Education Limited, 2001), 121–122.

20. *Los Angeles Times*, April 18, 1906.

21. A brief biographical sketch of Romana Carbajal de Valenzuela can be found at the website of the Unit for Historical and Social Studies of the Autonomous University of Ciudad Juárez. http://www.uacj.mx/UEHS/Mapa/IglesiaApostolica.htm.

22. A biography of Nava Castañeda can be found at the website of the charitable foundation that bears his name. http://www.acnavafoundation.com/biography.aspx.

23. Scott, *La sal de la tierra*, 140.

24. Ibid., 46.

25. Ibid., 35–36.

26. Interview with the author, December 15, 2005, Mexico City.

27. The statistics on Assemblies of God membership in Mexico can be found at the church's website. http://www.worldmissions.ag.org/downloads/PDR/CFH/agwm_current_facts_2_05.pdf.

CONCLUSION — AN INVADED COUNTRY

1. Interview with the author, November 26, 2005, Puebla.

2. Remarks by Jorge Yoma delivered at a breakfast in honor of Argentina's President Néstor Kirchner, Mexico City, August 1, 2007.

3. Alan Riding, *Distant Neighbors: A Portrait of the Mexicans* (New York: Alfred A. Knopf, 1985), 365.

4. Ibid., 371.

5. Alma Guillermoprieto, *The Heart That Bleeds: Latin America Now* (New York: Alfred A. Knopf, 1994), 244.

6. *Reforma*, December 18, 2003.

7. Interview with the author, May 14, 2005, Mexico City.

8. *New York Times*, July 4, 2005, A6.

9. John Mason Hart, *Empire and Revolution: The Americans in Mexico Since the Civil War* (Berkeley: University of California Press, 2002), 466–469.

10. *Reforma*, July 31, 2005.

11. Interview with the author, July 24, 2007, Mexico City.

12. Andrés Manuel López Obrador, *Un proyecto alternativo de nación: Hacía un cambio verdadero* (Mexico City: Grijalbo, 2004), 143.

13. Robert Pastor, "North America's Second Decade," *Foreign Affairs* 83 (1) (January/February 2004), 131.

14. *New York Times*, March 28, 2005, A17.

15. *Miami Herald*, August 26, 2007, 16A.

Selected Bibliography

Alarcón Segovia, Donato, and Samuel Ponce de León Rosales, eds. *El SIDA en México: 20 años de la epidemia.* Mexico City: El Colegio Nacional, 2003.

Babb, Sarah. *Managing Mexico: Economists from Nationalism to Neoliberalism.* Princeton, N.J.: Princeton University Press, 2001.

Camp, Roderic Ai. "Learning Democracy in Mexico and the United States." *Mexican Studies/Estudios Mexicanos* 19 (1) (Winter 2003).

———. *Mexico's Mandarins: Crafting a Power Elite for the Twenty-first Century.* Berkeley: University of California Press, 2002.

Castañeda, Jorge G. *Ex Mex: From Migrants to Immigrants.* New York: The New Press, 2007.

Cerutti, Mario. *Propietarios, empresarios y empresa en el norte de México.* Mexico City: Siglo Veintiuno Editores, 2000.

Christensen, Carol, and Thomas Christensen. *The U.S.-Mexican War.* San Francisco: Bay Books, 1998.

Cline, Howard. *The United States and Mexico.* New York: Atheneum, 1973.

Cosío Villegas, Daniel. *The United States versus Porfirio Diaz.* Lincoln: University of Nebraska Press, 1963.

Davidow, Jeffrey. *The U.S. and Mexico: The Bear and the Porcupine.* Princeton, NJ: Markus Wiener Publishers, 2004.

Davids, Jules. *American Political and Economic Penetration of Mexico, 1877–1920.* New York: Arno Press, 1976.

De la Garza, Rodolfo O. "Foreign Policy Comes Home: The Domestic Consequences of the Program for Mexican Communities Living in Foreign Countries." In *Bridging the Border: Transforming Mexico-U.S. Relations*, ed. Rodolfo O. de la Garza and Jesus Velasco. New York: Rowman and Littlefield, 1998.

De la Madrid Hurtado, Miguel. *Cambio de rumbo: Testimonio de una Presidencia, 1982–88*. Mexico City: Fondo de Cultura Económica, 2004.

De Zavala, Lorenzo. *Journey to the United States of North America*. Houston: Arte Público Press, 2005.

Fox, Vicente, and Rob Allyn. *Revolution of Hope: The Life, Faith, and Dreams of a Mexican President*. New York: Viking, 2007.

Frum, David. *The Right Man: An Inside Account of the Bush White House*. New York: Random House, 2003.

Fuentes, Carlos. *Nuevo tiempo mexicano*. Mexico City: Aguilar, 1994.

Garner, Paul. *Porfirio Diaz*. London: Pearson Education Limited, 2001.

Guillermoprieto, Alma. *The Heart That Bleeds: Latin America Now*. New York: Alfred A. Knopf, 1994.

Hale, Charles A. *Mexican Liberalism in the Age of Mora*. New York: Random House—Knopf, 1968.

———. *The Transformation of Liberalism in Late Nineteenth-Century Mexico*. Princeton, NJ: Princeton University Press, 1989.

Hart, John Mason. *Empire and Revolution: The Americans in Mexico since the Civil War*. Berkeley: University of California Press, 2002.

Hughes, Sallie. *Newsrooms in Conflict: Journalism and the Democratization of Mexico*. Pittsburgh: University of Pittsburgh Press, 2006.

Huntington, Samuel. "Clash of Civilizations." *Foreign Affairs* (summer 1993).

Kahlo, Guillermo. *Mexiko 1904*. Mexico City: Universidad Iberoamericana, 2002.

Katz, Friedrich. *The Life and Times of Pancho Villa*. Stanford, Calif.: Stanford University Press, 1998.

Krauze, Enrique. *Mexico: Biography of Power*. New York: HarperCollins, 1997.

———. "Mirándolos a ellos: Actitudes mexicanas frente a Estados Unidos." *Letras Libres* (June 2007).

López Obrador, Andrés Manuel. *Un proyecto alternativo de nación: Hacía un cambio verdadero*. Mexico City: Grijalbo, 2004.

Lowry, Malcolm. *Under the Volcano*. New York: J. B. Lippincott, 1965.

Masferrer Kan, Elio. *¿Es del César o es de Dios? Un campo antropológico del campo religioso*. Mexico City: Plaza y Valdés Editores, 2004.

Meyer, Lorenzo. "La visión general." In *Una historia contemporánea de México: Transformaciones y permanencias*, ed. Ilán Bizberg and Lorenzo Meyer. Mexico City: Océano, 2003.

Monsiváis, Carlos. *Los rituales del caos*. Mexico City: Procuraduría Federal del Consumidor y Ediciones Era, 1995.

———. *Mexican Postcards*. London: Verso, 1997.

———. "Muerte y resurrección del nacionalismo mexicano." *Nexos* 109 (1987).

Mora-Torres, Juan. *The Making of the Mexican Border: The State, Capitalism, and Society in Nuevo León, 1848–1910*. Austin: University of Texas Press, 2001.

Morris, Stephen D. *Gringolandia: Mexican Identity and Perceptions of the United States*. Lanham, Md.: Rowman & Littlefield, 2005.

Nava, Julian. *My Mexican-American Journey*. Houston: Arte Público Press, 2002.

Oppenheimer, Andrés. *Bordering on Chaos: Guerrillas, Stockbrokers, Politicians, and Mexico's Road to Prosperity*. Boston: Little, Brown, 1996.

Orme, William A., Jr., ed. *A Culture of Collusion: An Inside Look at the Mexican Press*. Miami: North-South Center Press, 1997.

Pastor, Robert A., and Jorge G. Castañeda. *Limits to Friendship: The United States and Mexico*. New York: Vintage Books, 1988.

Pastor, Robert. "North America's Second Decade." *Foreign Affairs* 83 (1) (January/February 2004).

Paz, Octavio. *The Labyrinth of Solitude, the Other Mexico, and Other Essays*. New York: Grove Press, 1985.

Preston, Julia and Samuel Dillon. *Opening Mexico: The Making of a Democracy*. New York: Farrar, Straus and Giroux, 2004.

Riding, Alan. *Distant Neighbors: A Portrait of the Mexicans*. New York: Alfred A. Knopf, 1985.

Riva Palacio, Raymundo. *La prensa de los jardines: Fortalezas y debilidades de los medios en México*. Mexico City: Plaza Janés, 2004.

Rubenstein, Anne. "Mass Media and Popular Culture in the Postrevolutionary Era." In *The Oxford History of Mexico*, ed. Michael C. Meyer and William H. Beezley. New York: Oxford University Press, 2000.

Scott, Lindy. *La sal de la tierra: Una historia socio-política de los evangélicos en la ciudad de México (1964–1991)*. Mexico City: Editorial Kyrios, 1991.

Index

Abrams, Elliot, 26, 27
Acá las tortas (film), 76–77
acquired immune deficiency
  syndrome. *See* AIDS
Aeroméxico, 160
agriculture, NAFTA's impact on, 96–99
Aguilar Camín, Héctor, 57, 61
Aguilar Zinser, Adolfo, 53, 56–58
AIDS (acquired immune deficiency
  syndrome), 7–8, 176–177, 210–214,
  218–219
Alamán, Lucas, 66–68
Alarcón Segovia, Donato, 211
Alemán, Miguel, 73
Alfa, 113
Almaraz Montaño, Gustavo, 50
Alonso, Manuel, 39
al Qaeda, 51, 60
Álvarez Reyes, Tadeo, 174
A.M. (newspaper), 124
American Association of Retired
  Persons (AARP), 144
American Biblical Society, 194
American College (Guadalajara),
  22, 105
American Express, 188
Americanization: acceleration of, with
  NAFTA, 83; as agent of change, 82;
  described, 6–7; efforts to contain,
  47–48; evolving Mexican attitudes
  toward United States, re globaliza-
  tion, 11; history of, 8–12; influence of
  U.S. traditions, resources, values, 7,
  42–50, 236–238; symptoms of, 48;

technocrats and, 4–6; term described,
  45–46; and U.S. domination of
  Mexican economy, 7
American University, 78, 242
Anderson, Jack, 25
Aramburuzabala, María Asunción,
  108–109
Arango family, 6–7
Arellano Félix, Benjamín, 54
Aronson, Bernard, 41
Asarco, 107
Aspe, Pedro, 5
Assemblies of God, 231–233
Associated Press, 126
Austin, Stephen F., 137
Autonomous Technological Institute of
  Mexico (ITAM), 58, 111–113, 115
Autonomous University of Zacatecas,
  167, 169, 171, 172
Ávila Camacho, Manuel, 73
Ayala, Ramón, 74
Azcárraga Jean, Emilio, 103–108, 114, 115,
  125–126
Azcárraga Milmo, Emilio, 103–106,
  115, 125

Babb, Sarah, 112–113
baby boomers in Mexico, 142–147
Banco Azteca, 110
Banco de México, 112
Bank of America, 188
Barahona, Rosaura, 197
Bartlett, Manuel, 40
Basañez, Miguel, 78

Becerra Mizuno, Rodrigo, 114–115
bin Laden, Osama, 51, 60, 153
Black, Roger, 122
Blanco Pasillas, Delfino, 173–174, 174–175
Blockbuster, 93
Bodega Aurrerá, 91–92
Boeing, 149
border fence, 178–179, 243
Boston University (BU), 114–115
Boy Heroes, 57, 71, 73
bracero guest-worker program, 168
Breton, André, 239
Brokaw, Kaye, 149
Brokaw, Rick, 149
Bronfman, Marío, 212–213
Brooks, Tatiana, 154–155
Buffet, Jimmy, 106–107
Buffet, Warren, 100
Burger King, 93
Burnet, David G., 65
Burton, Richard, 161
Bush, George Prescott, 138
Bush, George W., 49, 51–54, 58, 62, 138,
    146, 165, 178–179, 182, 225, 231, 239,
    242–243
Bush, Laura, 109
businessmen, new breed of, 103–117

Cabo San Lucas, 141, 160–161
Calderón, Felipe, 4, 49, 97, 123, 126, 129,
    165–166, 179, 226, 241
Calles, Plutarco Elías, 71–72, 76, 226
Camarena Salazar, Enrique "Kiki," 25, 34
Cambio de rumbo (A Change of Course;
    de la Madrid), 27
Camp, Roderic Ai, 80, 108, 114, 181
Canada, 41, 51, 79
Cancún, Mexico, 151, 161, 163–164
Cantú Treviño, Manuel, 193
Carbajal de Valenzuela,
    Romana, 229
Cárdenas, Cuauhtémoc, 225
Cárdenas, Lázaro, 47, 72–73, 226
Cárdenas Guillén, Osiel, 54, 198
Cargill, 97
Carlson, Marianne, 144–146
Carnegie Endowment for International
    Peace, 96
Carranza, Venustiano, 71, 75
Carso conglomerate, 10
Carter, Jimmy, 10, 20, 78, 242
Carville, James, 49

Casagranda, Mark, 160–161
Casey, William, 26
Castañeda, Jorge G., 10, 20, 27, 28, 37,
    51–54, 55, 58, 239
Castro, Fidel, 4, 44, 52–53, 56, 74
Catholic Church. *See* Roman Catholics
Cavazos Garza, Israel, 189
CBS News, 30
CEMEX, 99–100, 107, 115–116, 188
Center for Development Research, 14, 61
Center for North American Studies
    (American University), 78
Center for Nutritional and Health
    Research (National Public Health
    Institute), 217
Centers for Disease Control (CDC), 210
Centers for Juvenile Rehabilitation (CIJ),
    206–207, 219
Central Mexican Railway, 2
"Century of the Americas," 51
Cerda, Rogelio, 199
Cervecería Cuauhtémoc, 100, 193
Chávez, Hugo, 59, 240
Chavira, Ricardo, 36
Chiapas, Mexico, 224–226
Chicago Council on Foreign
    Relations, 79
"Chicano," 22
Chile, 6
Christian Friendship, 232
Chrysler, 188
Churchill, Winston, 1
Church of the Apostolic Faith, 229
Church of Jesus Christ of Latter-Day
    Saints, 137–138
CIE (entertainment company), 130
científicos (scientists), 2, 3–4, 5
Cifra, 91
CIJ. *See* Centers for Juvenile
    Rehabilitation
Citigroup, 7, 237
Civil War (U.S.), 184, 191–192
Clark-Alfaro, Victor, 208
Clayton, Powell, 3
Cline, Howard, 74
Clinton, Bill, 40, 42, 49, 131
Clouthier, Manuel, 195
Clouthier Carrillo, Tatiana, 195–196
CNN, 126, 209, 242
Coca-Cola, 39, 188
cocaine, 208. *See also* drugs
Colegio de México, 9, 112, 119

Cole Guerrero, Lizzie, 156–157
Collateral International, 140
Colombia, 24
Comercial Mexicana, 88, 92
Commission for the Defense of the
    Spanish Language, 47
Committee to Protect Journalists, 124
Communist Party, Mexican, 52
Companía Fundidora de Fierro y Acero
    de México, 32, 194
CompUSA, 116
Comte, Auguste, 3
CONADIC. *See* National
    Anti-Addiction Council
CONASUPO. *See* National Company for
    Popular Subsistence
Confraternice. *See* National
    Confraternity of Evangelical Christian
    Churches
Congregationalists, 227
Conley, Edward, 46
consumerism, 7, 9, 28, 42–50, 244
Contadora Group, 24, 32
Contreras, Caroline, 23, 29
Contreras, Claire, 35, 114
Contreras, Joe, 21–22
Contreras, Olga, 21–22
Contreras Castillo, Sergio, 98
Coolidge, Calvin, 72
Cornell University, 188
Cortés, Hernán, 11, 168
Cortés Camarillo, Félix, 125
Cortina, Jerónimo, 181
Cosío Villegas, Daniel, 70
Cosman, Madeline, 209
Costco, 88–92
Council on Hemispheric Affairs, 95
courtroom trials, 195
crack cocaine, 205–206. *See also*
    drugs
Creel, Santiago, 53, 225
Creevan, Nancy, 150
crime problem, 14, 146, 150, 159–161,
    177–179, 197–201
Cronkite, Walter, 30
crystal methamphetamine, 208–209. *See
    also* drugs
Cuauhtémoc brewery, 100, 193
Cuba, 6, 32, 52–53, 74
Cuban Revolution, 4, 240
cultural identity, 87–91, 238–240
cultural movement, 46–47

*Culture of Empire: American Writers,
    Mexico, and Mexican Immigrants,
    1880–1930* (Rodriguez), 46

Daniel, Jean, 61
Danilo Ruiz, Eduardo, 121–122
D'Artigues, Katia, 45
Dartmouth College, Tuck School,
    114–116
Davidow, Jeffrey, 54, 108, 128–129
DEA. *See* United States: Drug
    Enforcement Administration
de Alba Cruz, José, 162
de Ampudia, Pedro, 190
Dehesa, Germán, 120
de la Cajiga, Carolina, 147–148
de la Cruz, Manuel, 170, 172
de la Cruz, Marcial, 229
de la Garza, Rodolfo O., 79, 181
de la Granja, Juan, 96
de la Madrid, Miguel, 111, 155;
    anointment of Salinas de Gortari, 31;
    anti-American sentiment, 32–33, 42,
    54, 56, 198; economic challenges, 35;
    foreign policy stance, 24, 25–27, 30;
    GATT treaty, 36; *Newsweek* interview,
    39; reaction to emergency assistance,
    14; warming trend toward United
    States, 34
de Llano, Rodrigo, 126
de Montemayor, Diego, 189
dengue fever, 209
Derbez, Luis Ernesto, 23
de Zavala, Lorenzo, 64–66, 69
diabetes, 215
Díaz, Porfirio, 15, 229; and American
    population in Mexico, 137; Angel
    monument, 196; bilateral relationship
    with United States, 6, 42, 46, 68–89,
    244; economic dependence on United
    States, 93; embrace of globalization,
    1–2, 4; growth of positivism under,
    3–4; influence of *científicos,* 5;
    prescience of, 6–8; stance toward
    non-Catholic Christians, 228.
    See also Porfiriato
Díaz Negrete, David Bruno, 207, 219
Díaz Ordaz, Gustavo, 47, 74
Díaz Redondo, Regino, 30
Dinan, Stephen, 165
diseases, 205–234. *See also specific
    diseases*

Distant Neighbors: A Portrait of the Mexicans (Riding), 23, 237–238
Dobbs, Lou, 178, 209–210, 242
Doolin, Chris, 136–137
Dosamantes, María de Jesús, 190–191
Dow Jones, 118
Dresser, Denise, 57–58
Drug Enforcement Administration. *See* United States: Drug Enforcement Administration
drugs: as growth industry, 35; recreational use, 7–8, 205–209; tensions over drug trafficking, 25–26, 42, 54, 80, 159, 177–179, 209, 219; and violence, 159–161, 197–201; war against, 34–35

Ealy Ortiz, Juan Francisco, 124
earthquake (Mexico City), 14, 33
Ebrard, Marcelo, 240, 241
Echeverría, Luis, 75, 120, 155
economic policy, 4, 28, 57–59, 61, 93–96. *See also* North American Free Trade Agreement
Educating Your Woman (radio talk show), 197
education of Mexicans in United States, 4, 60–61, 78, 111–117, 118, 121–122, 130–131, 187
Eisenhower, Dwight, 74
Elektra appliance store chain, 110
Elizondo Jasso, Sofía, 185–186
El Salvador, 24
Emmanuel Evangelistic Center, 232
energy markets, 52
Enríquez Savignac, Antonio, 155
e.n.s.a.m.b.l.e (Internet blog), 11
Ensler, Eve, 147
environmental issues, 7
Episcopalian Church, 227
Este País (magazine), 77
European Union (EU), 242, 243
Evangelical challenge, 220–234
Excélsior (newspaper), 30, 119, 121, 122, 126
expatriate community in Mexico, 135–150

Falwell, Jerry, 225
Farela Gutiérrez, Arturo, 225–226, 231–233
Farías, María Emilia, 50
Fasci, Aldo, 199

fast-food culture, 214–218
Fastlicht, Sharon, 105
FCC. *See* Federal Communications Commission
Federal Agency of Investigation, 159
Federal Communications Commission (FCC), 104
Federal Constitution of the United Mexican States, 64
Federal Electoral Institute (IFE), 172
fence (border), 178–179, 243
Fernández de Castro, Rafael, 109, 243
film industry. *See* motion picture industry
El Financiero (newspaper), 119, 124, 126, 127
Florida International University, 111
Forbes (magazine), 100, 110
Ford, Henry, 110
Foreign Affairs (journal), 242; *Foreign Affairs en Español,* 109, 180
foreign debt, 72
foreign policy, 5, 23–24, 50–55, 57–59. *See also* North American Free Trade Agreement
Fortune (magazine), 188
Four Seasons hotel (Punta Mita), 162
Fox, Charles Parham, 228
Fox, Vicente, 80, 129, 220; advisors/cabinet members, 10, 28, 37, 49–50, 112, 115; AIDS prevention and control policies, 211; broadcast bias, 126; immigration agreement, 243; relationship with Cuba, 52; servility syndrome, 55–57; strategic relationship with United States, 50–55, 241, 242; television license lobbying efforts, 101; views on remittances, 166–184
Fox News, 242
Franco, Francisco, 6
freedom of information law, 7
free trade, 4, 7, 41. *See also* North American Free Trade Agreement
Free Trade of the Americas Area treaty, 59
free trade zone, 78–80
Frenk, Julio, 206
Frey, Butch, 231, 233
Friedman, Milton, 112
Frum, David, 52
Fuentes, Carlos, 70
Fuentes, Guillermo, 232
Fuentes-Berain, Rossana, 29, 119–120, 123–124, 197, 243

gang members, 177
García, Armando, 188
García, Gerardo, 158
García Castro, María, 79
García Medina, Amalia, 169, 171
García Sánchez, Leonel, 151
García Zamora, Rodolfo, 167–168, 169, 177
Gardner, Mary, 121
Garro, Elena, 89
Garza, Francisco, 188
Garza, Isaac, 193
Garza, Ramón Alberto, 118–119, 187
Garza, Tony, 55, 59, 108–109, 181
Garza Medina, Dionisio, 113–114
Garza Sada, Eugenio, 194–195
Garza y Garza, Marcelo, 198–199
Gavin, John, 25, 27, 34, 127–128
Gavras, Constance, 145–146, 150
General Agreement on Trade and Tariffs (GATT), 36
General Electric, 188
Germany, 6, 181
Gil Díaz, Francisco, 111, 112, 115
Giuliani, Rudolph, 14
globalization, 1–2, 11
global warming, 7
Goff, Charlie, 90
Gómez, Bernardo, 103, 106
Gómez, Pablo, 50
Gómez Zalce, Marcela, 129–132
González Parás, José Natividad, 186, 199–200
Good Neighbor policy, 72
Gore, Al, 49, 138
Gorman, Paul, 24–25, 31
Granados Chapa, Miguel Ángel, 130
Gran Fundición Nacional smelter, 193
Grant, Ulysses S., 69
Great Britain, 2
Great Depression, 138
"gringofication," 197
gringophile, 69
Una gringuita en México (film), 76
Grupo Cydsa, 113
Grupo Imagen (media company), 131
Grupo México, 107
Guerrero, Noé Gerardo Nicolás, 230
Guerrero, Vicente, 64–65
Guerrero Galván, Jesús, 89
Guerrero Goff, Flor, 89–93, 102
Guggenheim, Meyer, 193

Guggenheim family, 2
Guillermoprieto, Alma, 238
Gulf Cartel, 198
Gutiérrez, Abel, 157–158

Haar, Jerry, 111
Hair (musical), 47
Hale, Charles A., 64
Hart, John Mason, 240
Harvard University, 4, 57, 78, 82, 114, 131
Hearst, William Randolph, 69
Hechos de la Noche (television news program), 125
Helms, Jesse, 31, 32–33, 35
hepatitis, 209
Heredia Zubieta, Carlos, 95
Her Husband's Trademark (film), 47
Hernández, Jaime, 143
Hernández, María, 157
Hernández, Mariano, 191
Hernández Reseldes, Miguel Darío, 216
Hewlett Foundation, 80
Hickey, James, 227
HIV (human immunodeficiency virus), 177, 210–213, 218–219
homosexual couples, 149–150, 244
Honan, Gloria, 162
Hoover, Herbert, 138
Hotel Casino de la Selva (Cuernavaca), 87–90, 92
Houston, Texas, 183
Huerta, Victoriano, 70–71, 127
human immunodeficiency virus. See HIV
Huntington, Samuel, 57
Hurricane Dean, 164
Hurricane Gilbert, 156, 163
Hurricane Katrina, 163
Hurricane Wilma, 163–164
"hybridization" of Mexico, 11

Iacono, Francesco, 163–164
Ibero-American University, 130, 206
IBM, 188
ICON Vallarta (condominium project), 139–140
IDB. See Inter-American Development Bank
IFE. See Federal Electoral Institute
Imagen News (television news program), 131–132

IMF. *See* International Monetary Fund
immigrants, 12, 51–52, 171–173, 243. *See also* remittances; Two for One program; undocumented workers
El Imparcial (newspaper), 124, 194
Independent Pentecostal Christian Church, 222
information, freedom of, 7
Institute of the Americas, 129
Institutional Revolutionary Party. *See* PRI
Inter-American Development Bank (IDB), 167, 181
Inter-American Mutual Assistance defense treaty, 53
Interdenominational Christian Church, 226
Internal Revenue Service (IRS), 105
International Business Ethics Institute, 116
International Court of Justice, 53–54
International Monetary Fund (IMF), 5, 34
International Research Center (IRC), 208
Iran Contra scandal, 34, 35
Iraq, 56, 58, 242
IRC. *See* International Research Center
Islas, Jesús, 227
Islas Medina, Raúl, 176
Israel, 63
ITAM. *See* Autonomous Technological Institute of Mexico
ITESM. *See* Monterrey Technological Institute for Higher Education

Jackson, Andrew, 64, 65
Jeter, Derek, 176
Johnson, Lyndon B., 47
José Cuervo (tequila), 106
La Jornada (newspaper), 30, 119, 121, 124, 127, 128
Journey to the United States of North America (de Zavala), 65
Juárez, Benito, 3, 67, 227–228
judicial process, 195, 244
JUMEX, 108
Junco de la Vega, Alejandro, 118–122, 124
Junco de la Vega, Rodolfo, 119, 187
Junco family, 118, 187
junk-food culture, 43

Katz, Friedrich, 75
Kennedy, John F., 1, 54
Kerry, Diana, 138
Kerry, John, 138, 225
Kirchner, Néstor, 237
Kissinger, Henry, 42
Kosovo, 63
Krauze, Enrique, 5

Labastida, Francisco, 39, 49
The Labyrinth of Solitude (Paz), 19, 82
language, 7, 20–21, 39–40, 42, 45, 47, 129–132, 146
Leno, Jay, 44
Limantour, José Yves, 3, 5
Lincoln, Abraham, 191
Lindbergh, Charles, 72
Living in Mexico (television news program), 131
Loaiza, Esteban, 176
lobbyists, 49–50
López, José Manuel, 217
López Mateos, Adolfo, 74
López Obrador, Andrés Manuel, 10, 14, 49, 98–99, 101, 123, 126, 220–221, 226, 239–242
López Portillo, José, 27, 30, 120
Los Angeles Times (newspaper), 118, 228
lower classes, 77–78, 81
Loweís, 189
Lowry, Malcolm, 87–88
Loza, Francisco, 162
Lozano Muñoz, Reyes, 174
Luxor, Egypt, 164

machismo attitude, 146
Madero, Evaristo, 68
Madero, Francisco I., 69, 70–71, 113, 127
Madrazo, Roberto, 226
Maid of Monterrey, 191
Mancera, Miguel, 112
Manning, Peyton, 59
Marcos, Subcomandante, 239–240
Market and Opinion Research International (MORI), 77–78
Martí, Fernando, 153, 157
Martínez, Enrique, 225
Martínez, Javier, 158
Maseca, 97, 99
Masferrer, Elio, 222
Massachusetts Institute of Technology (MIT), 113, 195

Maximilian (emperor), 67, 227
Mayan culture, 11
MBA degree, importance of American, 113–117
McDonald's, 90–91, 93
McKinsey (consulting group), 115
McVea, Susan, 163–164
Medina Mora, Eduardo, 209
megastores, invasion of, 89–91
Mena, Damaris, 158
Méndez, Mary Carmen, 236
Menges, Constantine, 25
Methodists, 227–228
Mexican Council for Science and Technology, 55
Mexican Diabetes Federation, 215–216
Mexican dream, 135–147
Mexicanization, 13, 75
Mexican National Restaurant Chamber, 216
Mexican Revolution, 73, 173; and Americans living in Mexico, 137–138; anti-American sentiment of, 69–70, 75; eruption of, 2, 3–4, 46–47; exodus of people during, 229; height of, 36; overthrow of Díaz, 68; religious clauses following, 223
Mexican War, 8, 12, 26, 63–66, 71, 184, 189–190, 192
Mexico: ambivalence toward United States, 63–83; American immigrants in, 135–150; businessmen, new breed of, 103–117; cultural differences, 9; cultural identity, 87–91, 238–240; democratic reform, 82; direct investment in United States, 106–108; diseases from United States, 205–234; exports from, 7; feuds with United States, 23–31; Health Ministry, 206, 215; independence from Spain, 3, 63; influence of U.S. founding fathers on, 63–64; new media, 118–132; Public Education Ministry, 207; religious challenge, 220–234; role of U.S. companies in economy, 7, 188–189; Spanish heritage, 10–11; ties with Cuba, 6; tourism industry, 151–164; views on democracy and foreign policy, 79–80
Mexico—My Dream program, 140
México Unido Contra la Delincuencia, 206, 207

Meyer, Lorenzo, 9–10, 94, 238
Meyer L'Epee, Consuelo, 113
Miami Herald (newspaper), 127
Michoacán, Mexico, 165, 167–168, 182
Microsoft, 116
middle class, 28–29, 75, 82, 109–111, 237
Milenio (newspaper), 129–130
military assistance program, 74
Milmo, Patricio. *See* Mullins, Patrick
Minello, Nelson, 212
mining companies, 69
minorities, rights of, 82
Minsa, 97
Miss Universe beauty pageant, 60
MIT. *See* Massachusetts Institute of Technology
Moctezuma Longoria, Miguel, 171–172
Modelo brewery, 99, 106–109, 116
Monsiváis, Carlos, 5, 12, 60, 80–83, 236
Monterrey, Nuevo León, 183–201
Monterrey Daily News (newspaper), 194
Monterrey Era (newspaper), 191
El Monterrey News (newspaper), 194
Monterrery Technological Institute for Higher Education (ITESM), 22, 106, 185
Montes de Oca, Luis, 72
Mora, José María Luís, 64, 69
Morales Pérez, Desiderio, 189
"moral renovation," 31, 35
Moreno Uriegas, María de los Ángeles, 225
Morera de Galindo, María Elena, 206
Morgan, J. P., 2, 72
MORI. *See* Market and Opinion Research International
Mormon Church, 69–70, 228
Morris, Dick, 49
Morris, Stephen, 76, 79
Morrow, Dwight, 72
Mota, Carlos, 45
motion picture industry, 47, 76, 81
Mullins, Patrick, 192
Múzquiz, Oscar, 197

NAFTA. *See* North American Free Trade Agreement
NAFTA's Promise and Reality: Lessons from Mexico for the Hemisphere, 96
Namibia, 32
Napoleon III, 67
narcotics. *See* drugs

NASCAR races, 44–45
Nassirzadeh, Amir, 161
The National (newspaper), 104
National Action Party. See PAN
National Anti-Addiction Council
    (CONADIC), 206
National Autonomous University of
    Mexico (UNAM), 111
National Center for HIV/AIDS
    Prevention and Control, 211
National Company for Popular
    Subsistence (CONASUPO), 97
National Confraternity of Evangelical
    Christian Churches (Confraternice),
    225–226, 231, 233
National Corn Processors Chamber, 216
nationalism, 5, 57–59, 79
National Population Council, 169
National Public Health Institute,
    215, 217
National Revolutionary Party, 76. See
    also PRI
National School of Anthropology and
    History, 222
Nava, Julian, 20
Nava Castañeda, Antonio, 229
Navejas, Rigoberto, 174
Nebel, Carl, 8
Negroponte, John, 40–42
Nepomuceno, Alejandro, 222
New Mexico, 70
The News (newspaper), 131
news media, 30, 31, 118–132
Newsweek (magazine), 20, 23, 25, 39, 122
The New Yorker (magazine), 9, 12, 238
New York Stock Exchange, 116
New York Times (newspaper), 23, 126,
    130, 167, 243
Nexos (magazine), 51, 61
Nicaragua, 24, 27, 32, 34, 42, 72
Nicklaus, Jack, 161
Nieto Silva, Daniel, 92
The Night of the Iguana (film), 61
Nixon, Richard, 55, 74
Norman, Greg, 161
El Norte, 118, 121–122, 187, 197
North American Free Trade Agreement
    (NAFTA): and acceleration of
    Americanization, 83; culmination of,
    36; double-edged sword of free trade,
    87–102; effect of, 7; flow of U.S.
    investment under, 48, 241; impact on

Mexican agriculture, 96–99; Mexico's
    direct investment in United States
    under, 106–108; Mexico's economic
    fortunes tied to U.S., 4–5, 76, 93–96;
    Monterrey as laboratory for, 189;
    negotiation of, 41; real estate property
    ownership laws, 141–142; signing of,
    38; summit, 243; tangible legacies,
    42–50
North American Union, 241, 243
Northern Episcopalian Church, 227
Northern Methodists, 227
Le Nouvel Observateur (newspaper), 61
Nuncio, Abraham, 184

Oasis Viva hotel (Cancún), 157
Obama, Barack, 244
obesity, 7–8, 214–219
Obregón, Álvaro, 47, 71
Ochoa-Reza, Enrique, 181
oil industry, 4, 12, 52, 71–73
Olympics (Mexico City, 1968), 47
Omni Cancún Hotel and Villas, 156
open markets, 4. See also North
    American Free Trade Agreement
Operation Intercept, 25–26
OPIC. See Overseas Private Investment
    Corporation
O'Reilly, Bill, 242
Organisation for Economic
    Co-operation and Development
    (OECD), 100, 215
Orme, William, Jr., 124–125
Orozco, Pascual, 69
Ortega, Daniel, 27
Ortega, Joel, 208
Ortiz, Francisco, 49, 147–148
Osorio Chong, Miguel Ángel, 220
Overseas Private Investment
    Corporation (OPIC), 55

pachucos (gang members), 19–20
Pacific Gas and Electric, 144
Palacios, Octavio, 106
Palavicini, Félix, 230
Palestine, 63
Palinski, Becky, 142–144, 150
Palinski, Julian, 142–144
PAN (National Action Party), 33, 39–40,
    49, 80, 126, 195, 220, 225, 240
Panama, 24

Paniagua, Eduardo, 159
Paranagua, Paulo Antonio, 47
Paredes, Mariano, 190
Party of the Democratic Revolution.
    See PRD
Pastor, Robert, 10, 78, 242
La Patria (newspaper), 68–69
Paz, Octavio, 9, 12, 19, 80, 82, 89
Peace Corps, 54–55
Pentecostalism, 222, 228–229
Perenchio, Jerry, 107
Pérez, Jorge, 138–140
Peronist party, 238
Perry, Rick, 186
Pershing, John J., 70
Petricioli, Gustavo, 111–112
Pew Hispanic Center, 167
Philadelphia Smelting and Refining
    Company, 193
Pipsa, 120
PNR. *See* National Revolutionary Party
polio, 209
Polk, James, 64, 66, 189–190
Porfiriato, 2, 3–4, 67–70, 137, 235. *See also*
    Díaz, Porfirio
positivism, 3–4
PRD (Party of the Democratic
    Revolution), 50, 95, 172, 220–221,
    225, 239
La Prensa (newspaper), 45
Presley, Elvis, 81
PRI (Institutional Revolutionary Party):
    challenges from PAN, 33; complicity
    with Cuban dictatorship, 53;
    -controlled union of newspaper
    vendors, 120; economic nationalism,
    4; elections, 38–40, 49, 186, 225, 230,
    240; favored in broadcast coverage,
    125–126; middle class and, 109;
    Newsweek censure of, 26; "perfect
    dictatorship," 244; policies toward
    United States, 4, 237–239; prominence,
    220–221; relationship with United
    States, 54; and remittances, 172; ruling
    in the 1970s, 9; views of Evangelical
    power base, 224–226, 234; voting
    fraud, 31
Price Waterhouse Coopers, 188
Primera Iglesia, 194
Primero soy mexicano (film), 76
privatization of government-run
    enterprises, 4

PROCAMPO program, 98
Proceso (magazine), 30, 41, 56, 109, 124,
    126–127
Procter and Gamble, 49
productivity (concept of), 29
Protestantism, 221, 228. *See also*
    specific churches
Puerto Vallarta, Mexico, 141
Pulp Fiction (film), 205
punctuality (concept of), 29
Punta Mita, Mexico, 141
Purdie, Samuel A., 227

Quakers, 227

racism, 20, 35–36
railroad age, 184
Ramones, Adal, 44
Ramos, Jorge, 44
Ranchos Unidos de Fresnillo, 170
Rankin, Melinda, 194
Reagan, Ronald, 24, 27, 31–36, 40, 42,
    128, 198
real estate property ownership laws,
    141–142
Realpolitik, 42
Rebeldes de Roc, 46
Reed, Ralph, 225
Reforma (newspaper), 109, 118–130,
    187–188, 208, 222, 238
Reform Laws (1850s), 227
regiomontanos mindset, 183, 186–189
remittances, 165–182, 244
Renau, Josep, 87
The Related Group, 138–139
Residencial Bay View Grand (Cancún
    condominium complex), 141
ReVista (journal), 82
Riding, Alan, 23, 26, 62, 237–238
Riley, Henry, 227
Rios, Lázaro, 119, 124
Rios Gutiérrez, Mario, 199
Rius Palace, 160
Riva Palacio, Raymundo, 123–124
Rivera, Diego, 81, 147
Rivera Carrera, Norberto, 223
Rivera Dommarco, Juan, 217–218
Rivero, Marcelo, 108
Rivero, Valentín, 191
Rocher, Pedro, 205–206, 207
Rockefeller family, 2

Rodriguez, Abelardo, 87
Rodríguez, Alejandra, 180
Rodríguez, Alfonso, 179–180
Rodriguez, Gilbert G., 46
Rodríguez, Hortensía, 180
Rodríguez Ruvalcaba, Silvia, 175–176
Rodríguez Saldaña, Joel, 215–216
Román, Edgar, 213–214
Roman Catholics, 67–68, 221, 222–226,
    228, 230
Roosevelt, Franklin D., 72–73
Rubio, Luis, 14, 61
Ruesga, David Genaro, 229
Ruiz-Palacios, Guillermo, 210–211

Saban, Haim, 107
Sada, Andrés Marcelo, 113
Sada, Francisco, 193
Sáenz, Moisés, 226
Saint-Simon, Henri de, 3
Salazar, Ana María, 131–132
Salazar Mendiguchía, Pablo, 225
Salinas de Gortari, Carlos: de la
    Madrid's anointment of, 31;
    economic policy, 57, 91; embrace of
    free trade, 7, 12, 41, 114; government
    control of news media, 120; legacy of,
    78–80; privatization programs, 110;
    rise to power, 4–6, 38; ties to Catholic
    Church, 226
Salinas de Gortari, Raúl, 110
Salinas Pliego, Ricardo, 110–111, 114, 116
Salt of the Earth (Scott), 229
Salvador Zubirán National Institute for
    Medical and Nutritional Sciences, 210
Sam's Club, 92
San Diego State University, 208
Sandinista regime, 24, 27, 32, 42
San José del Cabo, Cancún, Mexico, 160
Santa Anna, Antonio López de,
    65, 75, 137
Sayulita, Mexico, 161–162
Schwarzenegger, Arnold, 243
Scott, Lindy, 229, 230
Scott, Winfield, 191
SEC. See Securities and Exchange
    Commission
Securities and Exchange Commission
    (SEC), 110–111, 116
Sepúlveda Amor, Bernardo, 32
Seward, William, 192
Seymour, William, 228–229

Sheffield, James, 71
Sierra Méndez, Justo, 68
Sierra O'Reilly, Justo, 67
Silva-Herzog, Jesús, 11, 113
Simmons mattresses, 188
Sinaloa cartel, 199
Slim, Carlos, 10, 14, 100–101, 107, 116
Smith, Charlie, 149
Smith, John Henry, 228
Smith, Rachel, 60
social diseases, 205–234. See also
    specific diseases
Social Security and Services Institute for
    Government Employees (ISSSTE), 214
Society of Newspaper Design, 122
Solís, Leopoldo, 112
South Africa, 32
Southdown, Inc., 107, 187
Southern Peru Copper Co., 107
sovereignty, 79
Spain, 3, 6, 10–11
Spanglish, 77
Spanish International Network, 103
spring break tourists, 154–163
Stanford University, 113–114, 122, 187
Stephens, John L., 227
Stewart Title Guaranty Company,
    140–141
Stillman, Charles, 192
Suárez, Manuel, 87–88
subsidies, 97
Suburbia department stores, 92
La sucesión presidencial en 1910
    (Madero), 69
Superama supermarkets, 92
Suro, Roberto, 179

Tarantino, Quentin, 205
Taylor, Liz, 161
Taylor, Zachary, 190
technocrats and Americanization, 4–6
Teen Tops, 46
Telcel (cellphone company), 152
telecommunications, 43, 100–101
telenovelas, 103
Telesur, 240
Televisa, 30, 100, 103–108, 114–115,
    125, 237
television, 44
Telmex, 10, 100–101
terrorism, 51–52, 54, 56, 79, 157
Texas, 12, 65

Texas A&M, 130
Thalia (singer), 14
Thelen, David, 5
Thoman, R. J., 141
Three-for-One program, 170–171, 174, 180
Thurman, Uma, 205
El Tiempo (newspaper), 68
Tlatelolco massacre (1968), 47
To a Young Mexican Economist
    (Silva-Herzog), 113
Toledo, Francisco, 90–91
Torres García, Bertín, 98
tourism industry, 151–164
Townsend, W. Cameron, 226
travel advisory, 200
Travolta, John, 205
Treaty of Guadalupe Hidalgo (1848), 184
Trevi, Gloria, 111
Trujillo, Magdalena, 157–158
Truman, Harry, 73
Truth, Integrity, and Democracy,
    225–226
tuberculosis, 209
Turkey, 181
TV Azteca, 101, 110–111, 114, 125
Two-for-One program, 170

UNAM. *See* National Autonomous
    University of Mexico
Under the Volcano (Lowry), 87
undocumented workers: backlash
    against, 13; and border fence, 178–179,
    243; concerns over influx of, 26;
    legalization status of, 50–51; physical
    dangers of crossing U.S. border, 12;
    reduction of, 80; rights of, 53–54. *See
    also* immigrants
Unefon cellphone company, 110
United Nations: Commission on Human
    Rights, 52; Security Council, 58;
    strengthening of, 79; UNESCO, 235
United States: ambivalence toward,
    63–83; Americans living in Mexico,
    135–150; anti-American sentiment,
    31–33, 59–62, 70–72, 75–77, 149–150;
    attraction of, 12–15; bilateral
    relationship with Mexico, 51; border
    fence, 178–179, 243; Commerce
    Department, 107; Drug Enforcement
    Administration, 25; economic link
    with Mexico, 58; feuds with Mexico,
    23–31 (*see also* Mexican War);

influence on social mores, foreign
    policy, consumer tastes, health, 7;
    influence on trade and investments, 2,
    106; Mexicanization process, 13;
    Mexico's direct investment in,
    106–108; occupation of Mexico, 66–67;
    pop culture, 44; post–Mexican War,
    66–67; role of U.S. companies in
    Mexican economy, 7, 188–189; roots of
    Mexican Evangelicalism, 227–229;
    State Department, 138, 140; warming
    trend toward, 33–36
El Universal (newspaper), 60, 122, 124,
    126, 129, 230
University of California, 19, 60, 113,
    130, 131
University of Chicago, 112, 113
University of Houston, 240
University of Southern California, 179
University of Texas, 118, 121, 188
Univisión network, 103–107
urbanization and social ills, 159–161
USA Today (newspaper), 118, 122
U.S.-Mexican War. *See* Mexican War

The Vagina Monologues (Ensler), 147
Valenzuela, Fernando, 176
Vara, Abelardo, 155–157, 160
Vargas Llosa, Mario, 9
Vasconcelos, José, 47
Venezuela, 24
Victoria, Guadalupe, 64
Vidriera Monterrey, 193
25 Horas (television news program),
    125–126
Vigil, José María, 68–69
Villa, Pancho, 8, 12, 70–71, 229
Villamil, Jenaro, 126–127
Villanueva, Mario, 159
violence. *See* crime problem
Vips restaurants, 92
von Raab, William, 26
voting fraud, 31
La Voz del Caribe (newspaper), 158

Wall Street Journal (newspaper), 118, 130
Wal-Mart, 7, 55–57, 91–93, 237
War of the Castes (1847), 67
War of the Reform (1858–1861), 67
Washington Consensus, 5
Washington Post (newspaper), 25, 130
Washington Times (newspaper), 165

West, Emily, 65
Weymouth, Lally, 38–40
W Hotel (Mexico City), 139
Wilson, Henry Lane, 127
Wilson, Woodrow, 8, 36, 70–71, 75
women, rights of, 82, 244
World Bank, 5, 95
World Health Organization, 215, 219
World War I, 71, 75
World War II, 73
Wornat, Olga, 48

Yale University, 60, 111, 113
Yépez, Heriberto, 11
Yoma, Jorge, 237

Young Men's Christian Association
  (YMCA), 230
Yunus, Muhammad, 111

Zabludovsky, Jacobo, 30, 125–126
Zacatecas, Mexico, 167–169, 173–177
Zambrano, Lorenzo, 107, 188
Zapata, Emiliano, 71
Zapata, Eufemio, 71
Zapatista rebellion, 40, 78, 89, 224,
  239–240
Zedillo, Ernesto, 5, 39–40, 45, 60,
  112, 128
"zero tolerance" approach, 14

About the Author

JOSEPH CONTRERAS reported from over fifty countries on five continents during a twenty-eight-year career with *Newsweek* magazine. He is the coauthor of a 2002 biography of Colombian president Alvaro Uribe Vélez entitled *El señor de las sombras* (The Lord of the Shadows). The father of three college-age children, he is now stationed in southern Sudan where he serves as a public information officer for a United Nations peacekeeping mission.